P9-CMA-416

Twayne's United States Authors Series

Sylvia E. Bowman, *Editor*

INDIANA UNIVERSITY

John Dos Passos

Blairsville High School Library

JOHN DOS PASSOS

by JOHN H. WRENN

 9

Twayne Publishers, Inc.   ::   New York

13794 Budget 75

Copyright © *1961, by Twayne Publishers, Inc.*

All Rights Reserved

Library of Congress Catalog Card Number: 61-15669

MANUFACTURED IN THE UNITED STATES OF AMERICA BY
UNITED PRINTING SERVICES, INC.
NEW HAVEN, CONN.

To C. B. W. and E. C. W.

"*The danger to the survival [of] any kind of personal liberty anywhere in the world has become so patent, that those of us who care for liberty more than anything find ourselves continually seeking new ground on which to stand.*"

— JOHN DOS PASSOS, in a letter
to the author, March 1954

"*To be an American is of itself almost a moral condition, an education, and a career.*"

— GEORGE SANTAYANA, *Character and Opinion in the United States*

Preface

WHAT'S HAPPENED to Dos Passos?" has been the key question asked almost two decades now about this once famous novelist. It has meant variously, "Where is he? Is he still writing?" or, "What's wrong with him? What's happened to the artist in him?"

A part of the answer is that Dos Passos has been admired for characteristics which today, with a perspective of twenty years, appear to be superficial: for his success in the novel of protest; for his brilliant technical innovations in such a work as *U. S. A.*; for his contemporaneity—his grasp of the problems and events of the time as they related to individual characters in his fiction. When the novel of protest became all too familiar, the innovations of *U. S. A.* no longer new, and the events of his major novels no longer *current* ones, even his best work seemed to become no longer relevant.

Another part of the answer is that as a novelist Dos Passos has had, in a way, too great success. The power and conviction of his early writing made converts. Since then, any deviation in Dos Passos from whatever creed his readers inferred from his fiction has earned him the label of apostate.

As a result, his works are no longer considered by his proper audience—contemporary Americans—not because his best work is out of print, which it is not, but because of erroneous or only partly valid preconceptions by which he is viewed: rebel of the twenties, ex-communist, political novelist, disillusioned social critic, and so on. In short the author, even more than his work, became the victim of stereotyping, a process which always obstructs a just evaluation.

John Dos Passos is an attempt, therefore, to break the stereotypes, to take a fresh look at Dos Passos' work in the context of his life and times, to reconsider his literary works. The intention of this series, as well as of this volume, is to emphasize the author's work rather than his "life and times." Yet when the subject as well as the context of the writing *is* the author's life and times, we intend to give them their due recognition. When the author's times are our own and when his chief concern is how we may best live in them, they assume even added significance.

The first stereotype into which Dos Passos has fallen is that of his generation—Gertrude Stein's "lost generation" and Malcolm Cowley's "exiles"—from which I attempt to extricate him by examining distinguishing elements of his family background and early years. The second, and most firmly set by now, is that of the fellow-traveler novelist, a stereotype which is at least damaged by attention to what Dos Passos was actually writing in the *New Masses,* for example, and to his novels *as* novels rather than as propaganda. The third constricting category, that of ex-radical and apostate, is largely irrelevant. Dos Passos is, today, a Goldwater Republican; he has reached a political position into which few of his old adherents can follow him. But an examination of his fundamental views—in *Three Soldiers* (1921) or in *Midcentury* (1961)—will show a consistency in his career of both purpose and principle which will surprise many. As the novelist himself has been forced to point out, he has of course changed—changed with the times in the never-stable twentieth century in which he has lived.

The importance of the United States in this century to Dos Passos' art may give this study a secondary focus which is of special pertinence to a "beat" generation wandering today in the limbo between the artistic impulse and the need for standards from which to create. If sufficient light can be brought to bear upon the problem, "What's happened to Dos Passos?"—upon the making and unmaking of an artist—then some light may be reflected by implication upon the more general problem: that of the artist in twentieth-century America.

I wish to express my thanks to John Dos Passos for his always friendly cooperation—in reading and supplying marginal notations on an early paper of mine and in providing suggestions and answers to questions in letters as well as in conversations in Baltimore, in Denver, and in Boulder.

I am indebted to the Council on Research and Creative Work of the University of Colorado for grants enabling me

Preface

to complete this study. For its initial stimulus I am grateful to Professor Joe Lee Davis of the University of Michigan. For valuable suggestions and encouragement I am grateful to Professor Robert E. Spiller of the University of Pennsylvania. For sustaining me physically and morally during stages of its composition, I owe my largest debt to my family in Boulder, in Villanova, and in Baltimore.

JOHN H. WRENN

University of Colorado
May, 1961

Contents

Chapter

    Chronology   13

1.   A Modern Telemachus   19

2.   Peregrinations in Print   44

3.   Homeward Bound   62

4.   Art and Society—The Search for Form   79

5.   Art as Criticism   99

6.   Three Novels: Tradition and the Individual Talent   108

7.   Three Plays: Time, the Individual, and Society   132

8.   Architect of History   145

9.   U. S. A.   154

10.   The Constant Quest   167

    Notes and References   188

    Selected Bibliography   198

    Index   206

Chronology

1896   John Roderigo Dos Passos was born January 14 "in a hotel in Chicago," son of Attorney John Randolph Dos Passos and Lucy Addison Sprigg.

1896- Travel in Mexico, Belgium, England. First school in
1908   District of Columbia, some childhood years spent on farm in tidewater Virginia. Father a senior member of firm of Dos Passos Brothers in New York.

1907- Student at Choate School under name of John Roderigo
1911   Madison; first published writing as staff member of *Choate School News.*

1912   Entered Harvard College at 16, having completed his preparatory schooling over a year earlier.

1913   First story, "The Almeh," in *Harvard Monthly* (July), signed "J. R. Dos Passos."

1914   February, second *Monthly* story, signed "J. R. Dos Passos, Jr."

1915   April, became a "regular editor" of *Monthly;* October, secretary of *Monthly.* Contributed more stories, book reviews, a poem, an editorial.

1916   Further contributions to *Monthly.* April, mother's death. June, graduation *cum laude* from Harvard. Volunteered for ambulance duty overseas; father objected; went instead to Spain to study architecture. Nov., 1916-Feb., 1917, winter in Castille, studying Spanish culture and writing poetry. Oct. 14, 1916, essay, "Against American Literature," in *New Republic.*

1917   Jan. 14, twenty-first birthday in Spain; Jan. 27, father's death. Returned to America, re-enlisted in Norton-Harjes Ambulance Unit, ambulance duty in France. "Young Spain," first version of *Rosinante to the Road Again* appeared in Aug. *Seven Arts.* Dos Passos one of *Eight Harvard Poets,* published in August.

1918   Red Cross ambulance duty in Italy, after dissolution of Norton-Harjes. Excited by Italian painting. Back in

U. S., inducted into army, Allentown training camp, "washing windows," back to France in early November, clerical work and ambulance duty in Medical Corps, 1918-1919.

1919 Spring, received discharge from Army in France, on condition of waiving transportation home. December, writing in Portugal and Madrid.

1920 Completed *Three Soldiers* in Madrid. *One Man's Initiation—1917* published in October by Allen and Unwin in London. Publishing in *Liberator, Freeman, Dial, Nation.*

1921 Travel in Near East with Near East Relief. *Three Soldiers* published in September by George H. Doran in New York.

1922 Returned to U. S.; *Rosinante to the Road Again* published by Doran in March; Doran published *One Man's Initiation* and *A Pushcart at the Curb* (poetry). From 1922 to 1925, Dos Passos lived chiefly in New York.

1923 *Streets of Night* (Doran). Trip to Spain.

1924 "July"—Jimmy Herf's stagnant summer in tidewater Virginia before college—published in *Transatlantic Review.*

1925 *Manhattan Transfer* (Harper and Brothers); *The Moon Is a Gong* (*The Garbage Man*) produced by Harvard Dramatic Club.

1926 *The Garbage Man* produced in New York in March; published in July (Harper). Dos Passos helped found *New Masses* magazine, on its executive board, and a frequent contributor until the early thirties. Travel in Mexico and Europe.

1927 *Orient Express* (Harper) based on travels in Near East. In Boston, Dos Passos jailed for picketing State House in behalf of Sacco-Vanzetti defense; published *Facing the Chair* also in behalf of Sacco and Vanzetti. Dos Passos helped found New Playwrights Theater: 1927-1928, directing and helping design and paint scenery.

1928 Extended trip to U.S.S.R. In March, *New Masses* carried *Daily Worker* advertisement listing Dos Passos as "contributing editor." Play, *Airways, Inc.*, published in October (Macaulay).

1929   *Airways, Inc.* produced in New York. Back in U. S., married Katharine F. Smith, friend of Hemingway's first wife. September, asked *New Republic* to send him to cover textile strike in Gastonia, N. C., but he was considered too far to the left.

1930   *The 42nd Parallel* (Harper). Auto accident with Hemingway in Montana. Established home in Provincetown, Mass. From 1930 to 1934, periodical contributions chiefly to *New Republic*.

1931   Chairman of National Committee to Aid Striking Miners Fighting Starvation; with Theodore Dreiser, reporting labor disputes in Harlan County, Ky., and testing freedom of speech and assembly: indicted for criminal syndicalism.

1932   *1919* (Harcourt, Brace). Reporting political strife from Central America. Reported depression and national political conventions; cast "protest vote" for Communist candidates, Foster and Ford. Treasurer of National Committee for Defense of Political Prisoners. Joined staff of contributors to new *Common Sense* magazine.

1933   Play, "Fortune Heights," in April issue of *International Literature* (produced around this time in U.S.S.R.). Visited Scott Fitzgerald in Towson, Md. Summer trip to Spain.

1934   *In All Countries* (Harcourt, Brace)—travel and reporting; *Three Plays* (Harcourt, Brace). Reported New Deal and depression from Washington, D. C. Signed "Open Letter to Communist Party" protesting Party actions; elicited reply (March 6, *New Masses*): "Dear Comrade Dos Passos."

1936   *The Big Money* (Harcourt, Brace). "Grosz Comes to America" in September *Esquire*. Voted for F. D. R. with "enthusiasm."

1937   *Big Money* voted best of year by American Writers Congress; one-man show of 30 sketches by Dos Passos in New York. Trip to Spain to film documentary of Spanish civil war (with Hemingway, Joris Ivens), but quit project as too political. Back in U. S., published "Farewell to Europe" in July *Common Sense. The Villages Are the Heart of Spain* (Esquire-Coronet), reprinted from February *Esquire.*

1938 *U. S. A.* (Jan. 27) and *Journeys Between Wars,* travel and reporting—both volumes published by Harcourt, Brace.

1939 *Adventures of a Young Man* (Harcourt, Brace), a novel. Won Guggenheim Fellowship.

1940 *The Living Thoughts of Tom Paine—Presented by John Dos Passos* (Longmans, Green), selections from Paine. Second Guggenheim Fellowship; treasurer of Joint Campaign for Political Refugees (National Relief Organization); named representative of New World Resettlement Fund in contract with Ecuador to establish farm colonies for political refugees. Voted for F. D. R., later regretted it.

1941 *The Ground We Stand On* (Harcourt, Brace), an historical study of our Anglo-American tradition of freedom. September, delivered paper, "The Duty of the Writer," to P. E. N. conference in London; visited H. G. Wells.

1943 *Number One* (Houghton Mifflin), a novel. Reported war effort on home front, chiefly in *Harpers.*

1944 *State of the Nation* (Houghton Mifflin). Voted for John Dewey.

1945 Jan.-March, reported war in Pacific as war correspondent for *Life.* Back in U. S., reissued his first novel as *First Encounter.* Nov.-Dec., reported peace and Nürnburg trials from Germany for *Life.*

1947 September auto accident: Katharine Smith Dos Passos killed, Dos Passos lost an eye.

1946 *Tour of Duty* (Houghton Mifflin).

1948 Tour of South America for *Life.* Address: Palisades, Rockland County, N. Y.

1949 *The Grand Design* (Houghton Mifflin), a novel. Hired by General Mills, Inc., to write "objective and human" field report about that company. Now living on his family farm in Westmoreland, Virginia.

1950 *The Prospect Before Us* (Houghton Mifflin)—reporting and "lecturing" based on above travels; *Life's Picture History of World War II* (twelve *Life*-size pages of signed text, plus "Epilogue," unsigned); "The General," for General Mills, Inc. Married Elizabeth H. Holdridge.

1951 *Chosen Country* (Houghton Mifflin), an autobiographical novel. Dos Passos' only child, Lucy, born.

1952 *District of Columbia* (Houghton Mifflin), a trilogy containing *Adventures of a Young Man, Number One, The Grand Design.*

1954 *The Head and Heart of Thomas Jefferson* (Doubleday), a biographical study. *Most Likely to Succeed* (Prentice-Hall), a novel of communists working in the theater and in the movie industry.

1956 *The Theme Is Freedom* (Dodd, Mead), Dos Passos' own handbook with commentary on his development of this theme in his reporting.

1957 *The Men Who Made the Nation* (Doubleday: Mainstream of America Series), "The architects of the young republic, 1782-1802."

1958 *The Great Days* (Sagamore Press), a semi-autobiographical novel of a reminiscing reporter who is past his prime. Dos Passos received gold medal for fiction, National Institute of Arts and Letters (presented by William Faulkner).

1959 *Prospects of a Golden Age* (Prentice-Hall), an historical study of early American culture through integrated biographies. Adaptation (with Paul Shyre) of *U. S. A.* for New York dramatic reading.

1961 *Midcentury* (Houghton Mifflin), a "contemporary chronicle" of history, biography, fiction on the general pattern of *U. S. A.* In progress: second contribution to Mainstream of America Series (Doubleday), a short history of World War I.

A Modern Telemachus

WHEN HE REACHED his twenty-first birthday in 1917, John Dos Passos was in Spain preparing himself for a career as an artist. "Painting and architecture," he reveals in *The Theme Is Freedom* (1956), "were my main interests at the time." Within a few days of his birthday (January 14) he learned of his father's death (January 27) in the United States. Within a few months, after having returned to take care of his immediate responsibilities in America, Dos Passos was again in Europe—but as an ambulance driver in France. Those few months reveal the essential elements of an apparently irregular yet strangely integrated career: the artistic bent, an interest in both Spain and America, a sense of responsibility, the loss of a father, the desire to participate in events of his time.

Some of those elements were common to others of his generation whose careers Malcolm Cowley chronicled in *Exile's Return* (1934, 1951); but Dos Passos lacked the one essential element of Cowley's thesis—the process of "deracination," of being uprooted from his natural environment and set adrift as an "exile." And the fact that he was never an exile in any true sense of the word has been one of the controlling factors of his career. For Dos Passos was born unrooted to any plot of ground; and his life has been dedicated, therefore, to a search for congenial soil and climate—for "new ground on which to stand"[1] or in which to grow.

I *The Need to Belong*

John Roderigo Dos Passos, born in a hotel in Chicago in 1896, was the illegitimate son of Attorney John Randolph Dos Passos. And some of the characteristics of his early, general environment helped shape the artist to be. Chicago, 1896, was the place and date of Bryan's famous "Cross of Gold" speech. It was also the year that—with the issues squarely drawn—the country proclaimed itself in support of capitalism, industry, and gold as opposed to agrarianism and silver. In Illinois, liberal Governor Altgeld was going down to political defeat and Eugene V. Debs had just emerged from prison; and both were victims of the triumphant railroad giants supported by the Democratic President Cleveland. In New York City, a third reformer, Henry George, was making a second try for the mayoralty and the single-tax, only to die before the election the following year, while his idea lived on; Edward Bellamy was dying while completing *Equality* (1897); Thorstein Veblen was brewing his *Theory of the Leisure Class* (1899). In England Friedrich Engels had published, two years earlier, the final volumes of *Das Kapital;* and Herbert Spencer's completed *Principles of Sociology* was just appearing; Carnegie and Rockefeller were practicing the gospel of wealth. McKinley in 1896 was elected over Bryan, but the small Republican majority (little over half a million) and the emotional character of the campaign were evidence that the protests against industrialism and narrow concentration of wealth would not end in the 1890's.

Although the topical events of 1896 were lost upon the infant Dos Passos, they were important indications of the times into which he was born. American society was becoming characteristically urban-industrial. Americans' knowledge of the world they lived in—and especially of how to exploit it for financial gain—was rapidly increasing. The affluent among them had discovered Progress, and their recent experience and their reading of Spencer made it seem inevitable; but the less well-to-do were discovering class struggle and Karl Marx— and it seemed, with the passing of the frontier around 1890, that the old sectional controversies were completing a metamorphosis into those of class. To the well-off, Utopia was both here and just around the corner; to most of the rest, it was over the horizon.

Half a century before, at the height of American territorial and agricultural expansion, when Utopia had seemed achieved to the satisfied or to be available in the West or in the immediate future to the dissatisfied, Americans had expressed their optimism in a great wave of idealism: cultural nationalism, imperialism, expansion, and reform. After much of the more articulate idealism had been diverted into protest by the slavery issue and by the Mexican War, it was eventually preempted by the abolitionists; and it ended in a climax of sectionalism and in the Civil War.

Around the turn of the century and with the opening of new frontiers by industrial technology and scientific knowledge, Americans responded with a new optimistic expansiveness and idealism. Again the optimistic reformism of the more articulate—for whom the literature of idealism of the earlier wave was already classic—was diverted into protests against financial, industrial, and territorial imperialism and against industrial slavery. This time, however, no single cause had a single group of dedicated spokesmen to channel the protests. The moral indignation of Eugene Debs, Samuel Gompers, and Daniel de Leon was no less than that of William Lloyd Garrison; the oratorical fervor of Bryan no less than that of Wendell Phillips; and the writing ability and the factual knowledge of Ida Tarbell and all the other muckrakers were certainly equal at least to Harriet Beecher Stowe's. But their aims and appeals were scattered; even those of Bryan and de Leon lacked the emotional drive of abolitionism. Nevertheless, by 1896 America seemed to be again dividing, and the first bloody battles of a new civil war had been fought: the "Great Strike" of 1877; the Haymarket affair of 1886; the Homestead Strike of 1892; and the Pullman and the Cripple Creek, Colorado, strikes of 1894. In each of them, as in the election of 1896, capitalism, industry, and gold proved the winning combination.

By 1896 Dos Passos' father, John Randolph Dos Passos, was well on the side of capitalism, industry, and gold. He was a personal friend of McKinley, for whom he campaigned in Pennsylvania and Virginia in 1896. Then, at fifty-two, he had made a reputation as a successful criminal defense lawyer and was pioneering in the organization and development of the great trusts. In 1895 his efforts in developing the Sugar Trust—for which his legal fee was said to have been the largest then on record—were capped by an approving decision in the E. C. Knight case by the Supreme Court (which held that control of 98 per cent of the sugar refining industry was not restraint of trade).

From accounts of his life—chiefly in the slightly veiled biographies by his son where he appears as "Jack" or "He" (always with a capital) in the Camera Eyes of *U. S. A.* (1930-1938) and as "Dandy" or James Knox Polk Pignatelli in *Chosen Country* (1951)—the senior Dos Passos was a strong man. He was strong in physique, a great walker, a yachtsman, a prodigious swimmer; he was strong in mind, an impressive speaker, an outstanding corporation lawyer; he was strong of will. In some ways his was a typical success story of his era. A first-generation American, born in the mid-nineteenth century (1844) in a seaboard industrial center (Philadelphia), he reached maturity around the end of the Civil War. Through initiative, energy, and luck—including that of having been born at a propitious time and place—he made himself essential to the surging industrial forces and rose to a position of influence and esteem in society. Himself the son of a Portuguese shoemaker, he must have retained some sense of pride in the Iberian tradition—or defiance of it—for he named his son John Roderigo.

Of an expansive, extroverted personality and a man confident of his intellect and of the rightness of his well-considered opinions, we can imagine his pride at the birth of his son and his eager expectation that John R. Dos Passos, Jr., would prove to have been made in the image of his father. But the biographical notes by his son reveal a certain ill-concealed disappointment in the myopic, awkward, introspective boy the son became: "But Monsieur Dandy said he must learn to swim and grabbed him with strong hands . . . but it was too frightening and he was yelling and holding on to the hard arm . . . Monsieur Dandy was angry."

Although John's father was a self-made aristocrat, his mother, Lucy Addison Sprigg, was a born one—a Southern gentlewoman from a family of Marylanders and Episcopalians, whose father, according to Dos Passos, "was living in Va. and served as some kind of engineer on Confed. side during [the Civil] war."[2] Forty-eight years old in 1896, so engrained was her consciousness of her class that she later reflected her attitude when she related to her young son little stories about the past, such as this one from Camera Eye Three of *U. S. A.*: "one night Mother was so frightened on account of all the rifleshots but it was allright turned out to be nothing but a little shooting they'd been only shooting a greaser that was all." A kindly mother and a good woman, she had no malice in the telling of such a tale; she had simply made a casual statement of fact; for "workingmen and people like that laborers travailleurs greasers" could scarcely be considered human beings. But her puzzled son could never forget the story.

So this and other problems in his environment found their way after a quarter of a century into his stream-of-memory autobiography, the roughly chronological Camera Eyes of *U. S. A.* Many of these concerns had appeared in his earlier fiction and many recurred later in *Chosen Country;* but nearly all—up to 1931—are in the Camera Eyes. Most of these, as one would expect, are found in the first volume of the trilogy, *42nd Parallel,* which covers his formative years, about 1900 to 1917.

The young Dos Passos was subject to a number of influences which might have developed in him not only a growing inability to share his mother's attitudes toward "people like that" but also a penchant for puzzling about the meanings— the real ones—of what people said and did. From his paternal grandfather he might have acquired a certain Latin sensitiveness tending toward emotionalism; from his father, a keen mind alert for significant details; or from both, a certain restlessness of spirit which, combined with a love for the sea and its broad horizons, would keep him ever searching for the better society, the better way of life.

And he inherited a Latin name, John Roderigo, in a society all too predisposed—as was his mother—to be exclusive in its associates and to insist that they be of the "right" families, of the "right" races, of the "right" nationalities, and so on. Although his father was diligent in providing the best of schooling for his son, prominent attorney Dos Passos evidently felt that he could not yet afford to acknowledge John Roderigo publicly as his own. Even of his name, therefore, the boy could not be certain. As late as 1911, in his fifteenth year, he had been living under the name John Roderigo Madison for three and a half years at the Choate School, a New England preparatory school for boys.

The boy's congenital myopia and his unsettled childhood might well have induced his habit of first grasping details before he could comprehend the wholes. Beginning life in a hotel in Chicago, "carted around a good deal as a child," as he once recalled,[3] to Mexico, to England, to the continent, and living principally with his mother (or with governesses, with friends of his mother, or in private schools while his parents were away on trips) his mind and attitudes developed, of necessity, in relative independence of what might have been the influence of a home—an institution he never really knew.

Without the security of a home, of a constant, familiar environment; not knowing his father except to worship him from afar as an occasionally reappearing god; able to depend only upon the companionship—cherished, but perhaps not wholly adequate—of his middle-aged mother, it is not surprising that nearsighted John Roderigo Dos Passos was a shy and self-conscious child, highly sensitive to human relationships, and ready to respond intuitively and empathically to those with whom he had any community of thought or feeling. The rootless existence of his childhood left him longing for something to belong to, something to believe in: "What a horrible childhood . . . A hotel childhood . . . and being a double foreigner to all the little English boys wearing their schoolcaps and special neckties: A Man Without a Country. . . . Was it the bar sinister or the nearsighted eyes that made him always fumble the ball—what a terrible tennisplayer, no good at football or even at soccer—or the foreign speech or the lack of a home that made him so awkward, tonguetied, never saying the right word, never managing to do the accepted thing at the accepted time . . . all his life he'd hated everything but Petite Mère." Although presented as fiction in Dos Passos' novel *Chosen Country,* this quotation contains almost unquestionably, item by item, painfully accurate autobiography.

This was the boy whose earliest recorded experience of the outside world in the first Camera Eye of *U. S. A.* is of running with his mother down a Dutch or a Belgian street—despairing that, running, "you have to step on too many grassblades the poor hurt green tongues"—fleeing the threats and stones of the anti-British populace who had mistaken his nationality. As early as 1900 he had felt, in the indirect ramifications of the Boer War, the effects of British imperialism and the confusion of unwarranted persecution.

No wonder he was puzzled at the attitude of his betters toward "workingmen and people like that." He was too young to understand either the complexities of British or American imperialism around the turn of the century or the conflicts between the rationalizations of self-interest and the traditions of self-governing democracy which animated much of American politics until 1912. But he was old enough to be puzzled that the names "greaser," "bohunk," "polak" should be so opprobrious while apparently referring only to nationality and the fact that a person worked with his hands. And later, if he chanced to hear his father declaiming that "it is now manifest that to this great [Anglo-Saxon] race has been entrusted the civilisation and christianisation of the world"—as his father in fact wrote in one of his books, *The Anglo-Saxon Century* (1903)—it is doubtful that he was any less perplexed. He knew well enough his own Portuguese origins and that his grandfather had been a shoemaker who "spoke mostly Portugee" (Cam. Eye 15). We can imagine his framing the question, if he had not the temerity to ask it: "Was Grandfather a 'greaser'?" And if so, what was the grandson of a greaser?

Such a boy could easily identify himself with the hero of *The Man Without a Country*: ". . . I was so sorry I never remembered whether they brought me home or buried me at sea but anyway I was wrapped in Old Glory" (Cam. Eye 14). Nor would it have been difficult for him to identify himself specifically with the "greasers," and then with the "bohunks" and "polaks," and generally with the oppressed. Without the sense of belonging which for most boys is provided by the home and by a more or less consistent circle of friends of their own age, Dos Passos had to seek it elsewhere. And no greater sense of belonging can be found than in the community of thought and feeling of the oppressed—especially of the unjustifiably oppressed, whose unity is strengthened by a common aim and by the bond of righteous indignation created by a common enemy.

The boy's feelings did not necessarily take explicitly such a direction. But his nature and his environment were such as to make it possible, and even probable, that they should. And the tenor of the period, which was proclaimed by the progressive reformism of all the leading politicians, helped to point out both the sources and objects of oppression and to give a general moral sanction to its combatants.

By 1912 young John Dos Passos had not yet consciously espoused "the cause" or any cause. The acting political leaders old and new—Theodore Roosevelt, La Follette, Bryan, Debs, Wilson—were themselves vigorous reformers; and the people were behind them. Dos Passos, having graduated from the Choate School at fifteen in 1911, was completing a year out of school before going on to Harvard. He was a bright, sensitive adolescent who "grew flowers and vegetables and . . . liked books and Gibbon's *Decline and Fall of the Roman Empire* and Captain Marryat's novels and wanted to go away to sea and to foreign cities . . . and liked things to be beautiful and wished . . . I had the nerve to hug and kiss Martha . . . and little red-headed Mary" (Cam. Eye 19).

II *Aura of Idealism*

Closely related to the reformist idealism which characterized the United States from 1896 to 1912 was its spirit of self-conscious nationalism and optimism. Democracy was a panacea, and all agreed that it should be extended. The contented wanted to extend it abroad, so even imperialistic expansion was undertaken in the spirit of crusading democracy which liberated and protected her weaker neighbors. The discontented wanted to extend it at home, and the result was a period of labor unrest and of unprecedented support for liberal and reformist politicians. Beautifully symbolic of the period is the great Trust Buster's coining of the term "muckrakers"; inscribing it on their banner, many journalists rode joyous and triumphant into the new century. Virtually no one questioned the principle of reform: the only questions were where and how to begin. It was inevitable that this ideal-seeking *zeitgeist*, continuing unabated into the year 1917, should affect the attitudes and aspirations of the young men who approached maturity during its height in the early war and prewar years.

During the summer of 1912 the spirit of idealism swept the country, and its principles of reform were proclaimed from the housetops by Roosevelt and from the mountaintops by Wilson. In the fall of 1912 John Dos Passos entered

Harvard University where most were agreed about the need for reform—but thought they ought to start by reforming the strikers in nearby Lawrence: "what the hell they were a lot of wops anyway bohunks hunkies that didn't wash their necks ate garlic with squalling brats and fat oily wives the damn dagoes" (Cam. Eye 25).

In November, with the Bull Moose running interference and splitting the Republican opposition wide open, Woodrow Wilson charged through for a Democratic victory. But not just any Democratic ball-carrier could have achieved it, and only Wilson's high ideals, hard work, and clean living in the New Jersey state league could have provided the requisite conditioning. For the times and Mr. Bryan were demanding idealism in action as well as in words. As American historians relate, although "technically, Wilson was a minority President, . . . actually the progressive principles which he, Roosevelt and Debs alike espoused, commanded the support of over three-fourths of the voters. . . . No administration of modern times has been inaugurated with a greater passion for righteousness and justice."[4]

So a nation of idealists—with differing ideals, to be sure—prepared to make the United States safe for the fulfillment of their ideals. And Dos Passos—with his own ideals as yet uncrystallized, but wanting "things to be beautiful" and all too aware of the need for reform and of the lack of beauty around him—started drifting toward the beautiful where he could find it. His was bound to be a frustrating search because it was already virtually an underlying assumption of the times that beauty could scarcely exist in the sordid, urban world of a raw industrial society. Furthermore, he was searching for an Ideal Beauty; but, by his own assertion, he had not then the critical equipment with which to recognize it had he encountered it. "I must have been well along in college before I looked at a picture directly as an excitement for the eye," he reminisced in 1936; in the same article he suggested that "it must have been at about the same time" that he discovered music, through Debussy.[5]

Thus the search for beauty insensibly became instead a search for its conditions. For the time being, these seemed to be an escape from the vulgar importunities of the moment. Dos Passos, who had always been an avid reader, had found in the romance of other, happier times and places of Kipling, Marryat, Sir Walter Scott, Malory, Dumas, and Mark Twain, relief from the loneliness that had plagued his childhood. Now he turned naturally again to books, to exhibitions of art, and to drifting around the fringes of aestheticism and its concomitant Bohemianism.

As early as his first year at Harvard he published in the *Harvard Monthly* a short story laid in Cairo about a lonely artist who falls in love with the eyes of an Arab woman whom he paints from memory. His next contribution was "The Honor of a Klepht," a story about leadership and sacrifice and love in "the days before the War of Independence had won the freedom of the Greeks from Turkish rule." These were followed by other stories, book reviews, an occasional poem, two editorials, and by an essay, "A Humble Protest" (June, 1916), which criticized American civilization. In the non-fiction, beginning in 1914, we can see a sharpening of Dos Passos' critical powers—the tools with which to discover the conditions of beauty. In the stories, which are mostly either autobiographical tales of the yearnings and frustrations of a young boy or accounts of the tribulations of an artist, we can also observe—especially in the latter type—the growing tendency toward satire. But they are predominantly evocations of a vague idealism; the criticism is as yet barely apparent.

Even those Harvard contemporaries of Dos Passos who opposed strikes and strikers reflected the aura of idealism. They were not anti-idealistic: they were simply echoing the ideals of their class, but ones which conflicted with those of the workers. They too were seeking the conditions of beauty in reacting against the disharmony which the strikes produced. A minority of the undergraduates, however, reacted differently to the manifest need for more harmony and beauty in the world they lived in. Those were the young men of an intellectual and aesthetic bent who responded more specifically than their fellows to their environment. They wanted, individually, to help better the circumstances in which they found themselves; and they were wont to react to situations in terms of the individuals concerned—others with whom they could, in varying degrees, identify themselves—rather than in terms of mere situations or groups or classes.

Also attending Harvard in the fall of 1914 were Richard

Dana Skinner, editor-in-chief of the *Harvard Monthly,* and E. E. Cummings, who immediately preceded Dos Passos as its secretary; in the law school was Archibald MacLeish; about to arrive was Malcolm Cowley, who later became the critic and historian of his generation. At Princeton was Edmund Wilson (also '16), who had arrived there a year ahead of Scott Fitzgerald. Although a decade the senior of most of them, Randolph Bourne had just ducked out from under the academic "bell-glass"—leaving behind him some uneasy questionings among the undergraduates at Columbia —and was already in Paris; T. S. Eliot, who had just quit as an assistant in philosophy at Harvard in favor of another trip to Europe, was about to publish "The Love Song of J. Alfred Prufrock," which he had written in Paris three years earlier.

These young men, a minority more or less shunned by the majority, held general attitudes similar to those of Dos Passos. That he allied himself with them, or with some of them, was perhaps at least as much the result of his personal need for such an alliance as of his full accordance with their beliefs. For Dos Passos, like most of them, never satisfactorily adjusted to his life as an undergraduate. And the relationship, in any case, was a tenuous one which was maintained usually by only a common interest in a literary endeavor; and the groups, comprised of two or three or four arguing about books or art or religion in somebody's bedroom or over beers at a restaurant, were apt to be small and varied. Thriving rather upon differences of opinion than upon similarities, they exhibited a unity which was more apparent to the conventional majority than to themselves.

Various critics and chroniclers have since grouped a number of these and other young men under various not-too-flattering categories. Gertrude Stein called them all "a lost generation"; Cowley labeled them "exiles"; the columnist Westbrook Pegler not unexpectedly characterized them as "a queer bunch of . . . self-indulgent brats"; and a recent critic has collected them into a "cult of disillusion," quoting Cowley's observation that as undergraduates, "Everyone was reading Casanova's Memoirs, Pater, Petronius, and discussing the art of Aubrey Beardsley and the 'voluptuousness of the Church.' "[6] But these generalizations, though they may shed light on an era, do little to explain the specific individual; and the individuals themselves have largely ignored them (unless like their literary sires, the muckrakers, they have basked in them—as Hemingway basked in the gloom of "a lost generation").

Dos Passos at Harvard was more impressed with Gibbon's history than with the unwritten one of his own generation; and, like young Jay in *Chosen Country,* he was willing to overtax his eyes "to read the fine print of Froude" because of fascination with his biographies (the raw material of history in the lives of great men). Furthermore, Pater could be read for the history of the Renaissance as well as for the elements of Epicureanism; and Petronius' satire of the *nouveau-riche* could suggest Veblen's conspicuous consumption as well as the enjoyments of indolence and profligacy.

To Dos Passos, aestheticism was still only a substitute for action; and he was never a complete Bohemian. For Bohemianism, while it was partly a sincere protest against mere conventionality, was also not only an indulgence in mere sensuality for its own sake but also a gesture of intellectual snobbery aimed at the majority. Already, in the spring of 1915, he had entitled one of his stories in the *Harvard Monthly* "An Aesthete's Nightmare"—a satirical description of the mourning of a sad young man over his broken Venus statuette. It indicated something less than full participation in the movement which he satirized.

It is more than probable, as Camera Eye Twenty-five indicates, that Dos Passos' very attendance at Harvard was at least in some degree an acquiescence to parental pressure: "four years under the ethercone breathe deep gently now that's the way be a good boy . . . get A's in some courses but don't be a grind be interested in literature but remain a gentleman don't be seen with Jews or Socialists." Young John Dos Passos respected, admired, and stood somewhat in awe of his father; and he loved his mother, now an invalid, and would on no account have done anything that might hurt her. He had not yet learned the meaning of individual freedom—nor of rebellion. But at Harvard he was beginning to yearn toward something more than a humble protest: ". . . haven't got the nerve to break out of the bell-glass . . . grow cold with culture like a cup of tea forgotten between an incenseburner and a volume of Oscar Wilde . . . four years I didn't know you could do what you   Michaelangelo want-

ed   say   Marx to all   the professors with a small Swift
break all the Greenoughs . . . and I hadn't the nerve   to jump
up and walk out of doors and tell them all to go take a fly-
ing   Rimbaud   at the moon."

By 1916 the attainment of his ideals seemed still as far
off as ever. He still did not belong: not even to a family,
certainly not to Harvard, not even to a class, scarcely to his
country ("but anyway I was wrapped in Old Glory"). He
was born an outsider, and his shyness and his developing critical intelligence only increased the barriers between his
isolation and an easy acceptance of existing institutions. It
was becoming clear, perhaps even to Dos Passos, that he
would have to create his own attachments. It was no mere
matter of a name—of simply calling himself "American," or
"artist," or even "Dos Passos"; he had to discover that he
could accept the privileges and responsibilities of any title;
and he had to pass the tests of membership in the order.
Then he might at last be free of the anarchy of unbelonging.

After four years of the New Freedom, Dos Passos had yet
to find his own; but its beginnings were not far off. In April
of 1916 his mother died; and within a couple of months he
graduated—*cum laude,* having gotten his "A's in some courses"
—from Harvard. Almost at one stroke his principal ties of
affection and of filial obligation to his father to complete
his formal education were severed. Longing to act at last
in pursuit of his ideals, wanting to "belong," and clinging
faithfully to his principle of "constructive pacifism"—which he
argued in an essay in the *Monthly* in June, 1916—he signed
up the same year in the Norton-Harjes Volunteer Ambulance
Unit. But his father, who was still alive, reacted; he, as Dos
Passos notes, "very naturally didn't want me to get my block
blown off too soon." So, having decided that he would become an architect, Dos Passos embarked for Spain in order
to study, as he said later, "l'architecture à Séville. C'était peu
de temps avant la guèrre." But "Spain was a compromise."[7]

III   *Compromises*

"It was a short time before the war." When Dos Passos
left for Spain, the war in France was already two years under
way. What he meant, of course, was that it was shortly before

his participation in it. He added, on the same occasion, that he did not continue his study of architecture. Rather drastic further adjustments were soon to be required of him after his arrival in Spain—further efforts to balance the varied claims of ideals, responsibilities, desires.

But going to Spain was not the first compromise for Dos Passos. His very existence had been the result of a tremendous compromise on the part of his parents, two people of very much the "better" sort, who had dared to take the lonely middle path between the dictates of their heads and of their hearts in accepting all the varied claims to their responsibility and also the requirements of their love; their son represented both. As a result, his childhood too was a compromise— between all that his parents wanted for their son and all that their first compromise prevented them from giving him. Attorney John Randolph Dos Passos knew well enough that compromise breeds compromise; but it was not upon that account to be avoided. One thing at least need never be compromised—a man's responsibility to his essential self, his individual integrity.

If we note that the father failed for sixteen years publicly to acknowledge his son, we must observe also that he had two very good reasons: he never forgot his responsibilities to his legitimate wife, the former Mary Dyckman Hays, and a public acknowledgment not only might have hurt her unnecessarily but might also have ruined his law practice and destroyed his power to fulfill his financial obligations to all who were immediately dependent upon him. Both of these reasons are implicit in the thinly disguised autobiography of *Chosen Country*.

The novel reveals, finally, a certain consolation in the father at his boy's grasp of language, his love of history and of travel, the quality of his mind: "That's right . . . never go out without a book in your pocket. The secret of a well-stored mind is never to waste time." So we are not surprised at the delegation to the son of the father's dreams: "If we could form an Englishspeaking league this century that you . . . not I, will live to see, would be the greatest in human history." This dream can be documented as well from the father's book, *The Anglo-Saxon Century*.

The father consciously and unconsciously had set a for-

midable pattern for his son to aspire to follow. Of the great age of American rugged individualists, he fancied himself a free-thinker and humanitarian: "He kept saying What would you do Lucy if I were to invite one of them to my table? They're very lovely people Lucy the colored people . . . and He was holding forth in the parlor car Why Lucy if it were necessary for the cause of humanity I would walk out and be shot any day you would Jack[8] wouldn't you?" Although something of an intellectual bully and somewhat inclined toward braggadocio—to the evident discomfort of his son—he had a real desire to improve the institutions of his country; "and He talked about lawreform and what politicians were like and where were the Good Men in this country"; and he had the practical attorney's recognition of where he stood in relation to his times: "Why thinking the way I think I couldn't get elected to be notary public in any county in the state not with all the money in the world no not even dogcatcher" (Cam. Eye 16). What is more, he had a genuine interest in his son, an interest which his son reflected in respect and awe.

If Dos Passos was to follow the pattern set by his father, he would have to insist on the freedom of the individual; he would have to promote the unity and strength of the group which claimed his allegiance ("Englishspeaking league" or some other), to think for himself and accept the consequences, to advocate humanitarian reform (with or without his father's condescension).

His whole career, including *U. S. A.,* is a testament to his eventual success. Behind it is the pattern of values his father—not Karl Marx—had outlined. But the father and son differed markedly in background, in interests, in temperament; and they lived in very different times. Therefore, the pattern could be fulfilled only by compromises.

Harvard College was one of the first. His father, his childhood travels, his reading of Marryat had filled him with an inextinguishable love of the sea. Later he was to be able to indulge that love—in his travels, at his home in Province-town, in his eventual return to within sight of the Virginia capes of his boyhood; but not in 1912.

Upon graduating after years of bleak confinement in a New England boys' preparatory school—Choate or any other—any

boy with a modicum of individuality wishes finally to assert it, to get away, to express himself, to do all—or at least some— of the thousand and one forbidden things, to be free! It is interesting to speculate about the unintended contributions of these frequently sectarian institutions to the various rebellious causes of human liberty, atheism, anarchy. Dos Passos, on emerging into the world from Choate, would have preferred to go to sea. But recognizing that preparatory school had been an investment by his father to prepare him not for the world but for college, he had hoped to go to Annapolis. His bad eyesight denied him the satisfaction of that compromise; the next was Harvard.

By the time he reached his last year at Harvard, Dos Passos was so familiar with the problems of choice in his own life (though most often it was a choice of attitude rather than of action) that it had become an underlying assumption in his writing that the distinguishing characteristic of truly human life was a frank facing of these problems, and their tentative solution was by the method of intelligent compromise.

In "A Humble Protest," published in the *Harvard Monthly* in the month of his graduation, Dos Passos in effect proposed this method to himself and to his readers as the basis for a philosophy. The essay is full of direct questions—there are ten in the last five paragraphs—including "the inevitable, unanswerable, question: what is the end of human life?" His answer was an intentional though tentative dichotomy: "It might be possible," he suggested, "to divide life's aims . . . into two half-opposed ideals; thought and art; Plato and Michael Angelo. . . . One is the desire to create; the other is the desire to fathom. . . . Is there any other path to the fullness of life?" For him, at least, there proved to be no other, or none so valid. Sometimes, indeed, he has been closer to one ideal than to the other; and, overall, his movement has been from art to thought, or from heart to head—to use the alternate terms of Dos Passos' work on Jefferson, *The Head and Heart of Thomas Jefferson* (1954). Yet he has consistently followed a path between thought and art—"these twin guide-posts for humanity." His protest in this early essay was against their repression because of general worship of the industrial system.

Until about 1914 Dos Passos had been reacting to the cir-

cumstances of his life almost wholly in terms of emotional responses—just as the world around him seemed to be doing. But he was not aping the world; for he had always been fairly well insulated from it though he had become familiar with a fair amount of its surface. He reacted emotionally because he was young and because nearly everything in his life had contributed to the development of his sensitivity. In another nature, the same circumstances might have developed a protective dulling of feeling, a sort of compensatory insensitivity. But that other nature would probably have had to be less imaginative than was Dos Passos or less insistently inquiring as to the meanings of things. Until 1914, he, for all these reasons, had been reacting almost wholly from the heart.

Between 1914 and 1916 a gradual change in emphasis can be noted in Dos Passos' writing for the *Harvard Monthly*. He continued to draw heavily upon his own experience for the materials of his short stories and poems. Yet along with the introspection, there is an increasing use of satire (for example, in each of the last six stories he published in 1915) which is usually directed at his own activities; and there is also a significant change from the lyrical toward the critical in the form of his contributions. His sixteen contributions before 1916 included ten stories; among his thirteen contributions during 1916 he included only three stories; and his two final publications in the *Monthly* were serious essays about American domestic and foreign policies.[9]

Although his mother's death in April, 1916, was a release of sorts, it also threatened to destroy whatever equilibrium between his head and heart he had managed to achieve. Only three months before her death he had published "The Shepherd," a semi-fictional account of an experience in his sixteenth year, in which "as he thought of his mother his eyes filled with tears. . . . She was the center of his world. In spirit he prostrated himself before the shrine of her sweetness and gentleness." Her death was a terrible blow: "When the telegram came that She was dying the bellglass cracked in a screech of slate pencils (have you ever never been able to sleep for a week in April?)" (Cam. Eye 28).

Six of Dos Passos' contributions in the *Harvard Monthly* had been concerned with the war in Europe; and one of them was entirely devoted to reminiscences of Brussels—in a country then being widely referred to in America as "brave little Belgium." After his mother's death, Dos Passos, just graduating from Harvard and acutely conscious of the war and its implications and even of its terrain, almost immediately enlisted for ambulance service overseas. Knowing his background, we are likely to see in his enlistment something more than the dilletante's yen for adventure and escape from boredom which Cowley describes as the typical attitude of the "exiles."

His father, as has been noted, helped him to check, at the time, his more nearly emotional reactions (which involved, indeed, a desire to escape, though not from boredom) in favor of studying architecture in Spain. Despite a quite natural concern about the welfare of his boy, the father was perhaps as anxious as his son that they not be thrown too suddenly and intimately together. The life of each had revolved in its separate orbit around the woman who was now dead; their paths had not frequently been aligned; and, when they had, it may not have been wholly pleasant for the one eclipsed.

His mother's death, though stunning, left Dos Passos securely in possession of her. He had known her intimately, and she had become a part of him. But he had never really known his father, the other of the two strongest influences of his early life. If he were to know himself in his "desire to fathom," he would have to comprehend first that part of him that was his father. Perhaps from the perspective of distance and in the Iberian peninsula of the Dos Passos origins, he might best begin the search for understanding. Although he may have had no consciousness of such a quest at the time, he certainly had it by 1921 when he was writing in Spain of his experiences there just before and after his participation in the war.

"Telemachus had wandered so far in search of his father he had quite forgotten what he was looking for." This first sentence of *Rosinante to the Road Again* (1922) introduces the principal character of its fictional part.[10] A kind of travel book written in alternate sections—one allegory, the other critical exposition—it is an attempt to assess and interpret the culture of Spain. In the allegorical section, Dos Passos presents the adventurous wanderings in Spain of two young men, Telemachus and Lyaeus. Tel—as he is called by his friend—is a romantic, thoughtful, introspective young man somewhat preoccupied at first with death and continually restrained from action by the memory of the maxims of his mother Penelope. It is a satirical portrait; but once again, as in many of his *Harvard Monthly* stories, Dos Passos presents his own likeness.

Much more sympathetically portrayed is Lyaeus (loosener of care)—Bacchus, Dionysus. Freely indulging in the pleasures of the moment—drinking with abandon, flirting with the Spanish girls—he does all the things that Tel is afraid to do and laughs freely and loudly "with his head thrown back" in derision at the genteel preoccupations of Tel—at his ridiculous futile attempts to formulate and make permanent the characteristic gesture of Spain, the essential quality of which was its spontaneity. That laughter is heard again and again in Dos Passos, for the reader has not seen the last of Lyaeus in his dual character of impulsive hedonist and cynic—"a young man with hollow cheeks . . . about whose mouth a faint pained smile was continually hovering"—who could rapidly change so that his face "looked fuller and flushed, . . . lips . . . moist and very red . . . an occasional crisp curl in the black hair about his temples."

Lyaeus is not Dos Passos—he represents neither his head nor his heart, which are exercising such a futile tug-of-war in poor Tel. But he is his complement, the valued friend whom he envies a bit because he seems so much more at home in the world, because he has the gift of spontaneity, and because he doesn't think about things so much—too much. He is the twin of Jay's "old dream" in *Chosen Country*: "the old dream that he was twins sailing in a boat down the Mississippi. If you were twins it wouldn't matter if you were tonguetied. Each could say what he liked to the other. Each would do what the other wanted. There wouldn't be that constraint that held him fast in a vise." Lyaeus, the modern Sancho Panza, was content to accept the present for what it was worth and to obtain from it whatever enjoyment he could. He was moved neither by the desire to fathom nor by the desire to create; he could laugh at the futility of any such impracticable quest—but he was ready, like Sancho, to enjoy the promised isle if it ever materialized.

Telemachus, however, was dreadfully in earnest about his quest. In Greek myth, the reader may recall, Telemachus spent his childhood with his mother Penelope in the shadow of the fame of his absent father Odysseus. His early manhood was passed in active search of his adventurous father. Following him to Calypso's isle, Telemachus escaped that goddess's charms—on the advice of Minerva in the form of Mentor, his friend and adviser—by leaping from a cliff and swimming to a ship which lay becalmed offshore. After further adventures Minerva appeared to Telemachus to reveal to him that Odysseus, after twenty years' absence, was to be found at home. Dos Passos was to look as long and as far as Telemachus, and his search took him over most of the world and many times over the centers of the western hemisphere; it was to be concluded in as unlikely a place.

Meanwhile, he had been in Spain only a few months when he heard of his father's death: "when the cable came that He was dead I walked through the streets . . . climbed on the night train at the Norte station without knowing why . . . the architectural details the grammar of styles it was the end of that book" (Cam. Eye 28). It was also the end of parental authority, of his feeling of moral responsibility to the ideals of the class which his father represented, and of his boyhood. His twenty-first birthday, which had occurred a few days before the cable arrived, left him legally an individual in his own right and gave him the sense of freedom and of responsibility to himself and his own ideals which the attainment of majority almost invariably entails. But he had no sooner been relieved of his family responsibilities than he accepted permanently what were to him the much broader, more urgent ones of a civilized man. He lost little time—as soon as he had fulfilled his immediate obligations in America— in asserting his new freedom in behalf of the then most sharply suffering of the vast brotherhood of the oppressed— the wounded and dying of the war. He renewed his enlistment in the Norton-Harjes Volunteer Ambulance Unit.

IV *Disillusioning War for Ideals*

By 1917 America was already losing some of her idealism. Since the outbreak of war and with the growing threat of becoming embroiled, the tenor of the average American's politics already showed a switch from liberalism and reform to conservatism and even reaction. The important objective since early in 1916 had been to maintain rather than to achieve democracy; and to that end Americans were to remember the gospel of the Father of Our Country and avoid "foreign entanglements." So the Democratic Party's campaign slogan, "He kept us out of war," had been sufficient to reelect Wilson.

To Dos Passos and other young idealists, it was quite difficult to understand how the United States could maintain what she had never achieved. They had been ingenuous enough to take their own idealism seriously and to feel they had a right to expect the same of others—even of the President. As time passed, these young men saw none of the lessening of oppression which they had so hoped for and even expected. Instead, they became aware of increasing numbers of men—not only at home but abroad, and perhaps notably in Russia—who were suffering under various forms of despotism. Disillusioned with what appeared to be the mere promises of liberalism, they grew impatient. Some renounced their social consciences altogether and escaped into nonpolitical and even antipolitical aestheticism. Some withdrew into the security of their middle- or upper-class heritages. Some effected the conveniently opportune transfer of their social idealism into patriotism. A few, Dos Passos among them, began a search for a more expedient way to the achievement of their ideals; the way of Marx was tempting. Meanwhile, however, one could lend a hand where help was most needed, take advantage of the opportunity to observe life reduced to its bestial essentials, and perhaps be present at the final collapse which would clear the ground for the new order.

Malcolm Cowley makes a particular point of what he calls the "spectatorial attitude" among these young men, most of them driving ambulances in France, who formed the advance guard of American participation in the war. There was certainly a good deal of this attitude in Dos Passos; indeed, it might even be said that the war made a reporter of him. His first reputation as a novelist came from reporting what he had seen of war in *Three Soldiers* (1921); and he had evidently observed it sufficiently closely and clearly to be able to make it understandable for the first time to many of his readers. He has been observing and reporting contemporary events and places ever since.

But when Dos Passos arrived in France in the spring of 1917, he was not only observing but searching. Intellectually, he was looking for an understanding of the world he lived in. Emotionally (the immediate motivation of the larger search), he was looking for the male companionship, the sense of belonging, and the feeling of identity which his childhood had lacked. The war in France—the nation which had proclaimed as its motto the Liberty, Fraternity, Equality which were to be his lifelong preoccupation—was an almost inspirational choice of hunting ground. The camaraderie of the trenches became a cliché after the war, not before.

In fact, he seems to have found in the war a portion of what he was seeking. His finding companionship could fill for a time at least some of the emptiness which the death of his father in January, 1917, had raised to the level of consciousness. Some indication of the importance of the discovery may be seen in Dos Passos' frequent portrayal of it in his fiction. Its initial occurrence is in his first novel, *One Man's Initiation—1917* (1920),[11] in the relationship between Martin Howe, the central character, and Tom Randolph, his friend and companion in ambulance duty—the prototypes of Telemachus and Lyaeus and other pairs.

Martin, like Dos Passos at the time, is a young intellectual in rebellion. Tom Randolph—one can scarcely escape the connection with John Randolph Dos Passos—is from the South (which through his father's farm in northern Virginia represented for Dos Passos the nearest thing to a home that he had known). Tom is much more the man of the world of the two, and he has an easy and confident manner that Martin admires and envies. When Tom is out with a girl one night, Martin sits alone "dreaming of the woman he would like to love tonight. She should be very dark, with red lips and stained cheeks, like Randolph's girl";[12] and the next day he admits to Tom that "Notre Dame [the cathedral] . . . was my real love of the night."

These two are, to a degree, spectators at the war. Like Cowley himself, they compete good-naturedly for the shrapnel splinter which each wants for a souvenir. For a time they find a retreat in an untouched garden which has a fountain in its center and is adjacent to a war-ruined "little pale salmon-colored villa"; there they meditate about the tiny, surviving natural beauties and about the destruction caused by war. But Martin, at least, is a particularly thoughtful observer. It is he, not Tom Randolph, who upholds the American libertarian objective in the fervent political discussion with four philosophical French soldiers near the end of the book (Chapter IX). It is also Martin who finally summarizes their common conclusion: "Oh, . . . there is hope. . . . We are too young, too needed to fail. We must find a way, find the first step of a way to freedom, or life is a hollow mockery."

Almost the only participation of Tom in the argument is to offer a practical check to the despair of his friend who laments that "we are all slaves . . . willing slaves" of the propaganda machines: "But, Howe, the minute you see that and laugh at it, you're not a slave. Laugh and be individually as decent as you can, and don't worry your head about the rest of the world; and have a good time in spite of the God-damned scoundrels." Except for the injunction about the rest of the world, that is almost precisely the attitude of intelligent hedonism and of responsible nonconformity of John Randolph Dos Passos, as his son later portrayed him in *The 42nd Parallel* and in *Chosen Country*. And without the intellectual ironic elements in that laugh, it is also the outlook of Sancho Panza.

Martin Howe participated too fully and felt too keenly in behalf of "the rest of the world" to be able to laugh, even in irony. Yet partially for that reason, he achieved at the end of the book a purpose and a dedication in life. For all the other hopeful young philosophers were dead; Martin only, like Job's servant, was left alone to tell us and to "find a way."

When he described the futility and enslavement of war in *Three Soldiers*, Dos Passos was writing from somewhat greater perspective than in *One Man's Initiation*. But as he wrote in "A Preface Twenty-Five Years Later" to a reprint of the earlier book (retitled *First Encounter*, 1945), the novel had been written in 1918 "by a bookish young man of twenty-two who . . . was continuing his education driving an ambulance . . . in France." When he was finishing *Three Soldiers* in 1919, that part at least of his education was complete.

With the entrance of the United States into the war in a

temporary recrudescence of active idealism—to make the
world safe for democracy—the Norton-Harjes Ambulance
Unit was taken over by the Red Cross. This ceremony Dos
Passos satirized in *1919* and in *Chosen Country* with scornful
laughter at the Red Cross Majors. But it entered into neither
of his first two books on the war; the war was still too close
for laughter—even in irony.

After the dissolution of Norton-Harjes, he drove an ambulance for the Red Cross in Italy in 1918 and later served
as a private in the medical corps of the army in France until
his discharge in 1919. His two years of ambulance service were
indeed a continued education. He had returned to the United
States, apparently early in 1918 after a censorship scandal
such as produced E. E. Cummings' *The Enormous Room*
(1922) and such as Dos Passos described almost identically
in the careers of Dick Savage in *1919* and of Jay Pignatelli
in *Chosen Country*. Both had written frank but indiscreet
letters, which the censors had misinterpreted. After 1917,
any intelligent soldier or civilian with independent opinions
was endangered if he became articulate.

It was too difficult to maintain one's individuality: in dis-
grace in Paris, Dick Savage came home and succumbed,
pulled wires, and became a top dog; Jay stayed in France
and submerged himself in the physical discipline of the bottom
ranks of the army. Dos Passos seems to have come home,
enlisted as a private in the medical corps, and returned to
France about the first week in November, 1918. His own story
is in his writing. In the preface to *U. S. A.* he recalls the
loneliness of "the training camp at Allentown"; and early in
1919, "washing those windows" at the same camp; and then
on board ship, assigned to the most menial duty of carrying
and emptying swill, "the November gale . . . Hay sojer tell
me they've signed an armistice . . . latrine talk. . . ."[13]

In Europe his almost daily contact with suffering and death
and senseless destruction and his awareness of the contagion
of the social disease in which virtually the whole not-very-
civilized world had become embroiled by 1917 were enough
to make less thoughtful and socially conscious men than he
ponder—as did Martin Howe and his friends—its causes and
the possibilities of their elimination in a society better organized than any that had existed before the war.

In his progress from "gentleman volunteer" to Army private, Dos Passos had seen more and more of his own individual liberties curtailed: *"No there must be some way they taught us Land of the Free conscience Give me liberty or give me Well they give us death . . . to hell with 'em Patrick Henry in khaki submits to shortarm inspection and puts all his pennies in a Liberty Loan or give me"* (Cam. Eye 30). He knew well enough that in April of 1917 making the world safe for democracy meant also to the politicians back home protection from revolutions like the one that had already started in Russia—no matter how oppressed nor how justified the revolutionists. He knew that after November, 1917, it meant making the world safe from Marxism, bolshevism, communism—not because they had been proven inefficient or oppressive, but because they were new, "radical," and "revolutionary." (How, then, had American democracy been born?) The war was not, after all, a war of principles but one of words, a semantic monstrosity in which a quixotic nation fought gallantly and bloodily against a bundle of terms in order to make the world safe for another term whose very meaning it had long since forgotten.

After the Armistice, Dos Passos endured with others the long, embittering winter of petty jobs and petty authority as casuals of the army—casualties of the peace. In that winter in France he had seen the failure of the peace amid the wrangling of the politicians and the disintegration of idealism—except for the futile idealism of Wilson's "faith in words" ("Meester Veelson," *1919*).

In the spring of 1919 Dos Passos willingly waived transportation home and accepted his discharge in France. And he rejoiced that same spring on the first of May, the day scheduled for the great Paris strike that was to begin a great revolution of the downtrodden to establish world-wide liberty, fraternity, equality: "the dates fly off the calendar we'll make everything new today is the Year I . . . We . . . step out wideawake into the first morning of the first day of the first year" (Cam. Eye 39). Here would be participation on a grand scale. But the revolution and even the strike fizzled out in the general post-war apathy. To Dos Passos, as to many others, the year 1919 had already shown itself as a year marked by anticlimax, frustration, disillusionment.[14]

CHAPTER 2

Peregrinations in Print

M ARTIN HOWE in *One Man's Initiation* had expressed his intention in 1918 to go to Spain after the war. The aloof, uncrowded promontory of the peninsula had already become for Dos Passos the place to retire to for a clearer view of the world whenever the turmoil and pressure of events threatened to obscure his vision. In Madrid in December, 1919, he wrote for the *Liberator* the first of his postwar contributions to periodicals, "In Portugal," in which he briefly reported his trip to that country and his hopeful impressions of the imminence of revolution there.

In the six years following the publishing of this article (April, 1920) until the appearance of the *New Masses* in 1926, Dos Passos contributed some thirty-eight pieces, of which a third were poems, to fourteen separate American journals. Although one offering appeared in the New York *Tribune*, the journals were with few other exceptions artistically or politically radical—and many were also ephemeral. The contributions other than poems were nearly all a kind of critical, impressionistic reporting of cultural and political events; and most of them were later included in what are usually called his "travel books": *Rosinante to the Road Again* (1922), *Orient Express* (1927), *In All Countries* (1934), and *Journeys Between Wars* (1938).

I *Search for Allegiance, Escape*

Although, from the standpoint of the periodicals, this might be called Dos Passos' radical-experimental period, the political ideas of his contributions seem scarcely extreme. He did seem hopeful about communism and revolution in

"In Portugal"; but in "The Caucasus Under the Soviets," an article written in Tiflis in the Soviet Republic of Georgia late in 1921 and published in August, 1922, in the same radical periodical, the *Liberator* (the successor to the Communist-Greenwich Village *Masses*), he was very cautious. He was, as before, hopeful about the social prospects of the area; but he was hopeful because of the tendency of the Communist government towards an "untheoretical attempt to conserve what's left of the old civilization"—and despite his "impression that communism in Russia is a dead shell." Although he submitted a plea for American relief for the "40 millions starving in the Volga Basin," he was frankly concerned about the lack of old people—had they all "been shot by the Tcheka"? And he was strongly critical of the terrorism of the Russian court system under which the continuance of military tribunals in peacetime made the "lack of security . . . intolerable."

Probably the most politically interesting of his writings of this period is the article "America and the Pursuit of Happiness," printed in the last issue of the *Nation* of 1920. In it Dos Passos speaks of "the duty of the individual to his conscience, in the good round 18th century term" as of more importance than all the cant about the citizen's duty to his government:

> Not until a large and aggressive body of our citizens has formed the habit of loudly and immediately repudiating every abuse internal or external of the government's authority and every instance of bullying mob intolerance will we as a nation show that "decent respect for the opinions of mankind" necessary to reconquer the confidence of the . . . [essential, freedom-loving] body of foreign opinion. . . . Somehow, in these dark days ahead, a compact Opposition must be built up which shall keep up contacts with the outside world. . . . And particularly for the sake of our peace with our nearest neighbors the Latin Americans, Spanish-speaking peoples must be made to feel that there is . . . in the United States . . . a body of opinion that puts humanity before national interests and class interests."

All this does not seem particularly revolutionary today. In fact his search for "the 'liberty and pursuit of happiness' of that original too long forgotten declaration of our aims" is very like a plea for a return to the-good-old-days.

One of the points of interest in the article is that it rather closely resembles in content an editorial Dos Passos had published four and a half years earlier in the *Harvard Monthly* for June, 1916. In "A Conference on Foreign Relations," he had mentioned a spirit of "discontent with the spineless and cowardly temporizing which has become the tradition of our foreign policy." As a remedy he had called for a "strong and organized public opinion" to bring "order . . . into the desperate chaos of our Euorpean world," but he had also warned that we must steer clear of "the Scylla of grape-juice moralizing and the Charybdis of long-haired ultra-socialism" to achieve "a middle course of forceful common sense."

His father in *The Anglo-Saxon Century* had declared the motive of his writing to be "the elimination of war and the advancement of civilisation." These were clearly Dos Passos' aims in his early articles. The difference was that civilization presumably having been achieved at home among "the most worthy" (i.e., Anglo-Saxons), the elder Dos Passos had felt that it was "now manifest that to this great race [was] entrusted the civilisation and christianisation of the world." But the son could admit no such presumption; to him all of this had yet to be achieved at home.

Moreover, he had not yet found his national allegiance. The search for one was, of course, a principal reason for Dos Passos' peripatetic inquiries into the natures of peoples, their lands, and their institutions during these and later years. That is why he accepted his discharge in France in 1919 and went to live in Spain; why he visited Portugal and the countries of the Near East, including Georgia in the U.S.S.R., while traveling for the Near East Relief; why, back in America in 1923, he published in the March issue of *The Arts* a poem of disillusionment, "In the Tents of the Agail," in which he contrasted the simple freedom of the desert with the constricting superficialities of life in America. His search is also the reason that, as the periodical noted, the author of *Three Soldiers* and *Pushcart at the Curb* (1922) had just sailed for Spain but would contribute to *The Arts* from that country.

In spite of his wanderings, however, he had written *Three Soldiers* while in Spain in 1919; he had completed *Streets of Night* (1923), which he had probably begun while he was still at Harvard; and, living mostly in New York from

1923 to 1925, he had written *Manhattan Transfer* (1925). These books are worth examining in some detail in a later chapter, but for the moment it is enough to look briefly at some of their protaganists, for each of the novels is the narrative of Telemachus searching for Odysseus so that both may return home.

Although *Three Soldiers* deals with the lives during the war of three young men—Fuselli, Chrisfield, and John Andrews—the last of these is the real protagonist. John Andrews, "when he had been a child . . . had had so many dreams; lying under the crepe myrtle bush at the end of the overgrown garden he had passed the long Virginia afternoons, thinking. . . ." His mother had taught him to play the piano when he was very small. "She and I lived alone in an old house belonging to her family in Virginia. . . . My mother is the only person who has ever really had any importance in my life."

Doomed to be a misfit in the army, John Andrews, within hours of his induction, "was washing windows." This humiliating, boring, deadening work became for him the symbol of his slavery and his humiliation. He was forced to perform the same chore over and over again in his nagging conscience from the second chapter to the last. They were the same windows that Dos Passos again washed in the first Camera Eye of *1919,* and finally recalled specifically at the beginning of *Tour of Duty* (1946), a nonfiction account of his reporting of the next generation's war: "Recollections . . . memories of other lonesome waits . . . of the time when I had to wash all those windows at the camp in Allentown." After enduring a number of humiliations for which they provided the symbol, John Andrews had asserted to a friend, "I'm going to write a book on slave psychology." This was Dos Passos' second such book, and he was to write more about the same theme; for all of Dos Passos' novels and his three plays deal at least in part with this subject.

But Andrews had deliberately enlisted in the faceless unity of the army: "This was what he had sought. . . . It was in this that he would take refuge from the horror of the world that had fallen on him. He was sick of revolt, of thought, of carrying his individuality like a banner above the turmoil. This was much better . . . to humble himself into the mud of common slavery. [But] he was still tingling with sudden anger at the officer's voice that morning. . . . 'Ain't this some film?' Chrisfield turned to him with a smile that drove his anger away in a pleasant feeling of comradeship."

John Andrews was twenty-two—just Dos Passos' age in January, 1918. Chrisfield was twenty, a strong, healthy country boy, passionate and physical in his responses; and with him Andrews shared most of his army experience. Chrisfield rather admired and followed Andrews than the reverse—and his admiration and support were essential to the older boy. But Andrews had other acquaintances, after he separated from Chrisfield, who filled in other ways the role of confidant and comrade and who even provided inspiration.

Among these was Henslowe, a brilliant voluptuary and a laughing cynic who transgressed all the barriers and invariably got away with it; he was A.W.O.L. when Andrews met him. Another was Marcel, a French farm boy. Possibly most important was the Kid who knew Andrews simply as "Skinny" when both of them were prisoners; for Andrews had been charged, unjustly, with desertion. The Kid gave Andrews the sudden courage to escape by swimming the Seine—truly to desert, a thing which Andrews later considered the only manly thing he had ever done. Andrews could then resume his own name, having not only asserted his identity by purposeful action but undergone his baptism—like Huck Finn before him and Frederick Henry after him—by total immersion in the river which was the means of his escape.

We might note, however, that this fairly common symbol of regeneration by water is not necessarily consciously used as such either by Clemens or by Hemingway in *A Farewell to Arms* (1929)—despite the striking similarities between their two books and Hemingway's admitted debt to Clemens. But in *Three Soldiers* it is clearly intentional; for Andrews specifically imagines much earlier in the book the regeneration he later undergoes. "He thought of himself crashing naked through the film of ice into water black as Chinese lacquer. And when he climbed out numb and panting on the other side, wouldn't he be able to take up life again as if he had just been born?" But first he must get to "the other side" —discover the symbolic father missing from his childhood, and so return home to begin life anew. John Andrews—like his friends Chrisfield and the Kid—never got to "the other side." Chrisfield succumbed to fear of the military police; the Kid drowned trying to escape them; and Andrews, at the end of the book, is rearrested for desertion.

Wenny, or David Wendell of *Streets of Night*, which is centered almost wholly in Boston, also made his escape in the river—but in the Charles instead of the Seine. He considered it in advance as his only courageous act, but it was premeditated suicide (much as Andrews' enlistment had been): he was unable to cross his Rubicon. Physically and temperamentally Wenny was the natural, sensuous man: "passionate impulsive hot," his friend Fanshaw thought him. The following shows how he affected Nan, the third of the three friends whom the book is about: "Somewhere at the end of a long corridor of her mind she ran through the dappled shadow of woods, naked, swift, chased by someone brown, flushed, goatfooted. She could feel in her nostrils the roughness of the smell of Wenny's damp homespun suit. Aprèsmidi d'un Faune." But Wenny, the son of a minister with whom he had almost nothing in common, had been brought up by a maiden aunt—"She was a fine woman. She died the year I went to college"—and educated by her and by Harvard into a timid, strait-jacketed conformity. His whole education had frozen his ability to act as his real self— except in his occasional honest, sometimes cynical laughter at all the pettinesses of life. When it came to purposeful action, he was a marble faun.

Fanshaw Macdougan, Wenny's friend, was a timid aesthete —almost identical with those Dos Passos had satirized in his *Harvard Monthly* stories—who had stayed on at Harvard as an instructor in fine arts. To him, Wenny represented all the natural manly virtues that he, Fanshaw, lacked. Tied by affection and inanition to his invalid mother (his father had died in Fanshaw's childhood), he had needed Wenny to teach him whatever courageous impulses he had had in his inconsequential life. In the same way, Whitey—a skinny, carefree young bum Wenny had met—had given Wenny the courage to try to escape into life, and, failing in that, to escape the futility of living.

II *Other Images of Self*

Jimmy Herf of *Manhattan Transfer* we first meet as a small boy on shipboard in the care of his mother; he is returning from Europe to what he has been told is his country, although he has forgotten it. It is July Fourth as they sail by the Statue of Liberty, and Jimmy feels the need to express his attachment to his country. The flag he would have liked to be able to wave like the other little boys has been packed away in the shawlstrap; but, when someone tells him he looks glad to be home, he says: "Oh I am, I could fall down and kiss the ground." Grownups laugh at him; and, since he has not the nerve to do it, he does nothing.

Jimmy seems not to remember his father. When he finds mustard too hot for him at dinner one evening, his mother Lily Herf tells him he must " 'learn to like hot things. . . . He always liked hot things?' 'Who mother?' 'Someone I loved very much.' " That same evening, his mother has a stroke, and Jimmy finds his escape in books, and then must go back to boarding school—"He and Skinny coming back from playing with the hoptoads down by the pond." And there are other memories of school: "Herfy an the Kid are goin to fight . . . before lights." We could go on at length documenting characteristics that Dos Passos has given this image of the self that we have met before and will meet again.

Jimmy's friend after high-school age is Stanwood Emery, a wealthy ne'er-do-well who, however, does what he likes, drinking and whoring, laughing at the world to the admiration of Herf: "Gee you get away with murder Stan . . . in everything. . . . I never can get away with a thing." Stan gets all the girls, even Ellen Thatcher, the talented actress who is another principal character. He would like to be an architect, but he burns himself up, literally, as the whole city is doing (fire-engines are a principal symbol in the book). So Herf eventually marries Ellen while they are both overseas during the war in the Red Cross; and they return with a baby named Martin, after Jimmy's best friend, a socialist (whose last name, mentioned only once, happens to be Schiff rather than Howe). Martin Howe of *One Man's Initiation* is, however, reborn in the writer, Jimmy Herf; Martin Schiff has lost his nerve and so drifts aimlessly in the sterile sea of Greenwich

Village radicalism; the baby, Martin Herf, will have his own struggle to discover and affirm his identity in a hostile world —just as Jimmy is forced to leave his family in his desperate quest to know and to be himself.

Herf feels the whole world and his own marriage going to pieces, but he doesn't know the answer: "God I wish I could blame it all on capitalism the way Martin does." Finally, having thrown up his newspaper job, he imagines the loss of his twenties (in January, 1925, the year *Manhattan Transfer* was published, Dos Passos was twenty-nine): "James Herf . . . recently lost his twenties . . . they were remanded to Ellis Island for deportation as undesirable aliens. The younger four Sasha Michael Nicholas and Vladimir had been held for some time on a charge of criminal anarchy. The fifth and sixth"—1921-22, the years Dos Passos was wandering in Europe and the Near East—"were held on a technical charge of vagrancy. The later ones Bill Tony and Joe were held under various indictments. . . . All were convicted on counts of misfeasance, malfeasance, and nonfeasance."

In 1923, 1924, 1925 Dos Passos was living principally in New York; by 1925 he had written books about Martin Howe, John Andrews, Telemachus, David Wendell, Fanshaw, and Jimmy Herf, all of whom were, or were considered to be, or thought themselves guilty on all three counts—and particularly of "nonfeasance." Just before the end of *Manhattan Transfer* we meet two young boys, Joe and Skinny, who are scared by a crazy but friendly old tramp while they are playing in the park. Joe—Joseph Cameron Parker—reminds us again of the loss of identity symbolized by the change of his Latin name; Skinny—the second Skinny in the book—knows better who he is: "Antonio Camerone . . . de guys call me Skinny. Dis guy's my cousin. His folks dey changed deir name to Parker, see?" At the end, Jimmy Herf, who at least has begun to discover who he is not, has cut all his ties and is hitchhiking out of town, "Pretty far."

III   *"The New Masses"—To Its Left*

From 1922 or 1923 to 1925 Dos Passos lived in New York, but in February and March of 1926 he was in Mexico reporting the plight of the repressed, exploited peons. He found normalcy in Mexico no less distasteful than in the United States, and he came back to help launch the *New Masses*[1] in May and perhaps to keep a few ideas and ideals warm during the Coolidge era. His first two contributions to the *New Masses* appeared in June in the second number. The first was an indignant report, written the preceding fall, of police forbidding a meeting. The second was an editorial setting forth his views of what the magazine should and should not be.[2]

The editorial, "The New Masses [*sic*] I'd Like," is the more important. After admitting that he was "a bourgeois intellectual," he stated his misgivings:

> At this moment . . . the word-slinging classes, radical and fundamentalist, are further from reality than they have ever been. . . . As mechanical power grows in America general ideas tend to restrict themselves more and more to Karl Marx, the first chapter of Genesis and the hazy scientific mysticism of the Sunday supplements. I don't think it's any time for any group of spellbinders to lay down the law on any subject whatsoever. Particularly I don't think there should be any more phrases, badges, opinions, banners, imported from Russia or anywhere else. . . . Why not develop our own brand?

Having asserted his independence of communist doctrine, he proposed suggestions critical of communist practice:

> In these terribly crucial years . . . being clearsighted is a life and death matter. If we could ever find out what was really going on we might be able to formulate a theory of what to do about it. Why shouldn't the New Masses [*sic*] be setting out on a prospecting trip, drilling in unexpected places. . . ? I think there's much more to be gained by rigorous exploration than by sitting by the sidelines of the labor movement with a red rosette in your buttonhole and cheering for the home team. . . . The tendency of the Masses [*sic*] has always been to be more disciplined in thought than in action. I'd like to see that state of things reversed for once. I'd like to see a magazine full of introspection and doubt that would be like a piece of litmus paper to test things by. . . . November, 1917, is in the past. . . . The *New Masses* must at all costs avoid the great future that lies behind it.

There is the quest for knowledge—"general ideas"—and the familiar "Humble Protest," as in 1916, against its prostration

Blairsville High School Library

"before the popular gods of materialism, on the one hand, and the inner shrine of science, of divine fact, on the other." There is the challenge, again as in 1916 in the form of a question, to produce our own, contemporary phrases, opinions, banners. In "Against American Literature" in the *New Republic* of October 14, 1916, Dos Passos had expressed his opinion that "our only course is to press on. . . . Or shall we stagnate forever . . . absorbing the thought, patronizing the art of other peoples, but producing nothing from amid our jumble of races but steel and oil and grain?" And here still is the principle of doubt of the "Humble Protest": "Are we so certain . . . that there must be no discussion of the question?"

Granville Hicks, citing Dos Passos' participation in the *New Masses* ventures as evidence that he was close to the communist viewpoint, says: "The communists, as Dos Passos must have known, were running the show."[3] It appears that he knew very well that they at least *intended* to run it. Dos Passos' plea—containing in the whole article at least five pointed references to the impertinence of Russian communism—was that the magazine should devote itself to the interests of the working classes it purported to serve and that it discover those interests in contemporary life and not in any slavish adherence to doctrine. "I charge thee Cromwell, avoid dogmatism," Jay's (i.e., Dos Passos') father had quoted at him, a bit sententiously, in *Chosen Country*. Dos Passos' position at this time was—because of his greater faith in the real and potential ability of individuals among the non-communist masses and because of his attitude that "a theory of what to do" about conditions was still to be found—considerably to the *left* of that of the communists. And his statement of his position, all things considered, was perhaps even more courageous than the protest which landed him in jail about a year later.

IV *A Matter of Principles*

From 1920 to 1927 the mass indoctrination in conformity and nationalism—which George Creel had so successfully instituted during the war, and which Attorney General Palmer so energetically pursued after it—bore its fruits in one of many instances of militant intolerance: the notorious

Sacco-Vanzetti case. It was inevitable that this case, which enlisted the sympathies of men and women of all opinions both at home and abroad in behalf of its defendants, should have been of vital, almost personal interest to Dos Passos. The principles involved were nearly all those for which he then stood. And was he not—himself the grandson of a Latin immigrant—professing views which were at least as "radical" as those of Sacco and Vanzetti and which corresponded to theirs at many points? Was he not as "guilty" as they? For certainly, in the absence of proven guilt, it appeared plain that it was as "anarchist wops" rather than as murderers that they had been condemned.

Dos Passos' first play, *The Garbage Man* (New York, 1926) was produced at this time; and, as he says, he "started in 1926, I think,"[4] working intermittently to help design and paint stage scenery for the New Playwrights Theater. In 1926-27 the Sacco-Vanzetti case, however, undoubtedly absorbed much of the energy which Dos Passos was not expending upon his writing and for the theater. Indeed, in the later months of the case his concern about the oppression of Sacco and Vanzetti elicited some of his most eloquent prose.[5]

At this time, August of 1927, Dos Passos also achieved what must have been his nearest identification with the men (average citizens, particularly minorities) and the cause (freedom from oppression) that had always aroused his strongest sympathies. He was twice arrested; he appealed despite the threat of more severe charges if he did appeal, and he was finally jailed—in the same cell with the communist Michael Gold, editor of the *New Masses*—for demonstrating in behalf of the two condemned men. One can imagine, even had Dos Passos not expressed it (in Camera Eye Fifty of *U. S. A.*), his sense of frustration and his heightened disgust at the perversion of democracy in the United States when, on August 23, 1927, Sacco and Vanzetti were executed: "they have clubbed us off the streets   they are stronger   they are rich . . . they hire the men with guns . . . there is nothing left to do   we are beaten . . . our work is over   the scribbled phrases . . . the search for stinging words . . . America our nation has been beaten by strangers who have turned our language inside out who have taken the clean words our fathers spoke and made them slimy and foul . . . all right we are two nations . . . we stand defeated America."

Meanwhile, Dos Passos had been continuing his periodical contributions, chiefly to the *New Masses*; these included an editorial, "Lèse Majesté," of July, 1927, in which he protested the conviction of an eighteen-year-old author of a *Daily Worker* poem whose only crime was "saying 'Damn the United States' like the man in Edward Everett Hale's story." Another "Man Without a Country," Dos Passos himself had come to accept America as "our nation" at least as early as his writing of *Manhattan Transfer*. And he had come to understand and to love "the clean words our fathers spoke." But now in the gloom, the resentment, the frustration of defeat, when even the words, his stock-in-trade, his only weapon, had been "turned . . . inside out," he "seceded privately," he explains in *The Theme Is Freedom* (1956); and he did so "the night Sacco and Vanzetti were electrocuted."

In his "Open Letter to President Lowell," which appeared in the *Nation* the day after the electrocution, Dos Passos referred to "the coming struggle for the reorganization of society," which he foresaw as being either "bloodless and fertile or inconceivably bloody and destructive." In December, now devoting more of his time to the New Playwrights Theater in its second season, he wrote for the *New Masses* "Towards a Revolutionary [American] Theatre," in which he gave his opinion that it was not then possible "for a group to be alive and have no subversive political tendency." For "a group" he might have more characteristically substituted "an individual."

Although he had, at the end of April, contributed a similar article, "Propaganda in the Theatre," to the *Daily Worker* and was listed among "contributors" to it in its half-page advertisement in the *New Masses* of March, 1928, the advertisement seems to have been largely mere publicity. He was also a director of the New Playwrights Theater, and of his position he later wrote in fiction that Jed Morris, the protagonist of *Most Likely To Succeed* (1954), "was elected . . . because his was the best known name." But he was already familiar with the figurehead device in *Manhattan Transfer*: "Well Dougan's got to be president cause he's the best lookin."

At any rate, by June, 1928, his "subversive political tendency" had apparently eliminated him from the executive board of the *New Masses;* for he then and afterward appeared only as one of its contributing editors. And in "They Want Ritzy Art" of the same June issue Dos Passos published his review of the experience of the New Playwrights; he reserved his finest scorn for the *Daily Worker's* suspicious discovery of "deviations among the New Playwrights." "The socialist press," on the other hand, had "said we were communists in sheep's clothing," and the New York theatergoer's "first reaction [had been] . . . to get up and walk out at the first unfamiliar sight or sound; except when recent trips abroad [had] . . . planted a seed of doubt."

The United States was perhaps after all "two nations"; and Dos Passos had reason, by the spring of 1928, as a confessed "bourgeois intellectual," to question to which one he really belonged. He had been in the country a full year. His own seed of doubt had already blossomed into the full flower of scepticism; but it was time to stand off again, to take new bearings. "Who am I? What do I want? Where am I going?" he asked himself before leaving New York for Russia on the trip reported in his book *In All Countries* (1934). Furthermore, the life of the theater had been stimulating but wearing. He needed a rest; and to a lover of the sea and to a son of Odysseus, "There is no sleep so good as sleep in a ship's bunk."

Dos Passos tells a pathetic little story of his trip to Europe and Russia. His cabin-mate, Mr. Hansen, a small, aging bachelor who had saved a tiny fortune, had been brimming with enthusiasm at going back to Denmark after twenty-five lonely years in America. When Dos Passos met him again in Copenhagen, "he seemed a little too glad to see another American." Denmark had refused to remain static for twenty-five years; the people, the places, the customs, even the language were strange and uncongenial. A Dane in America, an American in Denmark, he thought he would "go back to the States" where "he could have his same job again." Dos Passos then went to a remembered Paris, where he found all the old wartime romance worn off: "often it's painful snapshots I seem to have taken myself some years ago . . . well it may have been always like that. I keep a timetable in my pocket all the time. You and me, Mr. Hansen."

Later, however, on the Finland sleeper, "it was fine . . . joggling toward the actual existing to-be-seen-with-my-own-eyes so bloodily contested Frontier between yesterday and tomorrow." In Russia, the air was exhilaratingly full of history made and a-making. There was the sense of vigor and youth and work among the people; the theater was full of life and growth. But there was the "Terror" (a whole subchapter of it), including the memory of the massacre of the sailors who had revolted at Kronstadt in 1921; and after Dos Passos' experience of this terror through an acquaintance, there was "that night I couldn't sleep." There was the Russian driver who complained of too much liberty and wanted a Hindenburg "to put every man in his place." There were the absurd though subtle dialectic distinctions between science and counterrevolution. There was the country place that "looked like home; but . . . there was none of the flare and the excitement of the American autumn."

And so the Americanski Peesatyel, as Dos Passos called himself, queried: "But speaking of home, how much do you know about home, Mr. A. Peesatyel?" He found "all the old habits of thirty years of life . . . straining away towards the west . . . and all the cheerful trivial accustomed world." For the first time in his voluminous travel writings, Dos Passos was showing distinct traces of homesickness.

Writing in *The Theme Is Freedom* of his "secession" in August, 1927, Dos Passos has said: "I wasn't joining anybody." It's clear enough that he wasn't joining the communists, much less the Russians; nor the French; nor the expatriates in Paris whom he encountered on his way to Russia, "the anachronistic phonies with long hair who sit in the little square on the top of Montmartre." But at home (we can use that expression of him now in spite of its ambiguity) in America in 1929, he had sufficiently discovered who he was and what he wanted to be willing to join in a permanent relationship. In September, 1929, he married Katharine F. Smith, an old friend and schoolmate of Hadley Richardson Hemingway, the first wife of Dos Passos' friend of those days, Ernest Hemingway.

At the time of his marriage Dos Passos was finishing *The 42nd Parallel*, which was to be published in February, 1930; and he was contributing also to the *New Masses* articles

chiefly concerned with problems of artistic form and craftsmanship. The last of these, published in December, is a
review in high praise of Hemingway's *Farewell to Arms,*
in which he took the occasion to comment: "As industrial society evolves and the workers get control of the
machines a new type of craftsmanship may work out." This
acceptance of the *evolutionary* concept of change may seem
a new one in a man who was even then associating with
revolutionaries and, in fact, stating his position in their periodical. It may seem odd that only months before, in "The Making
of a Writer" in the March *New Masses,* he had asserted a kind
of envious admiration for the communist Michael Gold—that
he was born "a worker instead of an unclassed bourgeois"
and that he could accept "the discipline of the Worker's
Party." Yet the important point is that Dos Passos could not
accept its or any other outside discipline on his thinking.
Even at the time of his "secession," his warning to President
Lowell and to Lowell's class had been that "the coming
struggle" must be bloodless to be fertile—that is, more or less
gradual.

In September of 1929 Dos Passos had asked the *New Republic* to send him to Gastonia, North Carolina, to report
the textile strike there (the first major labor battle by a communist union). But according to Edmund Wilson, then of the
New Republic, he was "thought too far to the left to be reliable from our point of view." The following month the
stock market crash started the swing of liberals and of the
New Republic to the left—much closer to the position of what
Wilson has since called the "imaginary Dos Passos" of the
communists' wishful thinking. This mythical Dos Passos,
Wilson explains while speaking of the early thirties, was
necessary to the "Communist critical movement in America"
before it could identify its ideal—as it tended to do—with Dos
Passos' work. This example of the extraordinary success of
the communists in creating and sustaining myths may account
in part for the attitude of the *New Republic* and of Wilson
himself in September, 1929;[6] it may also account for a political
influence which Dos Passos even then would have preferred
not to have had.

At any rate, by December 18 the *New Republic* had so far
accepted Dos Passos as to print as its lead article his essay-

review, "Edison and Steinmetz: Medicine Men." In it he was again protesting the pervasive American practicality "carried . . . to a point verging on lunacy," the piling up scientific miracles until, like the Sorcerer's Apprentice, the people were overwhelmed by them. Here also was his familiar protest that in America it was the "cashers-in" who were in control. Only the term "cashers-in" was new; but, though merely another name for "exploiters," it may have smelled sweeter to sensitive nostrils already irritated by the red pepper of communist phraseology.

I have implied that this article in the *New Republic* in December, 1929, indicates a slight leftward shift in the politics of that liberal journal. But it denotes also a shift in Dos Passos, not so much in his political outlook as in his conception of his relationship to the society in which he was living and working.

One stimulus to his shift may be seen, ironically enough, in the remark of Michael Gold which had prompted Dos Passos' first contribution to the *New Masses* almost four years earlier. When Gold had called him a bourgeois intellectual, Dos Passos had referred to the epithet as a "salutary truth." As late as March, 1929, he was still envying Gold's having been born a worker instead of "an unclassed bourgeois" such as he. But by the winter of 1929-30 he seems to have come to a fuller acceptance of his position in the social-economic scale—intellectually, he had admitted it all along—and to have conducted himself accordingly. (I should state here that I make nothing of the coincidence of this "shift" and his first marriage, except to suggest, as I have, that both—like many decisions of most of us—are related to emotional growth.)

During the five years from December, 1929, to November, 1934, Dos Passos was contributing principally to the *New Republic*. In his "Open Letter to President Lowell" of Harvard in another liberal journal, the *Nation*, in August, 1927, on the subject of the conduct of the class struggle, Dos Passos had said, "It is upon men of your class and position that will rest the inevitable decision." Now, in his third and fourth appearances in the *New Republic* and in his final contribution (except for early versions of portions of *1919*) to the *New Masses* until 1934, he was directing himself specifically to middle-class liberals and writing as one of them—as "a middle-class liberal, whether I like it or not." And he added for the benefit of the communists at the *New Masses*: "You can call 'em intellectuals or liberals or petty bourgeoisie or any other dirty name but it won't change 'em any." The last of these three similar pieces appeared as a letter in the *New Republic* on August 13. In it he concluded that it was "the business-class," the source of "that mysterious force, public opinion," that was the one important group which might be made to "hate cruelty or tolerate the idea of change."[7]

Meanwhile, throughout this five-year period (1929-1934), his writing almost without exception was in behalf of the laboring class. His sympathy with their privations and suffering in the depression and under anti-strike laws, vagrancy and right-to-work laws, criminal syndicalism laws, and so on made him champion the workers' cause—and not only in his writing. In 1930-31 Dos Passos helped organize the Emergency Committee for Southern Prisoners; and in the summer of 1931 he appeared as chairman—in a half-page advertisement in *The Left* and in "An Appeal for Aid" in the *New Republic*— of the National Committee to Aid Striking Miners Fighting Starvation.[8]

In the fall of 1931 he and Theodore Dreiser went with some other writers to report the strike in the coal fields of Harlan County, Kentucky, and to test the violations there of civil rights. Later Dos Passos, Dreiser, and others in the group were indicted under Kentucky's criminal syndicalism law. (Dreiser, in fact, had been arrested while in Kentucky, on a morals charge for which his ingenious defense was that he was an old man and impotent.) Dos Passos, though importuned by the communists—who, in common with other religious minds of a certain type, appear to cherish martyrs— to return to stand trial, refused: "They would have to come and fetch me. Of course they never did."[9]

In 1931-32 he reported the depression from Washington and Detroit and the national conventions from Chicago in five articles in the *New Republic* (reprinted in his book *In All Countries*), and he managed to sandwich in a trip before the June conventions that year to note the exploitations by United Fruit in Central America.[10] On August 24, 1932, there appeared a letter in the *Nation* (and another in the *New Republic*) in behalf of the Scottsboro boys: "The two youngest Negro boys of the nine victims of the attempted legal lynching in Scottsboro, Alabama, are still in prison. . . . We appeal to men and women of imagination and humanity. . . . Please send your check to John Dos Passos, Treasurer, National Committee for the Defense of Political Prisoners." And in October was yet another appeal, this one for contributions to the support of the new National Student League.[11]

In October and November, Dos Passos attended the Madison Square Garden rallies of the four principal contending parties; retired to Provincetown to cast his protest vote for Foster and Ford, the Communist candidates; and then wrote his observations for the first issue of *Common Sense*: "Where was the Forgotten Man in all these meetings, the citizen of Hooverville, the down and out guy. . . ? The forgotten man didn't go to the Socialist meeting . . . he isn't in evidence at the Communist rally and celebration of the Fifteenth Anniversary of the October Revolution, either." And so began the *Common Sense* division of Dos Passos' liberal period among the periodicals.[12]

The liberal band in the political spectrum is almost by definition a broad one which can contain a variety of political tints. And so it could contain Dos Passos for a decade— until about the end of 1939 when he ended his association with *Common Sense* in something of a bang with an appropriate peroration in appreciation of Tom Paine.[13] During this period when he was writing as a liberal, in liberal journals, and for a liberal audience, he maintained a steady progress in his unceasing quest.

CHAPTER 3

Homeward Bound

TELEMACHUS was homeward bound. In December, 1928, Dos Passos had spent a sleepless night in Moscow listening to the arguments of his Mentor—his skepticism, his intellectual bent—unwilling to commit himself for communism. Then he had made his leap onto the westbound train, had crossed the sea, and so had escaped Calypso's roseate isle.[1] But she would continue to mourn him. As late as November, 1944, Dos Passos reported in *Tour of Duty* that a Ukrainian schoolteacher he met in Vienna expressed to him his own and his nation's disappointment that Dos Passos "had not written any work saluting the achievements of the Soviet Union."

Telemachus was not yet home. But by 1929 Minerva, perhaps in the shape of Katharine Smith, had appeared to reveal to him that it was at home that Odysseus was to be found. Almost immediately Dos Passos established his first real personal home in Provincetown on Cape Cod—among other artists and in a town of Portuguese fishermen, where it is scarcely possible to be out of sight of the sea. There in microcosm was the objective of his quest begun in Spain between 1916 and 1921. As Telemachus in *Rosinante*, he had found some companionship in his friend and practical mentor, Lyaeus, who represented even then the Sancho Panza proletariat; but it was not enough. He had found a part of his heritage in the Iberian culture, but it was only a part. Now both were merging and enlarging.

I *To His Own Kind*

With the assured, intimate companionship of his wife and with friendships, if he chose them, among men of similar interests, he could afford to be more independent in his relationships with others. The winter before in Russia, he had commented that "like the leech a writer is a varmint that can't get any sustenance from his own kind. . . . Of course you can't help getting to be friends with some of them; then you stop thinking of them as writers and it's all right." He no longer needed their sustenance, and so it became easier to consider them "his own kind" and to find pleasure in their company. But his great capacity for love and human sympathy required an external object which could release and absorb it, as well as subjects to reflect and renew it. This object he found in the "workers travailleurs greasers" that had first awakened his sympathetic affection, then his indignation, and finally his admiration because of their stubborn resistance to oppression.

Lyaeus, till now, had been a frustratingly unsympathetic companion. Laughing at the vain idealism and ingrained repressions of his friend Telemachus, he had always taken his liberty and his pleasures as his rights, like the sun he loved and the air he breathed. Yet his practical common sense had been valuable instruction for Telemachus, who, profiting from it, had learned a good deal about himself and the world he lived in. Dos Passos had learned that he was not a Lyaeus himself, that he had been born "an unclassed bourgeois" and educated beyond the possibility of becoming otherwise; and he had come, with difficulty, not only to accept his position but to expect no return of affection or sympathy from those upon whom he expended so much.

For Dos Passos, this acceptance permitted at last his identification with a larger group of "his own kind"—middle-class liberals with whom, without necessarily liking them or even being like them, he could make some common cause. And this identification, in turn, released him from his futile struggle to become one of the proletariat. He could still love them, admire them, work for them—in fact, better than before because unburdened of his need for a response from them and, therefore, better able to see where their needs lay.

II   *"The Communist" Problem*

To say that by the beginning of 1929 Dos Passos had escaped Russian communism and that by the end of it he had freed himself of personal commitments to the working class is not necessarily, however, to say anything at all about his relations with the American Communist Party. Nor is it particularly important to an understanding of the man that these be minutely traced. But we can now draw a few conclusions as informed guesses, if no better, which may help to clarify this much-discussed subject.

Apparently Dos Passos was conversant with at least some of the principles of Marxism during his years at Harvard. His third and final contributions to the *Harvard Monthly* had been reviews of books by John Reed, whom he admired; and in his next-to-last appearance he was warning of "the Charybdis of long-haired ultra-socialism." Between November, 1917, and December, 1919, he seems to have accepted the identification between Russian communism and the world proletariat: "The story of Russia has spread among the peasants and workmen" in Portugal, and "the days of the politician and of the bourgeois seem numbered."[2] Although between his first trip to the Caucasus in 1921 and his third in 1928, he became less and less able to accept Russian interpretation and still less Russian dictation of Marxist doctrine, he seemed at the same time to be growing closer to the American Communist Party.

Although his own emotional needs were among the reasons, there were others. The break with Russia in no way seemed to imply a necessary break with Marxism and its ideal of a classless society to which all would belong. With the increase of reaction and of cycles of oppression in America, it seemed more and more necessary that something be done; and the communist organization appeared to him as the only one sufficiently disciplined and well organized to have a chance of accomplishing anything.

However, when he joined the communists—but not their party—in establishing the *New Masses* in 1926, he did so—as he made plain in "The New Masses I'd Like"—in the hope of making contact with the masses, of learning their needs, and not of preaching to them: "Wouldn't a blank sheet for men and women who have never written before to write on as no one has ever written before be better than an instruction book, whether the instructions come from Moscow or Bethlehem, Pennsylvania?" And his increasing activity in the early thirties among what later came to be known as communist-front organizations should probably be regarded as evidence of his willingness to work cooperatively for the immediate goals he believed in. His endeavor was unquestionably not evidence of his control by the communists.

Yet the myth of Dos Passos the Communist, assiduously propagated in the thirties by Granville Hicks and Michael Gold and others, took hold. Furthermore, it was upon the mythmakers themselves—as so often happens—that it took hold most completely. Thus we have from Gold in 1933 the revealing sentence: "Dos Passos has always been dangerously honest." He goes on to conclude that "the future" would find Dos Passos "enlisted completely in the service of the co-operative society. He does not retreat. He goes forward."[3] Gold was right, but he was whistling in the dark. Dos Passos was at the time moving rapidly forward, but directly away from communism and the particular kind of cooperative so-ciety—and especially from the methods of bringing it about— that Gold envisioned. And in 1950 (in the March *Antioch Review*) Granville Hicks, eleven years after his own renunci-ation of the faith, devoted thirteen pages to an attempted demonstration that in the 1930's Dos Passos too had firmly embraced communism.

In "The Politics of John Dos Passos" Hicks traces Dos Passos' political progression from what he calls "this pioneer fellow-traveler" to the contemporary conservative; in this progression he finds the source of "political confusion" and a "decline of literary mastery." The article is more valuable for biographical facts and dates (I find only one minor error—the statement that Dos Passos did not contribute to the *New Masses* after 1934) than for conclusions; but it is interesting as an honest and fair-minded attempt to review Dos Passos' career from the vantage point of familiarity with the man, with his writing, and with the Communist Party.

The conclusions are suspect not because of factual errors but because of two unproven assumptions upon which they are based—first, that Dos Passos was deeply involved in acceptance of the communist ideology; and second, that he later suffered a "traumatic" disillusionment with communism. If we accept the premises, we must also accept the con-clusion that disillusionment is a major factor which can explain Dos Passos. Hicks starts with these premises as self-evident facts; he looks, therefore, not for explanations but for proofs; and, of course, he discovers them.

The cause of this logical aberration is worth a brief investigation not because of the importance of refuting Granville Hicks, but in order to illuminate the bases of communist (or ex-communist) criticism, a major source of Dos Passos' critical reputation. The cause appears to lie in Hicks's purpose to corroborate and justify his own experience. For Hicks, who shared Dos Passos' Harvard and literary background, *was* deeply involved in acceptance of the communist ideology as a member of the Communist Party (which he admits Dos Passos was not). Associated with Dos Passos on the editorial board of the *New Masses*, Hicks continued on the staff much longer, and Hicks *did* suffer a profound disillusionment with communism and did resign from both the magazine and the Party in 1939 to protest the blind endorsement of the Russo-German Pact by the American Communist Party.

With this background, perhaps Hicks was too close, felt too much sympathy with his subject, and suffered too much guilt at having been so far behind Dos Passos in seeing the light. His article becomes then an exercise in political apologetics—an act of which Hicks may not be aware. And so the surprising intimation occurs to us that this article in which Hicks uses the first person singular not once is not about John Dos Passos but about Granville Hicks. And this revelation clarifies not only Hicks's motive but that of all the disillusionists and the disillusioned to reveal—even if they must invent it—the complicity or involvement of others in the original error.[4]

When we consider Dos Passos' "protest vote" for Foster and Ford in 1932, we should accept Dos Passos' explanation that it was just that. "So far as I can remember," he says in *The Theme Is Freedom*, "I hadn't quite recovered from the plague on both your houses attitude toward the two conflicting systems." In the summer of 1932, he had replied to V. F. Calverton's questionnaire about writers and the social crisis. Asked whether becoming a communist might deepen an author's work, he answered: "I don't see how a novelist or historian could be a party member under present conditions." As to socialism, he said: "I should think that becoming a socialist right now would have just about the same effect on anybody as drinking a bottle of near-beer"; and as to capitalism: "We've got the failure, at least from my point of view. What I don't see is the collapse."[5]

In another way Dos Passos expressed the same protest at the same time by associating himself with the new journal, *Common Sense,* which published its first issue a month later on December 5. Its "Platform" proclaimed it "an independent publication . . . not connected with any existing political party" which "believes that a system based on competition for private profit can no longer serve the general welfare." The platform also demanded the calling of a constitutional convention "to adapt the principles of the American revolution of 1776 to modern needs."

Early in 1933 Dos Passos made his protest even more explicit when he published in April his third play, *Fortune Heights,* and a commentary, "Thank you, Mr. Hitler," in the April 27 issue of *Common Sense.* In the play the protagonists are Owen Hunter, proprietor of a little filling-station-motel, and his attendant; the story is their futile struggle to resist the destructive forces of the depression. At the end the minor characters, Old Man Matheson and other farmers ("quiet, determined-looking men in overalls") who stick together to resist oppression come near to becoming the real heroes; yet it is Owen Hunter who states the theme. Having lost everything, he refuses to give up: "All we want to do 's to dope out some way to live decent. . . . We got to find the United States."

In the commentary Dos Passos thanks Hitler for clarifying America's position: "Americans who don't want to live in a society of slaves can no longer look to Europe for moral countenance. . . . We can rely only on ourselves and our past and our future. . . . We haven't got much civilization; but some of it is our own. . . . If it's going to be saved it'll be saved from underneath, by the workers and producers, manual and intellectual. It's the choice . . . of hanging together or else assuredly all hanging separately. Young men of the left . . . the tar and feathers" (of an American fascism) "are just around the corner!" Dos Passos warned that finding the United States was essential. If the people failed, one of the dedicated minorities would find it for them; but it would not be the United States they had been looking for.

That summer Dos Passos again visited Spain with his wife (he had no need now for the close companionship of Lyaeus) to investigate the new Republic. What he discovered he recorded under the slightly sardonic title, 'The Republic of Honest Men," in his book *In All Countries*. Alfonzo was gone; the liberals and intellectuals, all wonderful talkers, had come to power. But they had had "little training in dealing with the . . . realities of a country day by day. They could never span the distance between word and deed." When he published some of his observations about Spain in the *American Mercury* the following March, he entitled them "Spain Gets Her New Deal." The warning was plain.

That same month (March 6, 1934) the *New Masses* published "An Open Letter to the Communist Party," signed by Dos Passos and twenty-four other middle-class liberals, or bourgeois intellectuals. The *New Masses* feigned astonishment (although Dos Passos had not appeared on its masthead since early January when it became a weekly and began paying its contributors) and published in the same place a personal reply: "Dear Comrade Dos Passos: . . ." That was his last contribution to the *New Masses*, except for one in mid-December, 1936, "Grandfather and Grandson"; written for old times' sake, he reviewed in it the old *Masses* and the new: "Now we are on the upsurge of a new democratic wave," he concluded. "Perhaps under the influence of the time the *New Masses* will be able to break out of the narrow sectarian channel. . . . I for one hope so."

The "new democratic wave" he spoke of had been achieved during the second two years of Franklin Roosevelt's first administration. Roosevelt—despite his origins "in Groton and Harvard and in the Hudson River aristocracy" and despite his gift-of-gab which Dos Passos had always distrusted—had won his support. "On his first reelection in 1936," Dos Passos reveals, "I had voted for him with enthusiasm."[6]

U. S. A.—completed three months before the election with the publication of its final volume, *The Big Money*—did not, it is true, appear to reflect much of that enthusiasm. In his first trilogy, Dos Passos presented a kaleidoscopic view of life in the United States as he had lived it and as he saw it to have been during the years 1900 to 1929; for his view was only partially colored by the lens of the period, 1928 to 1936,

in which he wrote it. The picture of the United States which
he painted was no trivial or enchanting landscape in pastels
of a sweet land of liberty and hope; it was a grim and
lugubrious representation, Hogarthian in its cynically pene-
trating detail of the squalor and misery of a machine-domi-
nated, monopoly-ridden civilization.

III *Telemachus—Home*

The Marxist readers learned to applaud this "proletarian
novel" which presented the manifest "inherent contradictions
of capitalism." Many of the more conventional literary critics
lamented that "the gusto and delight of American living"
had been left out, and they despaired of a novel in which
the author seldom seemed able to conceive—or at least to
transmit—a whole character in a fictional person.[7] Dos Passos'
purpose, however, was neither to placate nor to offend either
group; his intent was to reveal a nation, the men and women
who composed it, and one man alone—all hurtling through a
third of a century, propelled by events and by complex needs
and stimuli, traveling too fast to get their bearings or even
to know where they stood.

The one man alone was Dos Passos himself, the clearly
autobiographical narrator, whose character and whose story—
separated from the rest of the work—remind one of Telemachus in *Rosinante*. But there is an important distinction between the two, for by 1928-29, when Dos Passos
was writing *The 42nd Parallel*, Telemachus had been seven
years longer on the road; Dos Passos had gained sufficient
self-confidence to be able to treat himself directly as the
narrator of his own story in the Camera Eyes of the novel.
In the first of these he referred to himself as "you" and "us,"
in the second as "we" and "Jack," in the third as "*il*" ("he")
and "the little boy" and finally as "I." Though he was known
to others principally as "Jack" and in school also as "Frenchie"
(eighth Camera Eye), he had at last attained the first person
singular.

In those seven years Telemachus had advanced considerably in his quest. Even before his travels in Spain in *Rosinante*, he had been, in the roles of Martin Howe and John
Andrews (1920 and 1921), an American chiefly in origin;

and the reader saw him almost wholly on foreign soil. As Fanshaw in *Streets of Night* he had been in an American setting at Cambridge, but he had lived in an unreal world largely composed of selected elements of the European past. In the lives of none of these young men was there any development or emphasis given to the father—except in that of Telemachus, who when we first met him had already forgotten that he was searching for Odysseus (whose name is not even mentioned in the book).

Dos Passos, however, had not forgotten. As a trial investigation in his search, he had partially and temporarily entered into the character of Wenny, Fanshaw's friend, and provided himself with a family, including a father. Wenny, apparently like the others (though we are not told of Martin Howe's background), had been reared as an only child by a lonely middle-aged woman who had been the only source of affection and meaning in his early life. As the "ugly duckling" of a sizable but poor family, he had been brought up by his maiden aunt. For in order to make Wenny's condition approximate his own, Dos Passos had had to insert a barrier between father and son. To make it as nearly insuperable as the barrier of his own quest, though quite different, he had also made Wenny an intelligent, freethinking extrovert at Harvard whose father was a hypocritical, introspective, Congregational minister upon whom Wenny was forced to depend to continue his education. Wenny had managed to declare his independence, but not to effect it: "God damn my father," he had said (as the Man Without a Country had said of his fatherland); "I will live him down if it kills me." It did; but first he achieved understanding of their relationship: "And I'm just like him. . . . A chip of the old block."

As the narrator of the Camera Eyes in *U. S. A.*, Telemachus has begun to grasp his father intellectually and emotionally. If he is "just like him," he had better discover in what respects; if to "live him down" is self-destruction, perhaps an alternate method of reconcilement can be found.

In the role of Jimmy Herf in *Manhattan Transfer*, Dos Passos had come closer than ever before to America when he returned to it twice and studied a cross-section of its life as a reporter in Manhattan. He had also expanded his comprehension of his own background and much of his life from the age of six or seven to the age of twenty-nine or thirty; his college and war experiences he had already assimilated. And he had finally left Manhattan, "walking west," to transfer his search to the nation at large. At that time, however, his father was still remote, remembered only distantly in a dream: "There was . . . a smell of pineapples on the deck and mother was there in a white suit and a dark man in a yachtingcap."

In the lens of the Camera Eye of *U. S. A.* all these remembered and reconstructed parts of a life previously detailed in earlier novels are focused into one life and then refracted back onto the swiftly moving background of twentieth-century America in the lives of the fictional characters in the narrative. They are particularly recognizable in the life of Dick Savage as he appears in *1919* until half-way through his wartime career, when he is commissioned.

"The years Dick was little he never heard anything about his Dad." Those are the first words of the story of Richard Ellsworth Savage. To one who remembers any of Dos Passos' previous novels, or *Rosinante,* or who is reading *U. S. A.*—or even *1919* alone—straight through, Dick is a familiar character. Like the narrator Dos Passos in the Camera Eyes and like Jimmy Herf, Dick did not know his father (Dick's father had been sent to prison). Like them, Dick was an avid reader; like them, he attended boarding school and a major eastern college, had a boyhood friend named Skinny, and took moonlight walks on the beach with a minister's young wife. Dick also wrote for his school paper and the *Harvard Monthly* and was a pacifist.[8]

Both Dick and the narrator joined the Norton-Harjes Unit in France. Both experienced a respite from the war with two soldier friends—like Martin Howe and Tom Randolph and their friend Russell in the "little pale salmon-colored villa" in *First Encounter.* The scenes of these rendezvous are clearly identical. As presented by the narrator in Camera Eye Thirty, "three of us sit in the dry cement fountain of the little garden with the pink walls in Récicourt . . . and the little backhouse with the cleanscrubbed seat and the quarter moon"—to Dick it was a "half moon"—"in the door like the backhouse of an old farm at home"—to Dick it was a "New England" farm. Both the narrator and Dick Savage admired Dick Norton's speech where he turned over the Norton-Harjes section to the army; then both headed south with the Red Cross to Italy, got back to Paris, were shipped home, joined the army, and were shipped back to France.

There the similarity ends: Dick went back to France an officer, soon to be a captain; the narrator spent some time "washing those windows," "in the training camp at Allentown"; and in France he filled out forms, piled scrap iron, was finally discharged, and received his baptism into freedom in a public bathhouse in Tours: "I strip myself naked   soap myself all over with the sour pink soap   slide into the warm deepgreen tub . . . in the suitcase I've got a suit of civies . . . the buck private in the rear rank of Uncle Sam's Medical Corps (serial number . . . I dropped it in the Loire) goes down the drain with a gurgle and hiss and . . . I step out into the linden-smell of a July afternoon . . . an anonymous civilian."[9]

In the earlier Camera Eyes is Dos Passos' childhood, starting —even younger than Jimmy Herf's—at about the age of four, or around 1900. The scarcely known father is referred to as "He" and also, like his son, as "Jack," whose biography was finally to be set forth explicitly in the fictional *Chosen Country*.

In Camera Eye Eight is the same fight Herf was forced into by the bullies at boarding school and with the same participants—"the Kid" he had to fight; the bully Freddy (spelled "Freddie" in *The 42nd Parallel*); the master, "Hoppy," listening in the halls; and its results are the same—the unfair fight, people calling him "girlboy," the shame, the tears. It is almost the same situation that recurs in the first chapter of *Adventures of a Young Man* (1939)—a variation of another experience of Jimmy Herf—when Freddy this time bullies Glenn, who is called "the Kid." It is clearly not the sort of experience one would be likely to forget.

In Camera Eye Nine, "it was Chrisfield," the town in Southeast Maryland, "on the Eastern Shore," across from the Virginia capes; "I got talking to a young guy couldn't have been much older'n me . . . he had curly hair and wisps of hay on it and . . . his body was burned brown to the waist." In this young Huck Finn we learn the source of Chrisfield, or Chris, John Andrews' friend, and of Whitey, the young bum Wenny had admired.

Then, in Camera Eye Ten, we are introduced to "the old

major who used to take me to the Capitol when the Senate and the House . . . were in session" and who "had been in . . . the Confederate Army." This is Dos Passos' first portrait of his maternal grandfather who, according to Dos Passos' notation (cited in Chapter One), "served as some kind of engineer on Confed. side during war." As Major General Ellsworth in the same relationship to Dick Savage in *1919*, his fame (though he had been long dead) is largely responsible for Dick's commission in the army. In *Adventures* he occurs as Old Soul, the guide and friend—and the maternal grandfather—of little Glenn; again he is a veteran of the Confederate Army. In *Chosen Country* the father of Kathryn Jay—the fictional counterpart of Lucy Addison, Dos Passos' mother—had been a construction engineer in Virginia in 1861.

More important than the old gentleman in *U. S. A.*, as we have already seen, is the boyhood friend of the narrator, Skinny, who had given him some valuable information: "and Skinny said if you'd never been baptized you couldn't be confirmed" (Cam. Eye 17). When he was older, of course, the author-narrator was to receive a variety of baptisms in different roles. One of these roles was as John Andrews of *Three Soldiers*—for the moment himself known as Skinny—given courage by an older Skinny (called the Kid) to escape their slavery by plunging into the Seine. In this incident John Andrews last saw his friend who had given him his manhood.

This invaluable friend had been with Jimmy Herf at boarding school: "He and Skinny coming back from playing with the hoptoads down by the pond." There, we learn much later, in *Adventures of a Young Man* when Jimmy has become Glenn Spotswood, had occurred another lesson in the facts of life: "They roamed round the pond . . . watching the hoptoads sitting on each other's backs all round the edges of the water. Glenn asked what the hoptoads were doing. Skinny threw back his head and laughed, shaking his sides the way he did and said couldn't he see?"

That laughter, honest and amused yet slightly scornful of ignorance, became increasingly scornful as Skinny matured to young manhood in the earlier fiction. It was the laughter of Lyaeus at Telemachus' futile chasing after gestures, "like a comedy professor with a butterfly net." It was the laughter of Tom Randolph: "But, Howe, the minute you see that and laugh at it, you're not a slave. Laugh . . . and have a good time in spite of the Goddamned scoundrels"; and of Henslowe, John Andrews' friend, with his "impudent little brown mustache" and his "faint Bostonian drawl": "Have a good time in spite of 'em. To hell with 'em." It was the sardonic drunken bleating of Herf's friend Stan: " 'Baa baa.' Stan . . . leaned back and laughed deep in his throat," and the ridiculing bray of Ned Wigglesworth, Dick Savage's friend at Harvard, in *1919*.

Finally, in Skinny's metamorphosis into Paul Graves in the same work, *Adventures of a Young Man,* the bitterness disappears. Paul, "a tall skinny young man with big knees and big elbows and a big adamsapple," is about two years older than Glenn and becomes a sort of older brother to him. He has a characteristic "heehaw laugh that always made Glenn feel good." But his is more nearly the laugh of the old childhood friend Skinny again; the scorn, the trace of condescension are gone; it is no longer sardonic, but sympathetic.

For *Adventures of a Young Man* marks the culmination —not the beginning, as it seemed at the time it appeared— of Dos Passos' progression toward his fatherland, the United States; of Telemachus' long quest for his own identity which was to be found in his identification with his father.

As early as 1933, in his article "Thank You, Mr. Hitler," Dos Passos had spoken in essentially conservative terms in his strong plea for "repudiation of Europe" when he also emphasized the need of the United States "to keep" what civilization it had achieved—of "retaining a few of the decencies built up through the centuries." Already he had foreseen the implications for it of the rise of European fascism. In his trip to Spain that summer he had seen evidences of the rise of fascism even there. In two articles in the *Student Outlook* of October, 1934, and of April, 1935, he wrote in conscious anticipation of "the next war," a phrase he used in both articles. In "A Case of Conscience" in *Common Sense* of May, 1935, he proposed "bringing out of the attic of the nation's past a certain amount of dusty equipment long forgotten there" which might still have some present uses.

As evidence that *U. S. A.* was only partially influenced by Dos Passos' political opinions at the time it appeared, one can note that *The Big Money,* published in August of 1936, made the whole trilogy available at that time. Yet despite the apparent pessimism in that work, we have in his article "Grosz Comes to America," published in *Esquire* the next month, September, a clear expression of satisfaction with events in America: "In the arts as in science America has become the refuge of the traditions of western Europe. . . . The fact that first-rate men who can't live in their own countries feel that they can breathe here makes you feel good about this country." By November he felt so good about his country that he could vote for the first time for the presidential incumbent—and "with enthusiasm."[10]

That his was not an uncritical acceptance is indicated, however, by an article that appeared in the *Nation* in October. "Big Parade—1936 Model," in part a description of "the traditional Legion whoopee now nineteen years stale," is also a serious indictment of the conditions in American life that made such fatuous organizations virtually the only ones which could supply "the comfortable feeling of belonging so necessary to people now that small-town life is broken up and the family is crumbling and people live so much by themselves in agglomerated industrial masses, where they are left after working hours with no human contact between the radio and the car and the impersonal round of chain stores and picture places." Dos Passos was, if anything, even more concerned than earlier at what he called "the American passion for a smooth-running machine, if nothing else," because he had been watching them in other rapidly industrializing countries—Russia, Germany, and Italy. He had studied efficiency rather thoroughly in *U. S. A.* and had learned its tendency, as he said in the *Nation* article, "to eliminate troublesome ideas, outstanding personalities, and dissenters who ask awkward questions about how and in what direction the parade is being led."

Yet this same "comfortable feeling of belonging" was what accounted for Dos Passos' enthusiasm. He understood that we were already "in the middle of the general conflagration" in the autumn of 1936, as he noted in a letter to Scott Fitzgerald at the time. His feeling of belonging and the "conflagration" itself had taken him out of himself and redirected his quest from his personal needs to those of his society. They had been his salvation; he hoped they might also help to save his friend Fitzgerald, who was even then publishing the story of his own "crack-up" in *Esquire*. Hence in his letter he suggested that Fitzgerald "get a reporting job somewhere."[11]

Fitzgerald, however, continued his "crack-up," and Dos Passos took the reporting job. Early in 1937 he went to Spain with another writer, his friend Ernest Hemingway, and "a brilliant young Dutch director," Joris Ivens, to film a documentary movie. This was the *Spanish Earth*, which was intended to place before the American people the case of the Loyalist defenders of Spain against Franco. The failure of the project and of the whole republican cause as a result of communist intrigue and sabotage Dos Passos outlined without names in *The Theme Is Freedom.*

If the contrast between developments in the United States and those in Russia and Europe had not already done so, this final Spanish experience in 1937 would have driven him to an acceptance of American political methods and institutions. What it did was to confirm him in the position he had already taken: Europe had become a desert, parched by tyranny and scorched by war; only in American soil could liberty and those dedicated to its preservation find room and nourishment for further growth. Furthermore, the Spanish experience cut off his last remaining roots in the Iberian peninsula and his last faint hopes that the Communist Party, even in America, might be anything other than a highly efficient and ruthless machine for power. He has not since returned to Spain, nor has he written about it except to impress upon us as forcibly as he could the lessons he learned there; he has retained, however, the interest he had expressed in December of 1920 in "our nearest neighbors the Latin Americans."[12]

"And Skinny said if you'd never been baptized you couldn't be confirmed." Dos Passos had begun to study in earnest for his confirmation in American democracy at least by the year preceding his last trip to Spain. He had referred to his studies in his oddly paternal letter, written probably in October, 1936, to Fitzgerald. "I'm trying to take a course in American history," he had said, hoping to instill in his friend some of his own sense of urgency by which Fitzgerald too might be saved, "and most of the time the course of world events seems so frightful that I feel . . . that I've got to hurry to get the stuff out before the big boys crack down on us." One of the things he was anxious to get out was probably his edition with its fifty-page critical appreciation of one of the founders of our democracy, *The Living Thought of Tom Paine,* which appeared in 1939-40. Another publication related to his "course in American history" was doubtless *The Ground We Stand On* (1941), which he managed to publish barely before "the big boys" did "crack down on us."

In the spring of 1935 he had quoted from conviction—it had been his lifelong conviction—the democratic creed of two martyrs to the faith, Paine and Ray Becker: "The world is my country, mankind are my friends, to do good is my religion."[13] Although Dos Passos' central beliefs had changed scarcely at all, he had sufficiently clarified by the summer of 1939 their political bearings upon the state of the world, as he then saw it, to be able to announce his own position as an American democrat. In June of 1939 Dos Passos published *Adventures of a Young Man,* his story of the martyrdom at the hands of the communists of Glenn Spotswood, who was in part autobiographical, in part Ray Becker, and in part Dos Passos' friend and translator José Robles Pazos, who had been similarly killed in Spain. In September and October he published his appreciation of Paine in the magazine *Common Sense.*

Between these dates, in July, 1939, appeared his signature as a member of the Committee for Cultural Freedom, which protested the "totalitarian idea . . . in Germany, Italy, Russia, Japan, and Spain," and the suppression of "intellectual and creative independence" in those countries and "even in the United States." As a member of the Committee, he was "pledged to expose repression of intellectual freedom under whatever pretext," and "to defend individuals and groups victimized by totalitarian practices anywhere." Certainly, he had subscribed to that pledge at least as early as his "Humble Protest" in 1916, which was itself such an exposure.[14] At about this same time Dos Passos offered his credo to the *Partisan Review: A Quarterly of Literature and Marxism* (summer, 1939): "I think there is enough real democracy in the very mixed American tradition to enable us, with courage and luck, to weather the social transformations that are now going on without losing all our liberties or the humane outlook that is the medium in which civilizations grow."

In the meantime, after his final return from Spain, he had published *Journeys Between Wars*, an updating and a reorganization of materials collected from his life of travel and reporting in Russia, the Near East, and particularly in Spain. When he reprinted, in the first section of the book, some of his adventures as Telemachus in Spain in 1916 and 1920, he dropped almost completely the old distinctions between the allegorical and the expository sections of *Rosinante*. Telemachus was now simply "the traveler," and Lyaeus, "the friend"; and the transition from "the traveler" of one section to the "I" of the next was now scarcely discernible. When he recorded in the final section of the book his most recent observations *en route* to Spain for the last time, he entitled a chapter which described an experience of his own "Odysseus among the Shades." That title (dated March, 1937) clarified the earlier change.

For Dos Passos, like Telemachus, had come home for good by 1937-38 and knew it. He had caught sight of Odysseus not far away, and he had suddenly discovered that he need seek for himself no further. He was home; it was enough. He had *become* Odysseus.

CHAPTER 4

Art and Society—The
Search for Form

WHEN DOS PASSOS left America for Spain in 1916 after
graduating from Harvard, he intended to study art and,
specifically, architecture. He had entered Harvard as a young
man highly conscious of inadequacies in his own life—though
he might not have been able to identify them—and aware, too,
of much of the sordidness and of some of the beauties of his
world. Seeking to fill the lack that he felt within him, "wanting
things to be beautiful," he had experimented in the collegiate
bohemianism of the time. He had tried aestheticism; he had
written autobiographical stories of sensitive young men and
a few poems and essays; and he had discovered a certain
satisfaction in the writing. Like John Andrews and Dick
Savage, he had intended from the start to become an artist.

Artistic intentions, however, do not make an artist. The
conditions of Dos Passos' nature and of his environment had
somehow equipped him with an artistic temperament, a term
usually left undefined. It can be defined broadly and tentatively, however, as an exceptional sensitivity to one's environment and a resultant feeling of a need to relate the isolated
stimuli into some kind of original pattern or form which is
meaningful or satisfying, if only to oneself. Yet even an artistic
temperament does not make an artist; there is a prior re-
quirement of a perceptivity, an insight into the relations of
things, and an inventive, synthesizing ability. But the artistic
temperament does demand a more or less conscious search
for significant pattern or form.

I *Internal, External Forces*

That general search for order and definition was at the core of Dos Passos' quest for his father. Given his rootless background, with scarcely an identifiable human connection except his mother (who died in his last year at Harvard), his search for pattern and form took, perforce, a social direction. His primary need was to forge his own link in the human chain.

He was not alone, of course, either in his feeling of a pressing need for order, or in its social emphasis. The aestheticism, the frustrated idealism, and the oversensitivity so often portrayed in American fiction (and deplored by the critics) in the first quarter of the twentieth century were real phenomena. The climax of industrialism, immigration, and urbanization after the turn of the century upset much of what stability and order had been achieved, and new patterns and forms were not yet established. Furthermore, the more evident accompaniments of the disruption (including industrial warfare, poverty, slums, crime, and finally the war) thwarted normal aesthetic and ethical inclinations in the young men of the time and thus provoked these inclinations into conscious effort.

In effect, their environment created a generation of a type which a British critic, referring to their fictional counterparts, has since defined as "the Sensitive Young Man" or "the S. Y. M."—though he made the mistake of assuming that the S. Y. M. was merely "a hangover from the English fiction of the time."[1] Such a young man indeed had his counterpart in England, where he was reproduced in part by the end of the Victorian honeymoon (and in Spain, where the results of the Spanish-American War produced the "generation of '98," which so closely parallels the American literary generation of '17); but in America the S. Y. M. was distinctly indigenous.

Among the results of this widespread sensitivity were a burgeoning of American art colonies in Greenwich Village, Provincetown, and Paris; the tremendous, naïve idealism in the period of Wilson's first administration; and the literary renaissance of the twenties. Idealism and even art had become necessary and therefore acceptable. The release of pent-up ethical and aesthetic expression was spontaneous and phenomenal. But like the sometimes extravagant physical and emotional release of boys after four years of repressions in a boys' school (which was in fact an additional goad to many of the S. Y. M.), most of it was soon spent. People settled into the various grooves and patterns of American industrial society; and they were to a degree happy to forget disquieting ethical and aesthetic urges—except to disapprove what seemed to be their overindulgence by others.

Nevertheless, the collapse of existing patterns had demanded immediate and vigorous action of the civilizing process—the creation of order out of disorder, or out of unordered and unassimilated elements: *e pluribus unum*. In response to that demand there arose a significant conscious minority of dissidents and seekers, of writers and social critics. They did not, of course, all become artists. But they had in common the artistic temperament.[2]

Although Dos Passos' nature and the conditions of his personal life alone could have been responsible for his artistic temperament, he was certainly subject to the external forces which affected so many of his generation. Those influences emphasized in two ways the relation between his social needs and his need for form. The want of harmony in the lives of others became a part of his own wants; and a satisfactory order for him became dependent on a larger, social order. Also, the external forces of his time created a community of men similarly engaged in the pursuit of form, so that an artistic career became in a limited way a step away from loneliness.

If it was through art—or through "art and thought," as he said in his "Humble Protest"—that he was going to create the order he required and discover and express his relations to the world about him, his first task was to find his congenial artistic form and then to become proficient in it.

II *Early Writing*

In July of 1913, at the end of his first year at Harvard, he had published his first story in the *Harvard Monthly*. While at Harvard, Dos Passos has recently recalled, he was "punctual in attending whatever theatrical productions came to Boston."[3] In "Satire as a Way of Seeing" he has listed other early steps in his artistic development. For example, in that same year

1913 there was the Armory Show in New York, exhibited briefly in Boston, which he later remembered as "a real jolt." Meanwhile, there was the Boston Art Museum nearby where he "first looked at a picture directly as an excitement for the eye." The painting was by Whistler, and the stimulus to Dos Passos' interest had been literary—the joyful, biting, anarchic satire of Whistler's *The Gentle Art of Making Enemies*. After seeing Whistler, Dos Passos "got hold of a box of pastels and began making dovecolored smudges" of his own. The music of Debussy was another of his discoveries at the time.

But the story writing continued, and the composition of a few poems, and increasing numbers of book reviews and serious essays. Dos Passos was discovering that he had something to say. The creation of visual beauty had its satisfactions, but "it soon became obvious that almost any combination of pastel blurs was as agreeable to look at as any other," and his "enthusiasm for that sort of thing began to flag." What he had to say, apparently, he could not communicate with dove-colored smudges. Expression in writing, however, was another matter; and his interest, or at least his success—as measured by publication—in certain kinds of writing was increasing.

In his last year at Harvard, Dos Passos published only three stories in the *Monthly*. Two of these, "The Shepherd" and "Les Lauriers Sont Coupés," were autobiographies of his boyhood; the third, "The Cardinal's Grapes," was a pastoral idyll. Altogether, he published only seven poems in the *Monthly*, and all of these appeared in his last year between November, 1915, and June, 1916.

Clearly, one of the things that Dos Passos felt a need both to discover and to express was himself; and he was achieving some success in autobiographical narrative and in lyric poetry. His needs could even be combined as in the poem, "Memory" from the *Monthly* of April, 1916: "I stood beside you in the bow . . . / Red gold was your hair. . . ." Or he could subdue the narrative to almost psychoanalytical purposes, as in a later, profounder poem from *A Pushcart at the Curb*:

In me somewhere is a grey room

. . . .

When I was small I sat and drew
endless pictures in all colors on the walls;

tomorrow the pictures should take life
I would stalk down their long heroic colonnades.

When I was fifteen a red-haired girl
went by the window . . .
to burn the colors of my pictures dead.

. . . .

I have bruised my fingers on the windowbars

. . . .

While the bars stand strong, outside
the great processions of men's lives go past.

(pp. 200-1)

Here, of course, is a repetition of the girl in the earlier poem; and this girl appears again—as do all of Dos Passos' most significant memories. In his story, or excerpt, "July"— from the *Transatlantic Review* of September, 1924—she is Kitty, her "red hair tied up in a blue bandana," whom Jimmy Herf instructs in swimming.[4] We meet her in *The 42nd Parallel* as "little red-headed Mary I taught how to swim," and yet again as Annie O'Toole, to whom Jay, in *Chosen Country*, had given swimming lessons when he was fourteen.

The more interesting aspect of the poem is Dos Passos' almost explicit statement of his predicament and of his intentions: his sense of isolation from society and from life; his determination to participate—somehow to get past the windowbars; and his effort to escape his isolation through art by creating the essence of life in form and color from within. This poem was published in the same year as his equally explicit statement of his quest as Telemachus in *Rosinante to the Road Again*. His was no idle, irrational, or merely subconscious quest: Dos Passos knew early what he had to do, and that his means was art.

For the moment (from about 1916 to 1919) his particular means was poetry, and it was closely related to painting. The poetry is highly pictorial and highly sensuous, especially, as in all his writing, in the response to color and to form and movement. It is predominantly lyrical, conveying the writer's responses to the world about him, as well as to the world within:

On icegreen seas of sunset
the moon skims like a curved white sail
bellied by the evening wind
and bound for some glittering harbor
that blue hills circle
among the purple archipelagos of cloud.

So, in the quivering bubble of my memories. . . .[5]

The "endless pictures in all colors on the walls" have become word-pictures; perhaps they had a better chance to "take life," to make contact with "the great processions of men's lives" beyond the grey room within.

Dos Passos' first small recognition was as a poet when, in August of 1917 while he was already with the Norton-Harjes section in France, he appeared as one of *Eight Harvard Poets* (1917), a book for whose publication he was largely responsible. And though he is not widely considered a poet,[6] he has written a great deal of poetry since. In 1922, of course, he published his only volume of poems, *A Pushcart at the Curb*. Perhaps more such volumes were intended, though the remaindering of 544 of the original 1313 copies doubtless discouraged Dos Passos, as well as his publishers, from further offerings labeled as poetry. Having something to say, for Dos Passos at least, implied the necessity of someone to say it to.

But he was far from discouraged with the possibilities of poetic expression. Readers of *Manhattan Transfer* are familiar with the short prose poems introducing the chapters of the book. Readers of *U. S. A.* have noted the poetic compression of its biographies as well as the lyric intensity of the Camera Eyes. Critics have commented—though usually unfavorably—upon the poetic interchapters or commentaries of *District of Columbia* (1952). Dos Passos is probably most poetic, however, in his early so-called travel-books. *Rosinante* is itself an ode to the spirit of Spain, and *Orient Express* is one to the spirit of travel. From these, as from *In All Countries* and from *Journeys Between Wars*, we can excerpt whole passages which could stand as independent poems. Although Dos Passos wrote most of his poetry after he left Harvard in 1916 and although much of it was stimulated by Spain, he had made his choice of another form before leaving Harvard.

III *Spanish Influence*

The implications of his choice to study architecture are not
difficult to see. He was following what he had concluded (in
his "Humble Protest") to be the only "path to the fullness of
life," which lay between those "twin guide-posts for humanity
. . . thought and art." Since he was concerned with "fullness
of life" not only for himself but "for humanity," he required
a form which could express and in part fulfill the needs of
both. As an architect his effort would be to create a work
of art, a building, which should have its own intrinsic validity
and beauty. But in addition, it should enter immediately and
tangibly into the lives not only of those who used the building,
but of all who lived near it, and, more remotely, of those
who saw it. If he could express what he had to say in architecture, the completed building was guaranteed an audience,
someone to say it to.

Even in the creative endeavor architecture is perhaps the
most social of the arts. There are the clients, including all
who may use the building, whose needs the artist must learn
better than they know them themselves. Among the clients
are those who commissioned the work, who must be consulted, informed, and instructed throughout the process. And
when the idea of the work has taken shape, there are those to
whom its execution must be entrusted, who must be taught
its meaning and its requirements that they may teach the
others—draftsmen, contractors, builders, workers. When we
consider the aptness of Dos Passos' choice, the extraordinary
thing seems to be not that he chose architecture, but that he
never became an architect.

Perhaps the explanation is in a plethora of interests and
in the importunities of time. For the lonely boy who seemed
to have interests to spare—who liked books, grew flowers and
vegetables, who wanted to go to sea and to visit foreign cities,
and who "liked things to be beautiful"—never renounced any
of them. In college, he simply added to them; he discovered
music and took up painting; he wrote fiction and poetry and
book reviews, and critical social and political essays. After
college he put off his desire to drive an ambulance in the
war in France, and he went instead to Spain; painting and
architecture, we recall from *The Theme Is Freedom*, were his

"main interests at the time." It is doubtful whether he has ever had a single "main interest." At any rate, these two were complementary.

Although he was in Spain to study architecture, it was important first to know the language. To that end, but principally to fulfill social needs, he had to know some of the people. The person he came to know best, largely because of their common interests and tastes, was a young man whose main interests were painting and poetry. This was José Robles Pazos, later shot in the Spanish Civil War. Quite naturally, they toured the museums together and studied Spanish painting—Velasquez, Goya, El Greco. As he recalled the effect in "Satire as a Way of Seeing," "The 'Count of Orgaz' in Toledo started to bite in, maybe." But if he were really to understand the painting, he must know what it explained about the life of sixteenth-century Spain, or of twentieth-century Spain, or about the lives of all men in all times.

When Dos Passos in *Rosinante* was attempting to formulate "the gesture of Castile," El Greco and Spain and all his own unanswered questions had been gnawing at him for three or four years. Meanwhile, during the war years he had greatly increased his acquaintance with painting—in Paris and on leave in Italy, where "the frescoes on the walls became suddenly more important than anything else" ("Satire as a Way of Seeing," pp. 11-12). When he returned to Spain after the war, in 1920-21, Greco's painting came again to his mind in *Rosinante* to explain both the present and the past and thus to illumine the nature of man. "The infinite gentleness of the saints lowering the Conde de Orgaz into the grave" revealed the individual: "men concentrated, converging breathlessly on the single flame of their spirit. . . . Every man's life a lonely ruthless quest." And it revealed the existing society, "these generations . . . working to bury with infinite tenderness the gorgeously dressed corpse of the old Spain."

Dos Passos' approach to the study of architecture seems highly casual and roundabout, even subterranean. Yet it would be difficult to think of a sounder approach to any art than his method of studying it through an effort to understand the culture which produced it and the human needs and impulses which it must continuously express to survive as art. For Dos Passos was studying not only the architecture and painting of Spain in 1916 but also her literature, ancient and modern, religious and secular—poetry and prose; her religious, social, and political institutions; her people and her history. In short, he was exploring the entire Spanish culture.

His tentative findings he published in the magazine *Seven Arts* in August, 1917, in a long article which he called "Young Spain." This was after his father's death in January had released him from his obligation not to get his "block blown off too soon"; he was already in France. The degree to which he had succeeded in assimilating and synthesizing his experiences during the four months in Spain before his twenty-first birthday can be observed in "Young Spain." "As I learned the language," Dos Passos reflects today in *The Theme Is Freedom*, "I began to feel enormous sympathy for the people of this nation." Without that reaction, his success—which seems extraordinary, considering the above factors of age, time, and language—would have been much less; but he would also have been less hopeful and less disappointed in the end.

On the same page on which he recalls his sympathy for the Spanish people, Dos Passos recalls also that he was first in Spain "at a most impressionable period of my life." Some of his impressions, therefore, may be worth examining. We might examine them fairly accurately as they appear in *Rosinante*; but, since that book was not published until after his second trip to Spain—when, having been tempered by the war, he was presumably less impressionable—we can see them more freshly in the more impressionistic preliminary report, "Young Spain," written five years earlier.

"The two great figures that typify Spain for all time," he found, were Don Quixote and Sancho Panza. "Don Quixote, the individualist who believed in the power of man's soul over all things, whose desire included the whole world in himself. Sancho, the individualist to whom all the world was food for his belly. On the one hand, we have the ecstatic figures . . . in whose minds the universe is but one man standing before his reflection, God, . . . the originals of the glowing tortured faces in the portraits of El Greco. On the other hand are the jovial materialists. . . . Through all Spanish history and art the threads of these two complementary characters can be traced." And through all of Dos Passos' fiction they can be traced—from Martin Howe and Tom Randolph

in *One Man's Initiation—1917* to the idealists and the materialists (often both represented in a single individual) in
the biographies and the fiction of *U. S. A.*, straight through
to Jed Morris and Eli Soltaire in *Mostly Likely to Succeed*
and to Ro Lancaster and George Elbert Warner in *The
Great Days* (1958).

In the immense variety of language and of topography in
Spain, he concluded, was "probably the root of the tendency
in Spanish art and thought to emphasize the differences between things." This tendency of Spanish artists he defined
as caricature. "Their image of reality is sharp and clear, but
distorted. Burlesque and satire are never far away in their
most serious moments. . . . The great epic, Don Quixote; such
plays as Calderon's *La Vida es Sueño*, such painting as El
Greco's *Resurrection* and Velasquez' dwarfs, such buildings as
the Escorial and the Alhambra—all among universal master-
pieces—are far indeed from the middle term of reasonable
beauty. Hence their supreme strength."

Because of Dos Passos' own Iberian heritage, he had an
almost natural affinity for Spain and her culture. His trip
to Spain simply deepened it into genuine affection and provided an appropriate object for his already well-developed
capacity for sympathy—which was a feeling with, as well as a
feeling for, others. Similarly, Spain seems not so much to have
impressed upon him new ideas and principles as to have shown
him a fuller expression of many of his own and to have provided a congenial atmosphere for the development of others.

Long before he reached Spain, Dos Passos had experienced
a great variety of language and of topography in his childhood
travels. In his "Humble Protest" of 1916, he was almost hyper-
conscious of "the differences between things"—between himself and other Americans of more conventional backgrounds;
between "the few at the top in the sunlight" and the rest
"in the filthy darkness of meaningless labor"; of the contradictions of Germany, "the Eroica Symphony and the ruins of
Rheims"—between what was and what ought to be. At Harvard
he had begun to express some of these differences in criticism
and satire.

But the tragic differences were not all in Germany and
America. Before he had left America in 1916, Dos Passos
had written "Against American Literature" for the *New*

Republic. There he berated what he considered the fruitless stagnation of America's literature which resulted from her people's having forgotten and lost "the lesson of the soil." They had lost it in "an all-enveloping industrialism" which had broken down "the old bridges leading to the past" and with which American writers had not yet learned to come to terms. In Spain, Dos Passos was learning the lesson of the soil. But Spain too was forgetting it.

Everywhere in "Young Spain" the emphasis is upon Spanish individualism, "the strong sense of individual validity, which makes Spain the most democratic country in Europe," which had been "born of a history whose fundamentals lie in isolated village communities." Yet what Dos Passos called "the present atrophy, the desolate resultlessness of a century of revolution" had arrived as the result of "the persistent attempt to centralize in thought, in art, in government, in religion, a nation whose every tendency [lay] in the other direction." And so he found himself applauding a "fiery reactionary speech" denouncing the modernization of Spain which was destroying her roots in her soil and in her past.

There was hope, however, in the present generation of Spanish writers who were "strangely sensitive and self-conscious, some despairing, some pressing on very boldly up the logical paths of Spanish thought—toward anarchism, toward a searing criticism of the modern world in general and Spain in particular. Gradually, laboriously, with unexampled devotion, these men are piecing together the tattered shreds of national consciousness. Not national consciousness wholly in the present capitalistic-patriotic sense, however, but something more fruitful, more local."

Nearly all of "Young Spain" reappeared five years later in *Rosinante to the Road Again*. In it may be found each of the important ideas of the original article, including the Spanish Jeffersonianism—which must have seemed ironically familiar to Dos Passos, who had read Jefferson at Harvard. In *Rosinante* the ideas of the article are considerably expanded, though much of the original phraseology is intact. One important expansion in this book had only been implied in "Young Spain" in the emphasis upon individualism and upon the values and joys of Spanish village life. It is Dos Passos' development of the Spanish tenet, or concept, of *lo flamenco.*

As he describes it in *Rosinante*, *lo flamenco* is the simple, unaffected pleasure in living which he sees in the donkey boy—to whom he devotes a chapter—and in the youth's explanations of why he has no desire to emigrate to America: "En America no se divierte"—"In America they don't enjoy life." Put another way, *lo flamenco* is a way of life dedicated to living; or it is its momentary spontaneous formulation: "the tough swaggering gesture, the quavering song well sung, the couplet neatly capped, the back turned to the charging bull, the mantilla draped with exquisite provocativeness." Or again, it is the simple sensuality of Sancho Panza.

In 1916 Dos Passos had discovered Spanish village life, and it had appealed to his romantic impulses in contrast to the frustrations in his personal life and to the squalor and misery he saw in American industrialism. In 1920-21 he was rediscovering Spain, with an equal sense of contrast, immediately after his experiences of the war. He seems to have had at the time no thought of reversing the American industrial process, for in "Against American Literature" he had denied "the possibility of retreat. Our only course is to press on." But in *Rosinante* one can see his reluctance to abandon completely this simple agrarian way of life that so attracted him, his effort to study it, analyze it, and abstract from it its essence, which he might formulate into some principle that would be valid for all life.

The end of his pursuit of *lo flamenco* in "The Donkey Boy" in *Rosinante* is this: "'Something that is neither work nor getting ready to work, to make the road so significant that one needs no destination, that is *lo flamenco*,' said I to Don Diego." Dos Passos had been acting on that principle, perhaps unconsciously, when he had decided to become an artist. The work of art and even the act of its creation would each have its own significance and satisfactions. It might be hoped that art would have other satisfactions, and even uses, for other people; if so, that was all to the good, but at least it should have its own.

It is interesting to note that in this doctrine of *lo flamenco* the four major quests of the book converge: Telemachus' quest for his father, which had imperceptibly become his quest for the essential gesture of Spain; and Dos Passos' pursuit of *lo flamenco* itself, and *his* attempt—in the book as a whole—to formulate the essential gesture of Spain. *Lo fla-menco* is the core of the other things sought, a principle of action on which they were founded and through which they might finally be attained. It is more nearly a means than an end, a means which contains its own end; and that is its very meaning. Not only is it the secret of the sensual enjoyments of Lyaeus which Telemachus so envies but also a philosophical premise—a categorical imperative, a principle of moral judgment.

Another distinction between "Young Spain" and *Rosinante* is that in the book Dos Passos studies more closely the work of individual Spanish artists. In it the emphasis is not upon her classic painters but upon her contemporary writers, "the generation of ninety-eight" whose common efforts he had surveyed before. The first of these writers whom he discusses is Pío Baroja, "A Novelist of Revolution." Dos Passos particularly admires Baroja not so much for his artistry as for the honesty and clear-sightedness upon which his art depends. He also esteems him because he "has felt . . . profoundly, and has presented" the contemporary spirit of the Spanish people "without abandoning the function of the novelist, which is to tell stories about people."

What Dos Passos has to say about Baroja is sometimes so close to what might later have been written of Dos Passos— and in fact to what has been written of him—that it is difficult to know just what significance to give his statements as they might relate to his own art.[7] One paragraph is particularly to the point; for, speaking of Baroja's anarchism as "an immensely valuable mental position," Dos Passos then describes it:

> He says in one of his books that the only part a man of the middle classes can play in the reorganization of society is destructive. He has not undergone the discipline [of a common industrial slavery] necessary for a builder. His slavery has been an isolated slavery which has unfitted him forever from becoming truly a part of a community. He can use the vast power of knowledge which training has given him only in one way. His great mission is to put the acid test to existing institutions, and to strip the veils off them. I don't want to imply that Baroja writes with his social conscience. He is too much of a novelist for that, too deeply interested in people

as such. But it is certain that a profound sense of the evil of existing institutions lies behind every page he has written, and that occasionally, only occasionally, he allows himself to hope that something better may come out of the turmoil of our age of transition.

Although Dos Passos accepted Baroja's attitude as "an immensely valuable mental position," the problem is to what extent it was then, or later, Dos Passos' position. Perhaps the most accurate answer is that, as Dos Passos phrased it, Baroja's attitude represents his own *as* one deliberately taken and tentative. He accepted it, as he implies Baroja did, as an intellectual and emotional discipline essential to maintaining his individuality and integrity and his sense of perspective as an artist. He must be, as he was, "deeply interested in people as such"; but he must, therefore, consciously avoid becoming emotionally involved in their struggles. He must "only occasionally" allow himself to hope "that something better may come."

For Dos Passos in *Rosinante* had already caught a wave of "the new spirit" of aggressive protest which he felt was "shaking the foundations of the world's social pyramid." The revolutionary dialogue at the end of his first novel, *One Man's Initiation—1917*, and his articles in the *Liberator* in 1920 were indications of his reactions to these new protests. Yet in his discussion of Baroja, and earlier, he carefully refrained from identifying himself with "the new spirit" and he conscientiously reserved judgment because it was "perhaps only another example of the failure of nerve, perhaps the triumphant expression of a new will among mankind."

So his role as artist was to be a lonely one after all. And he would have to postpone even further his architectural career. However, it was a very partial and mitigated sacrifice. The old desire of the boy who liked things to be beautiful and who needed to create significant form from the chaos about him was more important than its particular social content or even than his need to belong. The mere submersion of himself in the mass, however much he might desire it emotionally, would only frustrate other demands of his nature and training. Besides, he had already tried it; if not in joining the medical corps and, to a degree and earlier, in joining Norton-Harjes, then certainly and explicitly in the character of John Andrews in *Three Soldiers* he had experimented with belonging for the sake of belonging and with deliberate submersion of individuality—to "take refuge from the horror of the world"— and he had unequivocally rejected this escape.

Furthermore, a "part . . . in the reorganization of society" was precisely the role he wanted. Even though, like Baroja's, it were a destructive, critical part, was that not equally the role of the architect as planner? Did not slums have to be recognized and condemned before beautiful apartments could be erected in their place? He was no doubt quite willing to renounce his desire to become "truly a part of the community" after the catharsis of his war experiences. If he could become simply a contributing associate of a community, perhaps after the reorganization were well under way, that would be sufficient. Meanwhile, he would be fulfilling a "great mission." He could already detect a "shaking" in the "foundations of the . . . social pyramid."

In fact, Dos Passos had long since become a writer. Discounting *Eight Harvard Poets, Rosinante* was his third published book. By the time it appeared early in 1922, he was already known. John Peale Bishop, in reviewing *Rosinante* for *Vanity Fair* magazine in May, 1922, refers to *"Three Soldiers,* on which his reputation was made." He also notes, in the same place, having read the manuscript of *A Pushcart at the Curb* (1922). Possibly already well along, in some form, was *Streets of Night* (1923), the first part of which is more like Dos Passos' *Harvard Monthly* stories than any of the three earlier prose volumes.

IV   *The Critic*

While at Harvard, Dos Passos had become not only a writer but a critic. He was not yet an artist. His short stories, his essays and editorials, his book reviews, even his poems were all likely to be criticisms—of himself, of the world around him, of others' attitudes and their views of the world. Everything he wrote implied a search for the conditions of beauty, of form and pattern, and an attempt to isolate and expose the conditions which inhibited the search.

He analyzed closely, looking for facts, truths, movements by which he could judge the meanings of things. "Vatchmaker's eyes," Benny Compton's father, in *1919*, had murmured approvingly when his son was fitted for glasses. Eyes which could not see far could be trained to see minutely and exactly. Whether the fascination of facts for Dos Passos was caused more nearly by his myopia or by his critical intelligence, it has never diminished. In his work today as then there is an abundance of facts. Some would say an overabundance, a mass of irrelevant detail—a common criticism of his biography *The Head and Heart of Thomas Jefferson* (1954). But to one who has had to gain most of his knowledge of the world from isolated facts painstakingly assembled, there is likely to be a relevancy in a given fact not immediately apparent to others.

Some of the facts he acquired in his early criticism show the development of the artist from the critic. In his first published book review, in the *Harvard Monthly* of November, 1914, Dos Passos was delighted with Jack Reed's *Insurgent Mexico* because the author "neither dogmatizes nor puts forward any panacea for the ills of Mexico," but is content to describe what he saw in "some of the finest impressionistic descriptions of the life and scenery of Mexico that have ever appeared." Dos Passos was here abstracting principles of writing and hints of form; and it is not surprising that with a few changes—such as "Spain" for "Mexico"—his review could stand eight years later as an adequate comment upon his own *Rosinante*.

In his next review the following February (1915), Dos Passos found a novel he liked, *Small Souls* by Louis Couperus: "Without a trace of didacticism, the novel is a tremendous satire, cold and unemotional, on the life of a small European capital." Ten years later, Dos Passos was to write his own tremendous satire of the small souls in an American metropolis in *Manhattan Transfer*.

As a "regular editor" of the *Monthly* in July, 1915, he reported upon yet another form, a romance, in "Conrad's 'Lord Jim.'" He was impressed with the factual possibilities of imaginative writing in which "The reader has constructed for him actuality;—but actuality refined upon, laid bare, as it were, made transparent." What he called "the great joy of reading Conrad" came, he admitted—though he was a bit ashamed of it and called it "priggish"—from "the fact that his books act as a sort of mental grindstone." In this comment is another clue to Dos Passos' intention in his own fiction.

The fascination of *Lord Jim* was in the central problem: "Through pure excess of imagination . . . Jim's ability to act is paralyzed." It fascinated him, like all the other facts he delighted in, because of its corroboration of experience, which, of course, could work either way. The work of art could organize previously unassimilated experience, and it could present new experiences to be fitted into the patterns already achieved—and corroborated later. The joy was in the recognition of the new piece which would just fit in that impossible gap and clarify a bit more the pattern of the never-to-be-completed puzzle.

Whether Lord Jim's paralysis of will pointed to the gap or to the piece which might help to fill it, much of Dos Passos' early work—particularly *Streets of Night*—was preoccupied with variations of "the failure of nerve." Doubtless he was already aware of the problem in himself, given as he was to self-analysis and self-criticism. "There was a cynical smile about his lips as he thought about his life up to this moment," he wrote at twenty in "The Shepherd," of January, 1916, a description of his own reveries at the age of fifteen. From his other reading he got his phrase and a more general corroboration, as he wrote in *Rosinante*, of "what Gilbert Murray in speaking of Greek thought calls the failure of nerve."

The contemporary failure of nerve was a large and unpleasant fact to his critical eye; but if he could somehow find its relations with two even larger facts he had discovered, it would diminish in importance and the three might complete a significant portion of the pattern. The first of these other factual discoveries was, of course, himself—a fact not particularly attractive to him but inescapable. The second was society, or humanity, a fact so large and obvious that he might never have discovered it if he had not been born outside it, or if he had thought himself a sufficiently attractive object for contemplation.

His attitude toward society was ambivalent. If he equated society with humanity, he was a part of it; it could serve for the basic social unit, the family, which he lacked—the whole for the part—as an object for his love and affection. As a whole, it was, in a way, his parent, to whom he owed not only affection but respect and filial obligation. Its individual units could serve as brothers and sisters whom he could also love, and to whom he was responsible should they need his help. Since most of those he saw and heard of needed help, he could easily develop a parental affection for them—what he has called the "parental bent";[8] it became incumbent on him to find ways of helping. But humanity was so large that his part in it seemed insignificant; it made little difference whether one felt he belonged or not—one could not help belonging.

Society, however, if differentiated from humanity, became a particular entity with certain distinguishing patterns and forms. These might become obscured, or they might break down almost entirely, but they would have to be reorganized into similar or new patterns if the society were to survive as such. Born on the fringe of American society—though geographically almost in its center, Chicago—Dos Passos had at first no chance even to become aware of the social entity. His birth had disturbed a portion of the pattern; and his parents—anticipating the reaction which could hurt the child even if not directed at him—whisked him off to the protection of Europe. So the first society he knew was an old but relatively fluid one. "For me Brussels has filled that place of earliest known city," he wrote anonymously in the *Harvard Monthly* of April, 1916, in "Les Lauriers Sont Coupés."

Probably only Dos Passos knew the painful irony of what he said and what he left unsaid in this essay. It is apparently not even very personal—only a casual little piece of reminiscenses of traveling with his mother when he was very young; the title is from an old song his mother used to sing to him: "Nous n'irons plus au bois, / Les lauriers sont coupés" (We'll go no more to the woods, / the laurel is all cut down). But it is highly uncharacteristic of him to fail to sign his work, except when anonymity is the policy of the periodical (as in the Choate School *News*). The explanation is that Dos Passos conceived of "earliest known city" as a place within him to be filled and that by April of 1916 Brussels had virtually ceased to exist as a functioning society, or at least as the one he knew. In the middle of that month he had lost the single intimate attachment he had known when his mother died—apparently from complications of an earlier stroke, probably accompanied by aphasia, which had left her an invalid.[9] He was now cut off from humanity; there would be no more trips to the woods for laurel; the victories had become defeats; and poetry and art were dead. The joke was only for himself and the gods: he really was anonymous.

Whether or not this analysis is correct, the basic facts are. In that same issue of the *Monthly* appeared his poem "Memory" about the girl with red-gold hair, one line of which is "I never even knew your name." That sense of loneliness and lovelessness which accompanied him almost to the peak of his artistic career (until about the time of his first marriage in 1929) reached its climax in April, 1916. Yet even in that cruelest month he had the strength or the resilience to continue; perhaps he had discovered then when he needed it most what he later called "the secret magnificent pleasure of release through the written word."[10] In any case, by the May issue of the *Monthly,* he appeared fully fleshed as author of another poem, "Incarnation," and he was again digging for principles of art and understanding in a "Book Review" of two recently published volumes of verse, *The Catholic Anthology* and *Georgian Poetry.*

His review begins with his praise of imagism as "an attempt to add something, to impose a new trend of thought on current literature." He praises not the result but the attempt, and it may be that this was precisely the significance of imagism. That it had some effect upon the literature which Dos Passos was to produce is almost certain. He was in the right place at the right time to receive it. (Dick Savage, in *1919,* while he was still a Dos Passos alter ego, had been invited to dinner by the empress of imagism, Amy Lowell, who in fact occasionally listened to readings of their verse by young poetry club members at this time.) But the same impulses that had created imagism at the end of the first decade of the century were of course working independently in him. They were the need to create new patterns to express and make intelligible the confusing new forces and institutions and, if possible, "to impose a new trend" of order upon the current chaos.

The work of the Georgians he thought—as might be expected

—often too far removed from the contemporary scene; but he admired "the aliveness and closeness to the soil of much of the work . . . the triumphant earthiness expressed by Chaucer in the beginning of the Prologue." The chief merit in *The Catholic Anthology* he felt was "the sense of satire, of half humorous character-drawing," represented by Edgar Lee Masters' work. In the *Anthology* he also found "a certain atmosphere of city life, a really poetic feeling for it," that he himself was to show in *Manhattan Transfer*. In this same *Catholic Anthology*, though he nowhere mentions it, he read for the first time (if he had missed its appearance in *Poetry* less than a year before) T. S. Eliot's "The Love Song of J. Alfred Prufrock," of which there are echoes in *Streets of Night*. At the end of the article he asserted his conviction, despite the events of April, that "life is not an empty, and very unpleasant dream."

Yet the world he saw about him was full of empty lives and many unpleasant dreams. His own life had already served as the example. Only the past January he had confessed in "The Shepherd" that "except for books, his life had been a great bare room"—the same figure of barrenness used in a later poem ("In me somewhere is a grey room"). His proliferating memory supplied the unpleasant dreams; and they recurred as bad dreams do, until the internal analyst set them in order for "release through the written word." Later, perhaps, there could be pleasant dreams as well. But the dreams, the memory, were not life, though they were real enough; they once had been essential parts of life, but then they had not been dreams. They were still essential as the platform upon which real life could be built and lived today. The vital thing was to make the critical distinction.

The internal and external forces which impelled Dos Passos toward art, his early pursuit of form at Harvard and in Spain, and especially his perception of contrasts between what was and what might be, all led him gradually to the conclusion that his means was criticism and that the means might be also the end: the artistic form in which to express and make intelligible the various conflicting elements within and without. *Midcentury* (1961), like *U. S. A.* before it, is criticism given artistic form.

CHAPTER 5

Art as Criticism

DOS PASSOS' last three essays of June and of July, 1916, in the *Monthly* comprise a fairly systematic extension of the principle of the need for critical discernment. To understand the foundations of Dos Passos' art and thought we must constantly refer to these essays because in them he formulated the basis of a theory of art as criticism and discovered a critical form which he could later develop to the level of art.

I *Duality*

In "A Humble Protest" he develops his point in predominantly general terms. He is disturbed at the tendency of "humanity for following processions . . . comfortable in companionship . . . the tendency to believe, somehow, that what is, is right and must endure forever. Even in oneself it is hard to eradicate the idea." Thus he explicitly states the social basis of his dualism: "oneself" and "humanity." Having made that critical distinction, he then proposes a program of questioning which is in itself a dualistic critical system.

"Isn't it time, once more, to question . . . ?"—that is, for each of us individually and all together to do so. "What, we should ask, is the result on the life of men . . . ?"—on each man and on all. "What is the end of human life?" Dos Passos' tentative answer to the last is, as we have seen, also dual: "two half-opposed ideals, thought and art." They are only "half-opposed" because thought demands artistic expression, or organization and synthesis, and art demands thoughtful use and analysis of its materials. In order to accept that end or aim, we must question the alternative aim, which is also dual: "What are the results of our worship of this twofold divinity: Science and Industrialism? His answer suggests a further duality:

"From over-preoccupation with what is at the other end of our telescopes and microscopes . . . in this consuming interest in science, in knowledge of the exterior . . . haven't we forgotten the *Know thyself* of the Greeks?"

The first question—"Isn't it time to question?"—we must ask continually. The second—"What are the results on the life of men?"—we must ask continuously. In its light we may arrive at a tentative answer to the third—"What is the end of human life?"—but we must remember that it is only tentative and continue to question it, too. We must remove man from his constant position at the diminishing end of the telescope. It is not that we must seat him permanently at the other, but that we must restore the flexibility of the instrument. When we have discovered a fact on the exterior world, we should not, like robots, simply lay it on our fact pile and turn to look for another. We should rather reverse our attention and look inward to see where it fits ourselves and what its results are on the life of men. The objective of all this critical questing is the same at each of its stages: balance, proportion, symmetry, harmony—perhaps also the ultimate objectives of thought and art. So much depended upon a widespread adoption of "the sceptical frame of mind." Yet Dos Passos was hopeful; for the war, as well as other evidences of the contemporary disorganization, could "be used as an acid to sear away the old complacency" and establish the distinction between dreams and life.

In "A Conference on Foreign Relations," also in the June *Harvard Monthly*, Dos Passos turned his critical thought from general principles to the more immediate and practical ones of American foreign policy. Starting by taking encouragement from the evident discontent—or critical attitude—which "the very existence of such a conference proves," he advocated his policy of "constructive pacifism," which is a balanced outlook and purposeful, humane action. He was even more specific: "Yet order can only be brought into the desperate chaos of our European world . . . by the action of strong and organized public opinion in all the great nations." We must awake from "our old provincial slumbers" and must begin "to mould opinion in America, and to stir it into active life."

His final essay in the *Monthly* in July was once again an examination of an individual's artistic expression as he discussed once more a book by Jack Reed. As in his review of November, 1914, he admired the balance of Reed's perception and of his writing. Thus he began his first critical commitment on the subject of form with an approach which was characteristically dual. Reed's form, "half newspaper report and half personal narrative," he forthrightly approved. "If there is any perfected form in American 'near-literature,'—excepting always the O'Henry [*sic*] short story, rather threadbare of late,—it is this very descriptive narrative of places and events."[1] We feel that if Dos Passos had been deliberately searching for a book form in which he could best exercise the critical principles he had been outlining in his writing, he would have chosen one very close to that described here.

Actually, he was searching for form in general and for *a* form in particular—form as both end and means. He chose architecture as his medium, but he must have known, almost certainly by this time, that he would continue to be a writer, or at least that he intended to do so. Writing could be complementary to architecture, a more direct expression of the individual. As a complement, it could perfectly well be "near-literature," especially if the form were new and indigenous, arising from and expressing the needs of the American society in which he must eventually find his place. In the *Monthly* Dos Passos seems to have been deliberately searching for a congenial literary form, and testing the one (Jack Reed's) he had discovered at least as early as November, 1914. Attracted first to the writing of fiction, he seems to have abandoned the short story by April, 1916, when he published "Les Lauriers Sont Coupés." Even that, of course, though published as a "story," was not one in the usual literary sense. It is probably safe to say that he has not since published a single short story that was not originally intended to become part of a longer work.[2]

As he portrayed himself as a boy in *Chosen Country*, Dos Passos found difficulty, from whatever cause, in oral expression—"the foreign speech . . . tonguetied, never saying the right word." Even today a relative says of him, "Jack's so shy and has such trouble expressing himself when he speaks, and he writes so beautifully." In conversation with Dos Passos, I have found him extremely cordial and interested. He seems very responsive to others and to their ideas but

slow to initiate a topic himself. He speaks somewhat hesi-
tantly, perhaps partly from shyness, partly from an eagerness
and intensity which he communicates in conversation. His
accent is what is sometimes called "continental," noticeable in
those who have spent childhood years in a number of European schools. As a member of his Hamilton Street Club,
Baltimore, reports, "He seems like an awfully nice guy; he's
always right there in what's going on, but he doesn't seem
to *give* much."

The discovery that he could become articulate in writing
made it important to him. He knew that he had much to say
and that he must communicate it in one or another art form
to release himself from "the great bare room" within him.
By 1916 he had found a need "to mould opinion in America,
and to stir it into active life." He was discovering his audience
in the American people, the society with which he must
establish some bond of communication.

II *Artistic Compulsion*

After his two years at the war, his need to communicate
had become absolute. His indignation at the war itself, at
America's treason to his ideal of "constructive pacifism" and
to the expressed will of the people (Wilson's re-election on
the slogan, "He kept us out of war"), his resentment at the
institution of armies that made men into machines to kill
other men, and at the institutions of profit behind them—all
these had boiled within him until they erupted into his first
two novels, *One Man's Initiation—1917* and *Three Soldiers.*

In the first he implied his own dedication, in the character
of Martin Howe, to live on and tell the tale, to fight for the
ideals of the dead idealists, his friends. But in one slim book
he could not tell it all, and not even one of three would stop
to listen. So he told it again, at greater length, and this time
revealed in a subtler symbol his artistic compulsion.

John Andrews, the artist, the free personality, had allowed
himself to be made a slave. So the first act of his slavery,
washing barracks windows, became its symbol, and he was
forced to wash them over and over again in spirit until he
could make his own freedom and express that slavery and
humiliation in his art at the piano, develop it, give it its

proper place in the unity of his experience. It was a thing he very nearly achieved before his final arrest. "Skinny" of the labor battalion had become again John Andrews; and he had played at the piano "the theme . . . which had come to him long ago, in a former incarnation it seemed, when he was smearing windows with soap . . . in the training camp." Though he had made his own physical and even his own spiritual freedom, he had not yet found himself because he had not had time to make his two freedoms one—to unite the essential elements of his nature. He had completed the first movement of "The Soul and Body of John Brown," his masterwork, based on the theme of his slavery. But the tyranny of the modern world in the form of the military police too soon took hold of him again.

After he had written these two war novels, Dos Passos appears to have felt much better, for he had completed the first movement of his own masterwork. The difference is suggested by the contrast between *Three Soldiers* and *Rosinante*. The novel is bitter, ironical, seeming to reveal, in the defeats of Fuselli, Chrisfield, and Andrews, the inevitable defeat of man—unless one remembers that Andrews' friends, the French boy Marcel, the nonconformist Henslowe, and "old Howe in America," were still undefeated. But Marcel and Henslowe were men of action who knew what they wanted to do and did it, and Martin Howe of his first novel had not been absorbed by the army.

Rosinante, in contrast, is full of light and color and the harmony of completed works of art—Greco, Velasquez, Goya, all the best painting and writing of old and modern Spain. Yet the work which contributed most to the harmony in this book was *Three Soldiers*. Both works are critical of individual characteristics and particularly of the failure of nerve. In the war novel there is little or no hope; in the book which is an ode to Spain there is much.

For with *Three Soldiers* Dos Passos had finally found his audience, and it had stayed to listen. I have said that the war made Dos Passos a reporter, as in a way it did. More accurately, it confirmed in him his critical attitude, his need to report immediately, "to sear away the old complacency" while there was still hope; and it gave him an audience in America which he could not afford to lose. The time for beautiful buildings, for the luxury of architecture, might come later.

All of the essential ideas and attitudes he expressed in *Rosinante* had been implicit in his work at Harvard.[3] His closer observation of life in Spain before and after the war merely corroborated them. The war itself and his writing of it confirmed them. In *Rosinante,* however, he summed up and presented in relation to Spanish life and Spanish art his thought about life and art in general. He consolidated in artistic form his own perceptions critically examined.

Dos Passos had long since seen the necessary connections between art and society, as he had those between thought and art. To him, all were meaningless except in relationship to the conditions of human life, life which had to be lived now, in reality, or not at all. For this reason he interpreted his function as an artist to be a critical one. It is also why in *Rosinante* he interpreted the achievements of Spanish art as the highest form of criticism, the expression of "the differences between things." For to interpret a given condition of human life is to say first of all that it is a condition and then whether and how it limits or enhances the living of life. In short, art must not only mirror life; it must also be true to life. The most significant art will somehow perceive and express the permanent conditions of life and those of the profoundest or fullest living.

Thus Dos Passos found that the "burlesque and satire" of the greatest Spanish artists "are never far away in their most serious moments." Thus also Dos Passos himself satirized in the character of Telemachus the condition of how many lives of his time?—the young idealist in quest of life (his father or the characteristic living gesture of Spain), inhibited by his training and the traditions of his past ("the maxims of Penelope") and stumbling and barking his shins on the real life which he passes over. As background and contrast to that picture was the actual life of Spain, symbolized in part by Telemachus' friend Lyaeus. From these Dos Passos abstracted what was to him a permanent condition of the fullest living, which he called *lo flamenco*—"to make the road so significant that one needs no destination"—a quest which is also a gesture, fulfilled in its pursuit; a means and an end; and a way of life. In *Rosinante to the Road Again,* a little known and rather unappreciated book about Spain, is perhaps one of the profounder expositions in American letters of the necessary social and cultural implications of art.

Although there is always the danger that art, conceived as criticism, will become merely criticism and not art—as Dos Passos must have realized—he accepted the danger and the challenge in the effort to report and interpret the essential conditions of American life. Before he published *Rosinante*, he had already accepted the novel as his chosen form, and he had proved his ability to handle it authoritatively in *Three Soldiers*.

III *Why the Novel*

If fiction had not been his first choice of form as a writer— as it apparently was when he started writing for the *Harvard Monthly*—he would probably have come to it anyway by a process of elimination. In fact, he seems to have done that. At Harvard he wrote or reviewed just about every accepted literary form except biography and drama. But the complete, brief impressionistic biography suitable for publication in a literary magazine did not make its appearance until he invented it in the late twenties. And he seems to have been born at the wrong time to do his first serious writing for the theater. Eugene O'Neill, as it happened, was studying with Professor Baker at Harvard in 1914, but the Provincetown Playhouse was not even conceived until the next year, and even O'Neill has singularly failed to impress Dos Passos with his "sophomore philosophies."[4] There was no theatrical audience as yet for the kind of serious writing Dos Passos intended. There was, for the novel; and the audience was crucial.

Dos Passos entered Harvard in the year that *Sister Carrie* was finally published, but it had been written when he was four. In 1938 he inscribed a gift copy of *U. S. A.* to Dreiser: "Dear Dreiser—Just wanted you to know that I still feel that if it hadn't been for your pioneer work none of us would have gotten our stuff written or published."[5] In the year Dos Passos left Harvard, Sherwood Anderson's portrayals of real American speech added a bit to Dreiser's tremendous expansion of the vocabulary and materials of the American novel. In the same year Jack London's death left a gap in American fiction for the kind of writing Dos Passos had praised in Jack Reed; and Joyce's *Portrait of the Artist as a Young Man* raised the portrayals of the conflicts of the Sensitive Young Man to the level of art.

By the time Dos Passos began *One Man's Initiation*, probably in France or Italy during his war service, the novel as a form not only had the largest audience but was easily the most flexible form he could choose. In America the realistic novel had a certain "closeness to the soil" that he had considered the "redeeming feature" of the poetry of the Georgians. There was even, according to his later opinion, an American proletarian literature: "Theodore Dreiser is, and has been for years a great American proletarian writer. . . . Sherwood Anderson . . . too . . . [and] Jack London. We have had a proletarian literature for years"—and incidentally, "Walt Whitman's a hell of a lot more revolutionary than any Russian poet I've ever heard of."[6] Not exactly proletarian, but a part of the background for all young proletarian or revisionist writers in the United States was Edward Bellamy's Utopian novel *Looking Backward* (1888), which Dos Passos read at Harvard.

There is not much point in going further into precedents and sources except to note that apparently Dos Passos' reading while at Harvard in the modern literatures of England, France, and Russia was extraordinarily broad, especially in the novel, with the emphasis, respectively, on H. G. Wells, Flaubert, and Dostoevski. But that is only a quantitative and probably misleading emphasis except in the instance of Flaubert, whom Dos Passos read through. Joyce, for example, offered him only *Dubliners* (1914) and *Portrait of the Artist* (1916), while Wells had written even then a great deal; and Dos Passos says today of Gogol's *Dead Souls,* which he read at Harvard, that it "still seems to me about the best novel ever written."[7]

If we look in Dos Passos' work for repeated mention of authors, we will find Whitman, Joyce, Dreiser, and Reed mentioned by name here and there, and not much else. He does not even mention Crane or Hawthorne, whose influence, though partially negative, is plain. If we look for precedents in a certain style of technique or set of ideas, we are likely to find the source we suspect, or else nothing. Had Dos Passos continued his architectural career, he would probably have been, like Zeke Harrington in *Chosen Country,* a modern eclectic, as he has been as a novelist. One of the most widely traveled and widely read of his generation of writers, with an almost limitless fund of sources at his disposal, he has been also perhaps the most experimental and inventive in techniques and form.

One Man's Initiation—1917 is not highly inventive. The pair of men adventuring together, the one an idealist, the other more practical, have clear parallels in Mark Twain and Cervantes—and almost anywhere else we might look, providing we look deep enough. The school of war, the emphasis on the impersonality of armies, the futility of war suggest Stephen Crane's *The Red Badge of Courage* (1895). Some of the description and narration also is reminiscent of Crane: " 'What do you think of all this, anyway?' said the wet man suddenly, lowering his voice stealthily."

But even in his first book, Dos Passos is much more personal, less objective than Crane. Nearly everything is seen through the consciousness of the person seeing, although the distinction between the narrator's eyes and Martin Howe's is not always maintained. The sense of adventure is there, but it is based mainly upon hope rather than upon the excitement of self-discovery by the youth Henry Fleming which is the essence of *The Red Badge.* One reason is that Dos Passos' book is too nearly an introspective exercise in self-discovery by the author; but its significance is also that it is an exercise in handling Crane's material and the basis for an original and creative critical study, *Three Soldiers.*

CHAPTER 6

Three Novels: Tradition and the Individual Talent

DOS PASSOS did not become an artist until after he had written his first novel. His individual talent is essentially an historical one seeking to align in intelligible perspective three sets of historical data—his personal history, the history of his time, and the tradition from which both of these derive. As his grasp of his own story became surer, his relationship to the social and institutional history of his time became clearer. We can trace, therefore, the parallel development of form and idea through *Three Soldiers* (1921), *Streets of Night* (1923), and *Manhattan Transfer* (1925)— three novels which are critiques both of American ideals gone sour and become institutionalized and of the chief naturalistic interpretations of those ideals or institutions.

I *Three Soldiers and Determinism*

In two related aspects of Dos Passos' first novel lay most of its promise. The first is the interplay of the disillusionment and hope which culminate simultaneously at the end in Martin's dedication to the ideals of his dead friends. The second is the remarkable conversation among those friends— Catholic, anarchist, socialist, and direct-action revolutionist— just before the end. Here are "the differences in mentality involved in . . . the various schools of revolutionary thought" about which Dos Passos wrote eight years later in his "Open Letter" to President Lowell. To Dos Passos ignorance of those "differences between things," combined with fear or failure of nerve, was responsible for the tragic deaths of Sacco and Vanzetti.

Although the distinctions outlined in his first book were not widely heeded, those in his second were heard. This story of three young men at war invites comparison with *The Red Badge of Courage* even more directly than does *One Man's Initiation.* Dos Passos even inserted in *Three Soldiers* a central episode which has an almost exact parallel in the famous seventh chapter of *The Red Badge* in which the youth, beset by fear, encounters a dead soldier in a chapel-like clearing in the woods. In *Three Soldiers,* Chrisfield, beset by fear and anger, comes upon a dead German while he is reconnoitering near the enemy lines. He, too, is in a hushed woods, with "the dark green of the leaves" overhead, while underfoot "the last year's leaves . . . rustled maddeningly with every step."

A pleasant Indiana farm boy who has lived close to the soil, Chrisfield lives almost instinctively by his emotions. He chafes under military discipline, scarcely knowing why. When he sees the dead man he is filled with an unreasoning, frenzied hatred at this thing which, because it is German and is dead, he instinctively feels is the natural enemy of the hunger for life within him. "He kicked the German. . . . He kicked again and again with all his might. The German rolled over heavily. He had no face. Chrisfield felt the hatred suddenly ebb out of him." It was not an enemy, after all. It was only another faceless machine, in a different uniform, in the vast no-man's-land of war. "Chrisfield felt his spine go cold; the German had shot himself." He had lost his nerve, his will to live, his hope. Somehow the awareness of suicide, the green of the forest, "the last year's russet leaves . . . underfoot" make Chrisfield dimly conscious that he, too, has nearly lost his nerve. Chastened, he hurries off to report that he has seen nothing.

The reader never really knows, after he has read this brief episode, whether Chrisfield's experience was real or a dream, or whether it was a dream within a dream or a dream of an earlier, real experience. That, finally, becomes the point. War, servility, uniformity were not life. They were an empty existence, a waking nightmare whose only end was death. Life was "not an empty, and very unpleasant dream." It was individual, spontaneous, free; but it took nerve to live it.

What, then, could a dedicated realist report of the war and

its aftermath—the war ends before the book is half finished—
its effects on the lives of men? Only that the nightmare was
not real life but a temporary though vastly destructive condition of life, which destroyed a man's will to resist it. It
might be argued from Darwin or Spencer that it was the
elemental struggle for existence; if it were, it was the further
removed from truly human life. Only the least human could
survive: officers and remote leaders who exploited the civilized order and used it to promote the war would survive.
The "Y" men—clerics strutting in uniform on the sidelines—
would survive, while they encouraged others to kill and die
for humanity and to keep themselves clean when filth, in
one way or another, had become a condition of survival.
Those who like sheep simply submitted, and the military
police who beat them into submission, would continue their
meaningless existence.

After the war, among the more nearly human of those who
had been engaged in it, there would be only the ones who
had learned to suppress central parts of their humanity. Henslowe, John Andrews' friend, survived by craftily dodging
authority, carefully suppressing idealism and thought by
vigorous action and a cynical opportunism. Heineman, Henslowe's friend, a sort of Bacchus in steel-rimmed spectacles,
would survive: " 'Don't think. . . . Drink,' growled Heineman."

The three soldiers did not survive. Fuselli, a second-gen-
eration Italian boy from San Francisco, had a natural instinct
for color, movement, and love. But he had been taught to
worship material success. "Oh, he wanted so hard to be pro-
moted. . . . He must be more careful not to do anything that
would get him in wrong with anybody." So the less careful
and the more ruthless walked over him, and he failed, miser-
ably alone.

Chrisfield, John Andrews' intimate companion until Andrews was wounded, should have been able to survive by
relying on his instinctive love of life—his will to live each
moment for what it was worth without thought for the next.
The army had caged and tormented him until, acting instinctively, he murdered one of his tormenters. Even so, he
should have survived, although perhaps brutalized, suspicious,
alert for the need to kill again. But something had made him
more human and less purely sensual than when he joined

the army. He discovered with surprise that he could remember, that he could mentally recreate scenes of past happiness and be aware of details he had never considered before. In the joy of the discovery he could forget his painful
swollen ankle and his sweating body rigid at parade rest.
"Funny he'd thought all that, he said to himself. Before he'd
known Andy"—John Andrews—"he'd never have thought of
that."

Something had touched him which made life more intense and gave it meaning. Shortly afterward, Andrews was
wounded. The two friends were separated, and Chrisfield
lost contact with the source of his inspiration. For him, it
was the spark of life; without it, he would never really have
lived. Though he might have been content, and even happy,
his would have been a bestial existence without contrasts
and without significance. Yet that spark was the one thing
which the forces of war must destroy. The war spared only
the dead, or those who had not yet begun to live. If they had
begun really to live, it attacked their will, destroyed their
nerve, and they succumbed. So Chrisfield was goaded into
murder; and he remembered it, re-created and brooded upon
it, until his nerve failed and he fled, a frightened, abject,
broken thing that had once been a man.

John Andrews, the artist, sensitive, intelligent, was also
broken. His very act of joining the army had been a failure
of nerve. He had failed to achieve his individuality and had
enlisted, seeking "refuge from the horror of the world that
had fallen upon him." Andrews was fully conscious of his
own weakness: his lack of initiative and his inability to act.
The war had claimed him from the start by providing escape
from responsibility, the easy way which he was too weak to
resist; and he knew that, too. His whole attitude toward the
war and toward himself was colored by the irony of that
knowledge.

His admiration and friendship for Chrisfield was, of course,
simply the complement of Chrisfield's admiration for him, the
other side of the coin:

> "Christ, Ah wish Ah was like you, Andy," said Chrisfield.
> "You don't want to be like me, Chris. I'm no sort of a
> person at all. I'm tame. . . ."
> "Learnin' sure do help a feller to git along in the world."

"Yes, but what's the use of getting along if you haven't got any world to get along in? Chris, I belong to a crowd that just fakes learning. . . . We're a tame generation. . . . It's you that it matters to kill."

"Ah ain't no good for anythin'. . . . Ah don't give a damn."

Chrisfield's natural, earthborn spontaneity, however, was not communicable. His own perceptivity was always latent and had only to be awakened by his association with Andrews. John Andrews' ability to act was not so easily released. He alone must sever the Gordian knot of inhibitions to become master of himself. When he finally accomplished it, it was not Chrisfield who handed him the sword but another like him: the Kid who persuaded Andrews to swim the Seine to freedom. And like the poignard of perception with which Andrews had presented Chris, it proved a two-edged weapon. For John Andrews found himself escaped, fully armed for action, into the still nightmare world filled with lingering tentacular shadows of armies and war. No action was possible until the world awoke—until he could find a "world to get along in."

When Andrews met Chrisfield in Paris after his escape, their earlier relative positions had been reversed. It was Chrisfield now who was oppressed by his obsessions of guilt and fear. He had depended upon finding Andrews, who would be able to think for him and tell him what to do; but his friend could only give him some money and the unavailing example of his own courage. To Andrews, Chrisfield had meant action and passion, the full, sensuous life; but he and Chrisfield had become separated forever.

Each had made his own first motion toward fulfillment: to establish within himself the conditions of truly human life. Each had begun to know and to mould the pattern of his own existence. But the anti-human conditions of the outside world proved too strong; its pattern was too rigid to admit of others than its own. In that pattern perception meant only pain, courage meant only frustration or death, and the only admissible arts were those of war and the management of men. John Andrews could only begin the symphony which was to be his masterwork. "The Soul and Body of John

Brown" could reach only its first movement; in such an environment they could be united only in the grave.

In *Three Soldiers*, Dos Passos appears to have accepted Crane's *Red Badge of Courage* both as a model and as a challenge. As realists, the common effort of the two writers was to present the surface realities of war as faithfully as possible and thereby to arrive at or to suggest whatever ultimate reality might lie underneath. Both were interested primarily in the effects of war on a young man engaged in the fighting. Crane had gone fairly deep into the psychology of war and the psychology of fear. The youth Henry Fleming's fear had been a broad but fairly specific one: that of the two unknowns which met in his first anticipation and experience of battle; the first unknown, himself, and the second, death. In the process of his flight, his shame, his return, and his final heroism (or courage), he learned what he needed to know about both self and death and achieved his manhood in a confident, unpretentious self-awareness.

Yet though *The Red Badge* is known as an early deglamorization of war, it was the war itself which had been the means of the youth's self-realization. Without the war, without the fortuitous wound, its misinterpretation, and the second chance at the same task in which he had once failed, Henry Fleming probably would never have become alive (in Dos Passos' sense). That, of course, is precisely Crane's point; for to him, a quest is an absurdity. All is meted out equally and unequally by an impartial universe. Tragedy is impossible; there is only irony. The best a man can hope is to be permitted to know himself; if he is given the occasion to perceive his own insignificance, he has a chance for he will learn also the unimportance of his death.

Dos Passos' view, clearly, is very different. Like Crane, he considers the problem of courage of central importance in war as in life. But to Dos Passos the courage that each man must attain is a courage to face life, not death; for life is the ultimate reality. To him it does not follow that a man who has faced death can walk forth with a kind of stoicism to face whatever life has to offer. Death is, rather, often a temptation to be resisted by those who have not attained the courage to face life; stoicism is passive and negative; and life demands action, response, and purpose. (Perhaps it should be pointed out here that what has been called in the discussion of *Three Soldiers* "existence" or "mere existence"—to differentiate it from what Dos Passos means by "life"—is apparently the only life that Crane conceives of.)

These differences in definition and attitude make the problem of courage considerably more complex in Dos Passos than in Crane, because they admit of various degrees or kinds of courage. Fuselli, for example, needed first the courage to doubt his own cleverness and the goals of material success. If he could have learned the truth about himself, he would have needed the courage to accept; that accomplished, he would have needed, then most difficult, the courage to act. As it was, having failed, he required the courage to reject defeat. What Chrisfield required first, on the other hand, was the possibility of courage. For courage, if it is not stoicism, implies deliberate action with a consciousness not only of alternatives but also of consequence known or unknown; mere spontaneity can not be courage. Chrisfield had to learn conscious awareness, then self-awareness. John Andrews, all too aware of alternatives and consequences and even of himself, needed only the courage to act; but because of his awareness, he had perhaps the most difficult task of all to acquire it.

Three Soldiers is, of course, a much larger and more detailed treatment of the problem than *The Red Badge*. The fact that Dos Passos treated all three of his soldiers in considerable detail, while Crane focused his attention upon only one, suggests another distinction. To Crane one soldier was sufficient; others might act and react differently in certain particulars—as indeed they did in his novel—but one would serve to illustrate the general principle. Each man was, after all, a mere speck in an indifferent universe; one speck should serve as well as another. Dos Passos, however, saw each man as a universe in himself, set in what was *at that time* a hostile environment. He therefore required a number of examples to illustrate the problem—he used, of course, many more than just the three principals—each of whom could be taken as more or less representative.

Both Crane and Dos Passos wrote about war with a sense irony. To both, war was an ugly thing, symbolized—in part—by a description of a dead soldier in the woods. In this symbol and its interpretation, again, their respective attitudes may be summed up. Crane erected a natural chapel to death, in which an ant "trundling some sort of a bundle" along the dead man's lip revealed the significance of life in a sort of consecutive inevitability. The ant was alive, the soldier was not. It made no difference how he had died or even whether he had felt fear or pain. Death had simply come to him as it must to all; one life laid down its burdens and ceased; the next trundled its bundle across him. Neither had any say in the matter. If any message was intended for the reader, it was futility of action—the more violent, the more futile; that the only attitude to take toward life as toward death was resignation, acceptance, stoicism.

To Dos Passos, as to Chrisfield, the central importance lay in the manner of death; all the difference was in the attitudes of the dead man before he died. Dos Passos stressed the difference between life and death, and Crane the virtual identity of the two. In fact their conclusions were not far apart, for what to Dos Passos was the living death beyond which man must reach toward "the fullness of life," to Crane was all of life. Dos Passos' message was intentional and vital. In terms of his "Humble Protest" of 1916, he hoped by applying the "acid" of his realism, "to sear away the old complacency" in which courage and action were stultified and life was smothered. In terms of his analysis of Baroja in *Rosinante,* he was engaged in his "great mission . . . to put the acid test to existing institutions, and to strip the veils off them." The institution then most flagrantly oppressive of the arts of life was organized military power. It was that, even more than war, that killed and that snuffed out the souls of men— the Chris in John Andrews, the Andy in Chrisfield—and stopped the march of the Soul of John Brown.

In the conclusion was the hint of why Dos Passos felt it necessary to rewrite the American classic of war. In his first published article after Harvard, "Against American Literature," he had pointed to the difficulty of learning "the lesson of the soil. . . . An all-enveloping industrialism has broken down the old bridges leading to the past. . . . Our only course is to press on." In *Three Soldiers* Chrisfield embodied the "lesson of the soil" which Andrews finally learned but was not allowed to use. The realistic portrayal of war repaired a plank in the bridge to the past between two major events of American experience and perhaps also in the bridges of her literature and her political tradition. For Dos Passos' criticism of Crane—though he evidently thought him a worthy model—was that he could have written a novel of the Civil War which left out both the Soul of John Brown and the vital, human spirit of Walt Whitman, "our only poet."

If we judge Dos Passos by some of the criteria of his "Humble Protest," he had some time before attained "the sceptical frame of mind required for the breaking down of the modes of thought inherited from the last epoch." Applying his scepticism to *The Red Badge of Courage,* he had hoped at least to damage the complete determinism of Crane—perhaps the one mode of thought most destructive of will and paralyzing to action. But Americans had inherited other modes of thought almost equally obstructive to "the vivider living of life" which Dos Passos aimed at. One of these was their Puritan heritage.

II *Streets of Night and Puritanism*

Begun during the authors' college years in New England, Dos Passos' *Streets of Night* (1923) and Nathaniel Hawthorne's *Fanshawe* (1828) are each centered about a scholarly ascetic named Fanshaw(e) who is one of two suitors of a girl whom he cannot bring himself to marry because of their essential incompatibility. The other suitor in *Streets of Night* and really its hero is David Wendell, or Wenny, Dos Passos' marble faun. The explicit connections to Hawthorne's last novel, *The Marble Faun* (1860) are the girl's impression of Wenny, already referred to, "someone brown, flushed, goat-footed . . . Aprèsmidi d'un Faune"—in short, Hawthorne's Donatello—and two widely separated references by Fanshawe, the instructor in fine arts, to the sculptors Donatello and Praxiteles (creator of the marble faun).

As in *Three Soldiers,* three young people are thrown together in an oppressive environment which frustrates or perverts their energies, their loves, and their hopes. Despite the seeming determinism of his naturalistic method, Dos Passos is again deliberately attacking a deterministic philosophy:

specifically, the doctrine of original sin, as well as Hawthorne's implied corollary of the virtue of a consciousness of sin.

Parallel to the irony of *Three Soldiers*—in which Dos Passos presented the absolute necessity of striving and learning to live fully, while revealing that it is their very striving or their approach to full living which brings about the destruction of the soldiers—is a similar irony in *Streets of Night*. Its characters are all very modern people (or at least they were when it was written), except for Aunt M., Nan's maiden aunt. None of them appears to believe in original sin; Dos Passos does not. Yet the doctrine, which is in the very air that they breathe, cramps and warps their lives. The scene has suddenly changed: we are no longer in France with Chrisfield and Andy, but in Cambridge and Boston, in the years between about 1910 and 1919 (and for a short time in Italy, about 1919). But we discover the same nightmare as we walk down the streets of night among the aimlessly wandering dead and hear the mocking laughter of Judge Hathorne and the Mathers.

Dos Passos provides an altogether unpleasant portrayal of his collegiate contemporaries. "Of course, it wasn't exactly intended as soothing syrup," as Dos Passos said of his later novel *Most Likely to Succeed;* and he might have said this of all of them. But it is partly its truth that makes *Streets of Night* so unpleasant; for we have known people like these, known them all, somewhere—perhaps in our mirrors. Afraid to live and clinging to outworn forms and traditions or unable to rebel against them, each is defeated. Reared under the shadows of Puritanism and living in a society still suspicious of the instinctive drives to action—particularly the sexual urge—they, like Dos Passos at the time, find themselves in "a gray room," bruising their fingers on the windowbars. Wenny, the nearest to a live person, kills himself in the struggle to escape into life. The other two scarcely struggle.

Only two very minor characters reveal the merely partial nature of Dos Passos' apparent determinism. Whitey, the young bum whom Wenny admires and envies, enjoys his independent life of elemental struggle for survival: "What I like is goin' round to new towns, hoppin' freights an' all that." Standing in the same relation to Nan as Whitey does to Wenny, Mabel Worthington escapes even the middle-class,

Back Bay environment into which she was born. Acting on impulse, she elopes with a handsome Italian, who proves to have already a family of his own. Undaunted, having made her escape, she marries a wealthy Dutchman; and all doors become open to her. But it is not wealth which opens them, but the escape: the willingness to act, even impulsively.

In contrast to these two unfettered spirits, Nan becomes a young old maid and turns, appropriately, to the ouija board for contact with the other dead—with Wenny, whom she had spurned while he lived because he had been too nearly alive. Fanshaw—Prufrock—returns from Red Cross duty in Italy, the chance of escape refused, to take up his meaningless old existence: "And I'll go back and go to and fro to lectures with a notebook under my arm, and now and then in the evening, when I haven't any engagement, walk into Boston. . . ."

No, he is not Prince Hamlet. Yet Dos Passos' generation of writers has made of Shakespeare's thwarted prince almost a symbol of themselves and their disjointed relation to their times, so that one comes to look for him in the work of each of them. In Dos Passos one finds him perhaps most clearly portrayed in Fanshaw's friend Wenny, whose words and conduct reveal the theme of the novel: "Thus conscience does make cowards of us all" (*Hamlet* III. i. 83).

An intelligent, sensitive person whose father, like himself, has been poisoned by the paralysis of cowardice, Wenny had, in effect, lost his father early because of their mutual lack of affection. When he runs out of money at Harvard, he makes the mistake of communicating with his father again. After that he cannot escape him: Wenny, drunk, awakes from dreaming of his boyhood, of being in church again, of listening to his father, the minister, pray—"I must pull myself together . . . for that face is my face and my father's voice is my voice. I am my father." So he decides that he can no longer be and shoots himself: "Maybe death's all that, sinking into the body of a dark woman, with proud cold thighs, hair black, black. I wonder if it shoots."

Despite his education, Wenny was a noble savage tamed. In fact, the corrupting influence of his false education, his own inhibitions, and those of the society about him prevented him from expressing his essential nobility. That is his tragedy; and, Dos Passos suggests, it is also ours. It is as if Hamlet had been deprived not only of the fortuitous occasion but also of the incentive for his final action. Wenny, like the others, was too much a part of the Puritan tradition to be able to be aware of one central wrong, much less to feel that he was born to set it right. All too aware that the time was out of joint, he could only curse the spite that he had been born at all.

In his contemporary review of the themes of Hawthorne, Dos Passos' attitude toward his model—as in *Three Soldiers*—was ambivalent. He accepted Hawthorne's premise of the immediacy of the past, even the specifically Puritan past, as controlling and shaping the lives of his characters. And he accepted also his concern not only with the effects of the consciousness of sin but with hypocrisy as perhaps the cardinal sin. Yet in Dos Passos' *Streets of Night* Hawthorne's emphases are subtly reversed. Where Hawthorne presented the past as an unequivocal fact controlling the lives of his characters, both strong and weak, Dos Passos presented it as a tyrannous force warping contemporary lives only because they had not the courage or strength to resist it. Thus where Hawthorne was sympathetic toward his weaker characters as innocent victims of forces too strong for them, Dos Passos scorned his in proportion to their weakness.

Both *The Marble Faun* and *Streets of Night* revolve about a single dramatic incident, or action: the murder by the "faun" of the persecutor of the woman he loves. In Hawthorne this was a central sin—if only because of his characters' consciousness of it as such—which could be studied in its causes and especially in its effects. In Dos Passos, however, Wenny's suicide (he is himself the persecutor of Nan), to which he was driven by Nan's ingrained frigidity and his own lack of courage, is almost the single affirmative and hopeful gesture in the book; and the central sin is not the suicide but the universal lack of courage which drove him to it. Wenny alone of the three protagonists is presented sympathetically because he alone was not a hypocrite and was capable of a definitive action.

Furthermore, if the suicide were a sin at all, it was Nan's sin and that of the bourgeois Puritan morality which had formed her and which she represented. The effect of this central incident on the girl was, indeed, as in Hawthorne, to bind her more closely to her faun. But far from having any regenerative effect, since Wenny is dead, it therefore alienated her irrevocably from the real world and left her, finally, a haunted devotee of the ouija board. To Nan and Fanshaw natural emotions and particularly their spontaneous expression were bad form and therefore suspect, the equivalent of sin. If Dos Passos could have agreed with them, he might then have agreed with Hawthorne that, since sin was an essential condition of humanity (original sin), its indulgence might be humanizing—as it was to Donatello or even ennobling, as to Hester Prynne.

But Dos Passos did not agree. Where Hawthorne's characters acted and then reacted in the consciousness of guilt, Dos Passos' characters started with a morbid consciousness of the effects of action which precluded action. Their sins, if any, were those of omission because of their unwillingness to use their wills to act. For the final implication of Dos Passos' novel is that will and its free expression—*not sin*—are the essential conditions of humanity. If to Hawthorne in the mid-nineteenth century the great evil was man's breaking of the human chain, to Dos Passos in the early twentieth it was his inability to forge his own link within it; and the fault was not entirely that of the individual.

In *Three Soldiers*, Dos Passos' characters were frustrated by the army, an impenetrable institution in the social structure. In *Streets of Night* a "generation of eunuchs," as Wenny characterized his own generation, was made impotent by confinement within an obsolete morality in an archaic and rigid social framework. Most of these characters seemed scarcely to have had a chance. Yet in each of Dos Passos' early novels there was both sympathy and hope.

In *One Man's Initiation* there was the hope of after-the-war; of the coming revolution based on the example of the Russian one already achieved; and especially the hope of one dedicated individual, Martin Howe, left alive. In *Three Soldiers,* there was no necessary assumption of the permanence of the army, either in the book or among Americans at the time. The hope of revolution had dwindled with the pathetic failure of the Paris strike in May of 1919, described near the end of the novel, but something could be expected of those who had avoided or escaped the army—Marcel, the French boy; "old

Howe in America"; and others like them. And it was not so much the army as John Andrews' fatal weakness in deliberately joining it that proved his undoing. In *Streets of Night* the constricting institutions, like the army in the other two books, formed only a part of the total social structure. Whitey, who had his origin in "a little jerkwater town back in South Dakota," was unaffected by them; his final decision was to return home: ". . . an' I aint been back since. I'm goin' though in about a year an' plant myself among the weeds. This aint no place for a white man." Mabel Worthington, acting upon emotions rather than mores, escaped even from within the rigid forms.

Dos Passos' position, then, even in these early works, was one of protest but not of despair. This objection against institutional repression, individual timidity, and their mutual destruction of individuality is the heart of all Dos Passos' writing. Protest is criticism; and criticism is Dos Passos' artistic method —the means which should have its own validity without necessary reference to its end.

III *Manhattan Transfer*

If criticism—"the desire to fathom" of his early "Humble Protest"—is one guidepost to Dos Passos' career, the work of art—the product of "the desire to create"—is of course the other. As both artist and critic, Dos Passos seems to have been aware almost immediately of a central weakness of *Streets of Night*—the fact that neither Wenny's suicide nor Whitey's escape into mere vagabondage was a valid solution to the problem of living. He also recognized that Whitey and Mabel Worthington were not strongly enough emphasized to carry convincingly the novel's essentially humanistic thesis. For *Manhattan Transfer*, his next work, was much more firmly integrated.

After completing *Streets of Night* in Spain, Dos Passos, as if fulfilling Whitey's promise, turned homeward in an effort to plant himself among the metaphorical weeds restricting individual growth at the nerve center of American life, New York City. Finally, neither Dos Passos nor his representative Jimmy Herf—a major character who finally does escape—could establish roots amid the granite and the choking economic undergrowth of the city. So New York emerged as a point of transit only—as Manhattan Transfer, a way-station and port of entry to the U. S. A.

Thus our first sight of Jimmy Herf and Congo, two central characters of *Manhattan Transfer,* is aboard ocean liners entering the port of New York. Everything in the book points to Manhattan as a place of transience: the emphasis on fire and destruction, the theme of "The Burthen of Nineveh" (the subject of the prose-poem introducing the second chapter and the title of the last chapter), the recurring motif of the song,

> Oh it rained forty days
> And it rained forty nights
> And it didn't stop till Christmas
> And the only man that survived the flood
> Was longlegged Jack of the Isthmus.

"Longlegged Jack of the Isthmus" is also a chapter title. The Isthmus may be translated as Manhattan Island, so closely bound to Europe by the ocean liner—such as that on which Jimmy arrives—and to the mainland of America by bridges and by ferries—such as that on which Jimmy leaves the city at the end of the novel. Or it may be translated as the Northern Neck of Virginia, the locale of Jimmy Herf's exploits—in the excerpt, "July," not included in the novel—and the childhood home of young Jack Dos Passos.

Manhattan Transfer marks an important stage not only in Dos Passos' progress toward his fatherland but in his development as an artist. In the preceding two novels Dos Passos had examined a rather special contemporary institution (the army) and a rather special area (Cambridge); but, in terms of form and of content, he had remained within the contemporary tradition of the art novel and of the story of the Sensitive Young Man: Martin Howe, John Andrews, Fanshaw and Wenny.[1] Living in Manhattan from 1923 to 1925, in the very center of our urban-financial society, he was ready for a broader view and a broader challenge. The book that emerged from these years was something new, a city-novel studying American social patterns from within and in a vertical cross-section in a single characteristic area.

Manhattan Transfer, like much of Dos Passos' later fiction, retains a number of characteristics of the so-called art novel.

"Thought and art; Plato and Michael Angelo," Dos Passos had observed, were the "twin guide-posts" not only for the artist but for all human life. If a novel followed Plato in probing the truths of life, then it must necessarily concern itself also with the essentially human "desire to create" of Michelangelo. This novel centers around the lives of two potential artists, Ellen Thatcher, a talented and beautiful young Broadway actress, and Jimmy Herf, a young newspaper reporter with ambitions to become a writer. Ellen achieves a brilliant success as an actress and a minor one after the war as a writer for a woman's magazine. Jimmy's one achievement is his marriage to Ellen, the dream-girl of all Manhattan. But these successes are ironic and superficial. At the height of her dramatic career Ellen feels frustrated at the insincerity of her role: "I hate it; it's all false. Sometimes I want to run down to the foots and tell the audience, go home you damn fools. This is a rotten show and a lot of fake acting and you ought to know it." And her success in magazine work coincides with the failure of her marriage to Jimmy, who has at first no job until he becomes an underpaid reporter on the night shift.

A major theme of the book appears to be the necessary failure of the artist in a materialistic, mechanistic society. Ellen fails successively as wife, daughter, artist, lover, wife (of her second husband Jimmy Herf), and mother. Jimmy's failures are less spectacular; even the failure of his marriage seems to be less his fault than Ellen's. He appears chiefly as a spectator at events who is caught up in the frantic whirlpool of the city until he is finally ejected into an eddy and drifts off across the river. The book is full of artists and would-be artists, of Greenwich Village radicals and intellectuals who hope futilely to achieve the good, the true, the beautiful. And the chapters are introduced by prose poems into the bargain.

Yet *Manhattan Transfer* is only superficially an art-novel, and it is deterministic only in method. Of the fifty or sixty or more characters whom we meet and whose lives intermesh in varying degrees throughout the novel, fewer than a quarter are artists or intellectuals, or even think they are. The Greenwich Village rebelliousness and intellectuality and the surrender of life to Art are presented as futile, unnecessary attitudes. They are futile because they are merely idealistic —the setting of visionary goals on the assumption that the goal is the important thing—and because they are poses and, therefore, escapes from the responsibility of immediate fulfillment. They are unnecessary because the only escape from the apparent horror and meaninglessness of life is to live life fully—or to die.

Thus the two heroes of the book are not Jimmy and Ellen, but *their* heroes. The first, Stan Emery, dominates the middle third of the book from his introduction to his death. With his zest for living and his gay, irresponsible nature, he wins Jimmy's affectionate admiration and a permanent niche in Ellen's Thatcher's heart. But he can find no place in the rigid social structure, largely because of the conditions of his birth; for he, like Dos Passos, is the son of a wealthy senior partner of a prominent New York law firm. He would like to be an architect, but there is no place to build. He is imprisoned within walls within walls of the dingy granite skyscrapers of Manhattan, as he cries out in his frustration, "in the City of New York, County of New York, State of New York." His life, which has been an ironically heroic attempt to escape the prison by living fully within it, ends in final escape in a magnificent drunken gesture (a subtler version of the suicide of Wenny). Dreaming of the city that might have been and that may yet be—"Steel, glass, tile, concrete will be the materials of the skyscrapers. Crammed on the narrow island the millionwindowed buildings will jut, glittering pyramid on pyramid, white cloudsheads piled above a thunderstorm . . ."—he sets fire to the building and himself. So he acknowledges the arsonist within him. The rest do not, though it is in them, too— the fearful fascination for fires, destroying, purifying, that runs with a motif of bells and sirens through the novel.

The career of the other hero, Congo, we can follow at intervals throughout the book. Though apparently a very minor character, Congo is probably more nearly the hero than even Stan. He is, in fact—like Stan, and for the same reasons—an alter ego of Jimmy Herf and therefore of Dos Passos. Like Stan, Congo is determined to experience at all costs as much of life as he can; but unlike Stan, who is tied to New York by his birth and by his dependence upon his father's money, Congo has achieved and maintains a real independence. With no memory of a family, without a country, having quit France with her military service for the sea, and without even a name, he is the only free person in the book. Like all of Dos Passos' heroes—or perhaps, rather, their heroes—he is a type of philosophical anarchist: "I won't go" (if the U. S. should go to war about 1916); "A workingman has no country. I'm going to be American citizen. . . . Moi je suis anarchiste vous comprennez monsieur." The explanation of this apparently confused point of view (no country— American citizen—anarchist) is that it is not so much a political position, or even wholly an intellectual one, as an instinctive attitude of intense individualism.

This philosophical anarchism—the insistence on individual liberty—has been Dos Passos' constant theme. In his first three novels and in *Rosinante* he expressed it in variations of his complementary characters: the natural sensuous man (Lyaeus) and the intellectual or seeker (Telemachus) who is dimly aware of an essential self to be found somewhere within the tangle of restrictive social forms in which he has become enmeshed. In each version of the seeker there is a distinctive autobiographical element which becomes increasingly identifiable as we approach the intimate personal narrative of the Camera Eyes of *U. S. A.*

Everything in *Manhattan Transfer* is more direct, but by no means less subtle, than in the earlier works. For the first time since *Rosinante* Dos Passos was writing of his immediate environment and directing his criticism not so much at partial or temporary or external oppressions—war, the army, the New England Puritan inheritance—as at the ubiquitous contemporary American success myth. It had become tyrannous when it had become predominantly a myth about the time of Dos Passos' birth (1896).

Published in the same year as *An American Tragedy*, *Manhattan Transfer* owes something to Dreiser's first novel, *Sister Carrie* (1900, 1917). Ellen Thatcher, a more modern Carrie Meeber, climbs to theatrical success; achieves fame, wealth, applause, and the world of men at her feet; and finds it all lonely, dull, and superficial in the end. There are other similarities; for the pictures of the down-and-outs Bud Korpenning and Jimmy Herf's Uncle Joe Harland, once king of the curb market, resemble George Hurstwood in his declining days, though they lack his stoic dignity. The differences are more important; Dos Passos is no Dreiser. For Dreiser believed in material success—not that it would bring happiness, which to him was a mirage, but that it would bring comfort and the satisfaction of physical desires, which were all one could hope to get in the grim business of life. His salesman Druet illustrates his point of view; utterly opportunistic and materialistic, unthoughtful and completely adaptable, he accepts expected rebuffs and genially turns aside toward the next best chance.

Like Dreiser, Dos Passos shows us characters going up and down in the economic scales as they pursue the god of success. But Jimmy Herf, finally, and Congo and even Ellen make decisions; Dreiser's characters principally drift as their fates direct them. The life which both writers portray is almost equally grim in their books; but in Dos Passos' it seems unnecessarily grim because men and women make it so: they have not the nerve to flout the forms and rules made by others or the strength of character to make their own places rather than passively allowing themselves to be molded to fit the institutions of their time.

Again in *Manhattan Transfer* the autobiography is expanded from Dos Passos' previous novel; and it is placed almost wholly within the life of a single fictional character, Jimmy Herf. The suicide motif is still there, but muted. None of the characters we know by name actually commits intentional suicide, though he may threaten to do so. Yet the underlying death wish is apparent in the theme of arson and in the deaths of Stan Emery and Bud Korpenning; the former dies drunkenly obsessed with fire and the latter, obsessed by fear, when each has reached a dead end in his life.

The father problem is also handled not only more directly but more subtly than in the earlier novels. In *One Man's Initiation* there was no mention of Martin Howe's family or background; and the handling of the problem was not intended for the reader's recognition, for it is obscured in the name of Martin's friend, Tom Randolph, whom Martin envies and admires—discussed in Chapter One, section IV. In *Three Soldiers*, as we noted in Chapter Two, section I, we were given a glimpse into John Andrews' childhood in Virginia, from which his father was conspicuously absent. In *Streets of Night* for the first time Dos Passos frankly investigated the problem of a man's resentment of his father, first in the character of Wenny (see Chapter Six, section II) and second in that of Wenny's hero, Whitey, who has been driven from home for rebelling against his drunken father's persecution of his mother.

In *Manhattan Transfer*, Bud Korpenning—a very minor character (another version of Whitey) whose story is complete by the end of the First Section (or book)—justifiably murders his inhumanly tyrannical father; and his fear of apprehension then destroys him. Congo's story is parallel but different: "When I first remember . . . a big man not my fader beat me up every day. Then I run away and work on sailboats." Congo's independent life, his broad experience, and his contempt for success as a goal mark his active career—he exploits rather than is controlled by the social patterns of Manhattan. Under a succession of aliases—as the nameless Congo ("dey call me Congo because I have curly hair an dark like a nigger"); as the select bootlegger, Marquis des Coulommiers; and as the millionaire Armand Duval, who lives in a palatial suite in Manhattan and is driven by his chauffeur in a Rolls-Royce—he alone achieves both an ostensible and a real success.

Although Stan Emery's desire to be an architect and his frustration as the son of a prominent New York attorney are taken from Dos Passos' life, Jimmy Herf is the author's true representative. Herf's own father is barely referred to as "someone" his mother "liked very much" and as the "dark man in a yachting-cap" whom Jimmy dimly, though resentfully, recalls in a dream as insistently urging him to perform, to succeed: " 'Jump, Yimmy, yump; you can do it in two yumps' . . . the dark man's beating him, yump yump yump." In all Dos Passos' fiction there is a subtle interpenetration between dream and reality (as in Chrisfield's encounter with the dead German in the woods in *Three Soldiers*). In this instance, Jimmy's dream, though it lacks the reality even of a memory, epitomizes the central problem of his career: having been born into the conventional pattern of success, he is supposed to have the tremendous advantage of starting at the top, and he is faced with pressure from all sides to succeed as his father and his uncle Jefferson Merivale did before him.

The reality of the dream is further augmented when we realize that it represents a very real American social problem

which is that of the rich man's son born in a society theo-
retically fluid and dedicated to the individual's achievement
of his own success. Moreover, it was very probably a real
dream of the author, which reveals his own predicament in
terms of the aspirations of his wealthy and successful father.
For how does one *achieve* the top when one starts there?
As Herf remarks to Congo almost at the end of the book,
"The difference between you and me is that you're going
up in the social scale, Armand, and I'm going down. . . .
My mother and father did all this Vermont marble black-
walnut grand Babylonian stuff . . . there's nothing more for
me to do about it. . . . If I thought it'd be any good to me I
swear I've got the energy to sit up and make a million dollars.
But I get no organic sensation out of that stuff any more.
I've got to have something new, different. . . . Your sons'll be
like that Congo."

Jimmy himself is, in a way, the first of these sons. For the
filial respect and admiration of Jimmy for Congo is recipro-
cated in the paternal concern and affection of Congo. Occasionally he praises him: "You never get drunk, Mr. 'Erf. . . .
Very good. No use spend a lot o money ave a eadache next
day." He instructs also: "But a feller like you, good education,
all 'at, you dont know what life is. When I was seventeen
I come to New York. . . ." And he tries to help him: "But
Meester 'Erf, if dere is anyting any time I can do for you,
money or like dat, you let me know eh?" On this occasion of
their last meeting, Jimmy remarks to Congo: "If I'd been God
and had to decide who in this city should make a million
dollars and who shouldn't I swear you're the man I should
have picked." If he could have picked his own father, his
choice would have been the same.

Not until a quarter of a century later did Congo reappear
in Dos Passos' fiction under the name of Nick Pignatelli—
a distant cousin of Jay Pignatelli, the clearly autobiographical hero of *Chosen Country*—who was a sort of guardian and
political mentor of Jay after the death of his father. In the
meantime Dos Passos published a brief, appreciative portrait
of the probable original of Congo and Nick as "Carlo Tresca,"
in the *Nation* for January 23, 1943. Yet only recently in the
non-fiction review of the development and practice of his
political philosophy, *The Theme Is Freedom,* did he reveal

at all explicitly the character of the relationship he had portrayed in *Manhattan Transfer* over thirty years before. On the eve of his trip to Spain in behalf of the republican defense against Franco early in 1937, Dos Passos sought out Tresca, who took him out to dinner. "Carlo Tresca combined the shrewdest kind of knowledge of men and their motives with profound information on the realities of politics he'd acquired in a lifetime of partisan warfare in the anarchist cause. 'John,' he told me 'they goin' make a monkey outa you . . . a beeg monkey.'" As it turned out, "Carlo Tresca, as he always did, had his facts right."

Whether or not it is the example of Congo that gives him the faith and courage he needs, Jimmy Herf at the end of *Manhattan Transfer* is able to perform very simply and casually a tremendous act. Granting Ellen the divorce she seeks, quitting his job as a newspaper reporter, determined to be neither a slave nor a hypocrite but himself, he strolls aboard a ferryboat before dawn and leaves the city. So he buries "his twenties" in "the City of Destruction" and crosses the river to a new life; and this time, like Congo before him, he starts as a homeless vagrant, without family, without money: "Carefully he spends his last quarter on breakfast. That leaves him three cents for good luck, or bad for that matter." He has discovered himself in transit through the gateway to America. The novel ends as he sets out joyously, "taking pleasure in breathing, in the beat of his blood, in the tread of his feet on the pavement," to discover his country.

Certainly the burly, carefree, independent figure of Congo—a success in spite of himself and because he works and lives outside of the conventional social patterns—provides an important unifying element in this grim satire of the American success myth. His example at once defines true success and illustrates the means of its achievement—even in Manhattan—in self-reliance, freedom, a joy in living, and a confident devotion to those means.

Yet even more important than the relative explicitness and optimism of his message, compared to his earlier novels, is Dos Passos' achievement in terms of form. What Dos Passos has done in *Manhattan Transfer* is to turn the well-made novel upside down. Superficially the form is chaotic—a succession of scarcely related or unrelated portraits of dying and dead souls seeking some meaning in existence as they are first sucked in and then whirled around and around, occasionally passing one another, in the whirlwind of the mad pursuit of success which is Manhattan. There is no conventional plot, and there is little or no significant action except in the deceptively casual release of Jimmy Herf at the end of the book. Most of the characters are rather acted upon than acting; for even suicide, unlike that of Wenny in *Streets of Night*, is presented as an unconscious surrender rather than an act of will. Almost none of the characters come alive, except as children; only Congo and Nevada Jones, an ex-prostitute and showgirl whom he finally marries, and Jimmy Herf are alive in any true sense at the end of the book.

In *Manhattan Transfer* the apparent chaos of the whirlwind itself provides the form and the action. Developing in tighter and tighter concentric circles until only three characters (those just mentioned) are left alive in the calm at its center, it acquires a centrifugal force which ejects one of these, Jimmy Herf. But it must be remembered that this is a manmade whirlwind, and that the force which ejects Jimmy is his moral conscience. Jimmy's lesson comes—like the voice Job heard—from within the whirlwind: it is the voice of the example of Congo bidding him gird up his loins now like a man, for his own right hand can save him.

This unity of form and idea in *Manhattan Transfer* parallels Dos Passos' increasing sense of his relationship to his society at the time, his consciousness of the nature of that relationship, and a new sureness in expressing it in his art. All of these are intrinsic in his handling of his own story in the character of Jimmy Herf. In the first place, Jimmy, unlike his predecessors, is not a rebel although some of his associates are. We recall his comment, when he first met him as a small boy aboard the liner, in reply to a remark that he looked glad to be home: "Oh I am, I could fall down and kiss the ground." His only error—which he realizes at the end—was in thinking that he could find his home within a portion of the society when he had not yet found it within the whole. In the second place, Jimmy's (or Dos Passos') story is tangential rather than central to the action of the novel; for his specific role is more nearly that of a reporter or an observer than that of a struggling participant in the life around him. Finally, Herf's story is Dos Passos' story with a new explicitness; it symbolizes the problem not only of Dos Passos' generation but, in fact, of almost the entire American experience. This story or problem is the search for individuality in a changing society in which the frames of reference seem never fixed; for they are either crumbling or so narrow as to mold the individual to a predetermined form; or they are so broad as to leave him indistinguishable from the democratic mass.

In effect, if not in intention, *Manhattan Transfer* is Dos Passos' tribute to Dreiser, who probably taught him most about the realistic city novel and the naturalistic method. At the same time it is Dos Passos' critique of Dreiser's portrait of life in America—a portrait which mocked the long American tradition of faith in the possibilities of pragmatic individualism and which accepted too readily the materialism of the present.

Taken together, *Three Soldiers, Streets of Night,* and *Manhattan Transfer* constitute a first trilogy by Dos Passos, which he might have entitled "American Perspective." By focusing his criticism at once upon contemporary institutions and upon their principal interpreters—Crane, Hawthorne, Dreiser—in our literary tradition, he developed his own thought and his own techniques in relation to theirs. He also added to his understanding of the whole American tradition and of his relation to it. In the process, he uncovered some interesting paradoxes: that fiction may help to shape the realities of the future; that a central reality today may be a fiction, a myth; and that today's fiction may shape the past by interpretation, by criticism, by new work which, if true enough, may alter the tradition into which it fits.[2]

These were heady discoveries for a novelist still in his twenties in 1925 when *Manhattan Transfer* was published. The possibilities of a profound long-range effect on his environment were opening up. But Dos Passos' social conscience was as active as ever, and there were plenty of things that needed doing and saying *now* in the America of Silent Cal Coolidge. At the same time, the possibilities of a more immediate effect were opening up in the theater; they were worth investigation.

CHAPTER 7

Three Plays: Time, the Individual, and Society

DOS PASSOS' picture of Jimmy Herf in the role of reporter and critic and with his associates from Greenwich Village and the theatrical life of Manhattan reflected his own pursuits at the time. He was not, of course, a reporter in the literal sense that Herf was; but much of the structure, style, and content of *Manhattan Transfer* are those of the daily newspaper; and the intent is criticism. Nor was Dos Passos ever an actor or apparently much in rapport with the theater crowd, which he satirized in *Manhattan Transfer* and elsewhere;[1] yet the first version of *Manhattan Transfer* was Dos Passos' play *The Moon Is a Gong*.[2] This play, an expressionistic pre-telling of the story of Jimmy Herf and Ellen Thatcher through the lives of its two principals, Tom Burns and Jane Carroll, inaugurated the period of Dos Passos' special interest in the theater.

I *The Larger Audience*

A relatively brief period, it reached its climax in 1926 and 1927, when Dos Passos was writing and producing plays and helping design and paint stage scenery as a member of the New Playwrights Theater group. Except for publishing his third play *Fortune Heights* in 1933, his active participation in the theater, interrupted during his trip to Russia in 1928, ended about the time of his first marriage in 1929. But his continued interest is indicated by occasional articles about the theater (including the Russian theater) through 1931 and by a group of articles in 1934 at the time of his publication of his *Three Plays* in a period of generally heightened interest in the possibilities of an American federal theater. His special preoccupation with the theater lasted only about a decade. But the years from 1923 to 1934 were, as I have intimated, crucial years in the development both of the man and the artist—and of the civilization in which he was trying to make his way.

The reasons for Dos Passos' interest in the theater are perhaps obvious enough even had he not made them fairly explicit in *The Theme Is Freedom* and more recently in "Looking Back on 'U. S. A.'" (New York *Times,* October 25, 1959). First, he had long intended to be an artist and more specifically a writer; and, in his search for his appropriate form, he had always been eclectic and experimental; but until 1923[3] the drama was one of the few literary forms he had not yet tried. Secondly, a primary consideration of his search had always been the size and availability of his audience. Moreover, two contemporary phenomena coincided that would have made it surprising had Dos Passos not experimented in the theater: one was the period of postwar reaction which reached a climax in 1926 and 1927 in the trials and execution of Sacco and Vanzetti, which symbolized for Dos Passos the imminent collapse of whatever tenable social structure he hoped to find in his country and which made it imperative to him that his anguished cry of warning be heard. The other was the success of the little-theater movement between 1923 and 1926 in creating an audience for serious, experimental drama.

He was already publishing, increasingly actively, in the weekly journals of dissident opinion. "The problem," he recalls in *The Theme Is Freedom,* "was how to reach a larger public. O'Neill and the Provincetown Players had opened up a path." Finally, his participation in the theater at this time offered him a release from his lonely art of novel-writing and the opportunity to join with other dedicated men and women in the hope that through art they might create, both directly and indirectly, a better world to live in.

II *The Moon Is a Gong*

In *The Moon Is a Gong* (1925) or *The Garbage Man* (1926), its later title, Dos Passos used the expressionistic method to present the most direct statement in his imaginative writings of many of his familiar themes. Tom and Jane, like

Wenny and Nan and like Jimmy Herf and Ellen Thatcher, are two young people ensnared by the institutions of their time. Although they are conscious of their predicament, they think they can escape it together: "When we get to Chicago it will be different. Our life will begin from tomorrow." But a train wreck on the next track convinces them of the futility of their dreams, of the easy obliteration of their tomorrows, and of the necessity of their finding their own ways. In Jane's words, "The only thing that can be done two by two is come out of the ark. We've done that. Now we are on our own. . . . There's no after, there's no tomorrow. . . . It's the same now. I will live now. . . . Have you forgotten how the moon would mean act not dream to you?" Tom goes off to "see the world . . . live every sort of life" and to achieve his individuality in action and in defiance of the Garbage Man and of the Voice of the Radio commanding obedience. Jane chooses acting rather than action and loses her identity as Janet Gwendolyn, the successful actress. At the end Jane is carried off by the Garbage Man, whose job is to remove the human offal—"all the dead-alive"—from the world.

This Garbage Man, as he appears in Part Two, Scene Two, is the central symbol of the play—at once a chorus and *deus ex machina;* he not only personifies but comments upon the significance of time. As the Family Practitioner when Jane's mother, Mrs. Carroll, dies, he serves as a sardonic reminder to Jane of her place in the pattern when he remarks upon her resemblance to her grandmother whom he had also attended in the same room. As the Man in Black Overalls, he helps carry off the dead from the train wreck, while he comments ironically about their hopes and ambitions: "Funny I call it."

And as the Man in the Stovepipe Hat who inveigles Tom and a young bum to participate in a robbery, he is complemented by a more nearly classical chorus in the Telescope Man who sells *"ten cent squints at the moon"* on Union Square and philosophizes (somewhat gratuitously) about time and the human comedy around him: "Every day they're tied tighter in ticker ribbon till they can't move, till they don't have time to look at the moon. . . . And time slips through among the garbage cans in the canyon streets. Time is a great snake writhing through gray streets, wearing away angles of stone cornices, wearing ornaments off marblefaced sepulchers. . . . Time is a gray ash dropping from the souls of fat men in swivel chairs. . . . Time has his undertaking establishment on every block."

Time, in short, is on man's side, if he will only use it to live in. The Garbage Man, in a sense, represents death, but he is also the force that removes all that is antithetical to true living. When at the end the Garbage Man carries off Jane, he makes possible her reunion with Tom in the final scene. Tom has escaped the Garbage Man through his own efforts by literally scaling the skyscrapers to the moon to beat on it with his two fists as on a gong. Jane, unable to escape by herself, had to be carried off as one of the dead-alive before she could begin to live.

Portions of Dos Passos' biography appear only vaguely in the lives of Tom, *"a skinny brownfaced young man"* (in his confused genealogy and in his quest), and Jane (whose mother's death, again associated with aphasia, has many parallels in Dos Passos' fiction). But one other character or symbol in the play that is worth mentioning is John, a Negro preacher to whom Dos Passos has given both his name and his purpose. Appearing only briefly and early in the play, John states the central problem of Tom and Jane and presents also its solution: "In dis world dey's many folks thinks dey's alive as ain't alive. . . . It's dem dat's felt tingle within 'em de breath o' de Lawd, like a bird, like a maukin' in de woods, a song full o' warm honey, and all de same ain't follered de call. . . . Hit's dem dat's dade!" After hearing him, Tom and Jane know that now they "are really seekin'." Although Jane loses herself in her success as an actress, Tom continues the quest and so saves himself and ultimately—with the help of the Garbage Man, who is the ally of life—even Jane.

The romantic and rather mystical elements of this play— the idea that to seek (devotedly enough) is to find and that love (if it is profound enough: a love of life) will find out a way—are balanced by the pessimistic implications of its conclusion: contemporary society is composed almost wholly of the "dead-alive"; and love, life, and individuality can be found, therefore, only outside it. Viewing the work by itself, we are apt to be puzzled about what to make of it. But by studying it in the context of Dos Passos' larger work, we can resolve the romantic quest into the more practical and realistic principle of *lo flamenco*: the road and the way one travels it determine the destination, rather than the other way around. Two further observations are, moreover, pertinent: first, Dos Passos, while he was writing the play, was moving toward a closer understanding of his society; second, at the end of the novel which he later made from the play, Jimmy Herf achieved his individuality and began to live his life as he moved *into* the United States and not away from it.

III *Airways*

In his later two plays, *Airways, Inc.* (1928) and *Fortune Heights* (1933), Dos Passos was still concerned with the problem of time and how an individual could use it to come to grips with himself and with the society in which he must live and move. But the time gradually becomes more specific, and the emphasis shifts from the need for the individual's integrity, which is more and more assumed, to the need for an environmental integrity which will permit man to exercise his own.

In *The Garbage Man* the time was abstract, for it ranged from "no time," as Tom threw his watch across the stage in the first scene, to "now's the time," as the Garbage Man remarked as he carried off Jane. *Airways,* based on two important myth-making events of the preceding year—the aviation accomplishment of Lindbergh and the execution of Sacco and Vanzetti—is, however, specifically contemporary in its emphasis.

The play opens as the Turner family awaits news of young Elmer Turner's record flight; a strike continues throughout the eight months of the play, and it halts not only progress in the industrial town but the construction of a house next door to the Turner home. The play ends as Martha Turner—still keeping house for her brothers in a now disintegrated family—awaits and meets the moment of execution of the man she loves, the radical Goldberg. Both the strike and the development of the airplane company, Airways, Inc., represent attempts to exploit time—the one for social equality and the other for monetary gain. At the end the strike appears to be broken with the electrocution of Goldberg, its leader; and the company declares a stock bonus.

In this play Dos Passos has also used a chorus in the person of the Professor, an old man who lives with the Turners and who is a refugee from "the collapse of the shining socialist dream" in his native Hungary and Europe in general. Like the Garbage Man, he represents time—specifically, past time in its bearing on the present. Nobody pays much attention to his rambling reminiscences of his early life as a radical intellectual, its hopes, its betrayals, and its disillusionments. But each one is a pointed but unintended commentary about the life surrounding him. He had come to America to escape: "I wanted to go far away." But technology, the airplane and the telegraph, have foreshortened distance, and "nowhere is far any more." And they have also foreshortened time, so that even the European past impinges directly upon the American present—as is emphasized again in Goldberg's comments about his racial memory as a Jew: "We've been in prison for two thousand years. I have the mind of a jailbird. . . . We were all jailed in poverty and Judaism and in old customs and hatreds and wornout laws." As in *Streets of Night* the emphasis is upon the presentness of the past, but it is focused in *Airways, Inc.*, on the vitality of a conscious memory.

In this play—which presents us with a picture of contemporary American society in microcosm, enacted about the Turner household—none of the Americans have any memory, except for the Jew Goldberg and old Dad Turner. The latter, however, remembers only his own failure in life, which is colored by his feelings of persecution past and present; and he hangs himself at the end of the first act. Of the others only an "Old German" and Amari, *"an old Italian,"* can relate the present to what has gone before. At the end, after the news of the execution, even the Professor's memory is gone: "I can't remember. . . . I can't remember." As Martha explains, "He had a stroke the other day, aphasia." Yet in the final, tragic speech of Martha a kind of hope emerges from her despair: "Now I'm beginning to feel it, the house without Walter, the street without him, the city without him, the future that we lived in instead of a honeymoon without him, everything stark without him. . . . What can I do now that he is gone and that he has left me full of scalding wants, what can I do with the lack of him inside me like a cold stone?" For Goldberg has given meaning to her otherwise drab, old maid's life. Now she must learn to live with only the memory to sustain her; yet one feels that it is enough.

The Garbage Man posed questions about the nature and use of time in general and suggested that life achieved validity only in individually conceived patterns of present action, as opposed both to dreams of the future and to social pressures to conform. *Airways*, although more concerned with the social context of individual life, maintained essentially the view of society of the earlier play and revealed the disintegration of the Turner family, the cramping tyranny of industrial-commercial society, and the frustration of potentially valid new patterns based on cooperative organizations of working people. But it went further in examining the context of the present in which action must be performed; for it implied that, since patterns of action extend into the past as well as into the future, truly conscious action can exist only within the framework of a conscious memory.

IV *Fortune Heights*

In *Fortune Heights* Dos Passos is even more concerned with contexts, social and temporal. In the first place, the play is a contribution to a "theatre of depression" that Dos Passos had called for two years earlier in the *New Republic*,[4] and it deals directly with that contemporary and very urgent social problem. As the stage directions indicate, *"The action takes place at a fillingstation on a national highway. . . . In the back are visible three of a row of overnight cottages."* What Dos Passos presents here is a rootless, transient, speculative society of bums, hitchhikers, vagrants, wanderers who pass by this prototype of the modern motel and who are looking for they hardly know what—but for something to belong to. There is little chance for individual growth since nearly all have lost their roots in the soil; even the farmers have been leaving the farms for the cities, and those who have stayed are threatened with foreclosures and evictions. There seems to be no adequate cohesive element to bind and to hold together even one man and one woman. Morry, the hero (also known as Slim), is unable to see his way to marrying Rena, whom he loves, so he walks out on her and on his boss Owen, whom he respects. Owen and his wife Florence, who have been separated for years and reunited, are now drifting apart again within the pattern of shabby overnight loves on which their speculation in real estate survives.

But in the final tragedy, in which Morry returns and is killed in a futile attempt to defend Owen from eviction, there is again hope. Common adversities of the depression are driving people together. The farmers of the neighborhood band together to stand behind Owen and to resist evictions everywhere on principle. This particular skirmish is a failure, yet the principle has held; and Owen and Florence are at last truly united as they join the vast procession *"straggling end-lessly down the road . . . the homeless and jobless on the march after a job, after a home, after a new order."*

More important, the people are discovering, not so much in the soil as in time, their roots and a common origin. They are discovering the American past, and their common efforts are directed at re-establishing its principles. As Morry says before he is killed, "Resistin' oppression was how this country was started. Our forefathers settled it so that they could live independent an' every man could have an equal opportunity." Or as Joe, one of the group of farmers, puts it, "We stand on the Declaration of Independence. In school they taught us . . . unalienable rights. . . . A country where a man who wants to work can't earn his own livin' ain't the United States. We're out to find the United States. One for all and all for one, we'll find the United States." And Owen's final words, as he and Florence join the marchers, are an echo of Joe's: "We got to find the United States."

V *Dramatic Themes, Techniques, Aims*

These *Three Plays,* then, have more than the fact of their common form to warrant their inclusion in a single book. Together they comprise a consistent, integrated development of the triple theme of the individual, society, and time. Although they have no common characters, they contain common types: a man and a woman struggling for identity and unity in the face of a society represented by parasitic speculators (real estate agents) and bullying authority (policemen and federal agents).

Technically, too, there are similarities. In each the radio is used as a sort of anti-intellectual voice of the nation urging conformity in promises and platitudes which emerge in ironic contrast to events on the stage. In each there is almost a minimum of scene detail and especially of scenery change, for *Airways* and *Fortune Heights* are designed for a permanent set. In all of them an attempt is made to bring the action closer to the audience than in the conventional theater. In the first, for instance, when Tom escapes the Garbage Man, he *"leaps across the footlights, and disappears up the aisle."* In *Airways*, according to the "Production Note" in *Three Plays,* "the pictureframe stage was done away with. . . . The action was followed and continuity established by a spotlight. . . . The apron was extended over the orchestra pit to bring the actors nearer the audience, and the slight changes of set between the acts were made in full view." *Fortune Heights* appears to have envisioned a similar production technique: the many scenes are differentiated only by changes in position of the actors and by exits and entrances; and the acts are terminated, mechanically, only by blackouts or dimouts.

Dos Passos' first extensive comment about the theater, like his first extensive comment on many subjects, occurs in *Rosinante to the Road Again.* In his chapter about the Spanish playwright Benavente, Dos Passos was particularly intrigued with the meaning and significance of the Spanish term, *lo castizo,* applied as a compliment to Benavente: *"Tiene el sentido de lo castizo.* He has the sense of the. . . ." He went on to explain: "The very existence of such a word in a language argues an acute sense of style, of the manner of doing things. . . . *Lo castizo* is the essence of the local, of the regional . . . refers not to the empty shell of traditional observances but to the very core and gesture of them . . . all that is acutely indigenous, Iberian, in the life of Castile. . . . The theatre in Madrid has been the refuge of *lo castizo"* (pp. 184-86). Thus the theater in Madrid was the nourisher of the roots of national identity and distinctiveness. Not only that, it was also an essential element in the remarkably public, communal social life of the area: "In Spain this social life centers in the cafe and the casino. The modern theatre is [the direct] offshoot of the cafe. . . . The people who write the plays, the people who act them and the people who see them spend their spare time smoking about marbletop tables, drinking coffee, discussing."

Dos Passos seems to have hoped to discover or to create some such significance in the theater in America. In December, 1927, at the height of his participation in the American theater, he published in the *New Masses* an article entitled "Towards a Revolutionary [American] Theatre." He began by defining his terms: "By theatre I don't mean a building or an idea, I mean a group of people, preferably a huge group of people: part of the group puts on plays and the rest forms the audience, an active, working audience. By American I don't mean that the group's interests must necessarily be limited to America, but that they should be as deeply rooted here as possible. By revolutionary I mean that such a theatre must break with the present day theatrical tradition, not with the general traditions of the theatre, and that it must draw its life and ideas from the conscious sections of the industrial and white collar working classes."[5]

To create this American version of the Spanish theater, which was to conserve national cultural roots and "the general traditions of the theatre," and to serve as "a real focus in American life," Dos Passos devoted much of his time during the decade from about 1923 to about 1933. His opinion of the importance of this period was stated in his first appearance in the *New Masses* in June, 1926: "In these terribly crucial years . . . being clearsighted is a life and death matter." One man acting alone could do little to achieve his "revolutionary American theatre"; but a dedicated group might do more: "If we don't do it, it will be due to lack of organizing skill." These words explain his association with the American Communist Party in the *New Masses* and in the New Playwrights ventures. This was probably the one group sufficiently dedicated, sufficiently concerned with "the conscious sections of the industrial and white collar working classes," and well organized enough to have a hope of achieving such a theater.

Of course, from one point of view the communists were too well organized from above to permit their being much influenced by such dissident associates as Dos Passos or even by their American leaders. But, from another point of view, their subservience to Moscow prevented their developing any real or effective organizing skill in America because their interests could never become "deeply rooted here." Neverthe-less, Dos Passos' ideal theater, as he described it in his essay—and even the Americanization of the American Communist Party—was worth a try.

When the communist organization and, therefore, its theater proved inadequate means to achieve "a real focus in American life," Dos Passos abandoned both in the spring of 1928 and left for his trip to Russia. But he maintained his contact with the social nucleus with which he had identified himself. And he continued his search for some institution which could serve as a cohesive social force and as a common meeting ground from which men of good will could direct their actions along meaningful paths.

The list of contributing editors and of contributors in the first issue of the *New Masses* (see Chapter Two, note 1)—nearly all of whom are better known today than they were then—defines fairly well the nature of the group of Americans with whom Dos Passos had finally aligned himself. For the most part artist-intellectuals, they were, if only by virtue of their artistic temperaments, highly conscious of the need for more meaningful forms than they perceived in the world around them. Although their stay with the *New Masses* was for the most part brief, they achieved a certain unity of protest and even of purpose, and they anticipated the more general quest a decade later in the depression-thirties. Like Dos Passos' Marchers in *Fortune Heights* and Steinbeck's Okies in *The Grapes of Wrath* (1939), they were out "to find the United States."

In the *New Masses* of December, 1929, Dos Passos used his review of Hemingway's *Farewell to Arms* ("the best written book that has seen the light in America for many a long day") as the opportunity for some remarks about craftsmanship: "After all craftsmanship is a damn fine thing, one of the few human functions a man can unreservedly admire. The drift of the Fordized world seems all against it. . . . It's getting to be almost unthinkable . . . that a man should enjoy doing a piece of work for the sake of doing it as well as he damn well can." From these reflections, Dos Passos went on to identify a new class in "Whom Can We Appeal To?" published in the *New Masses* of August, 1930. This was "the class that had the smallest stake in the [capitalistic] game . . . engineers, scientists, independent manual craftsmen, writers, and actors, technicians of one sort or another." These men, he felt, with "their technical education that makes them valuable to the community," were the key men in our industrial society. "They should be made to realize that they have power and that by intelligent organization they could make themselves respected." Claiming membership in that class, Dos Passos concluded that "most of us [are] too cowardly . . . to want to make events, but . . . we are the handlers of ideas. Ideas can't make events but they can color them. We can't affect the class war much but we might possibly make it more humane."

Almost by an act of will, or of definition, Dos Passos had placed himself, as artist and craftsman, within the middle-class majority of American society. He had defined a vocation both for himself and his group which was consistent with the principles he had all along maintained: the use of their craftsmanship—art and thought combined as a means valid in itself—to achieve first their own unity "by intelligent organization," and ultimately the larger social unity by their willingness "to think, talk, write, vote, act, in favor of toleration."[6]

By 1930 Dos Passos had not yet reached, or rather the United States had not, the stage where he could accept it as a fully participating citizen of the whole society. Within the next six years the course of her history moved the country sufficiently to the left to align their positions, so that Dos Passos could vote "with enthusiasm"—on probably the one occasion of his life—for the continuance in office of the existing administration. But in the early thirties Dos Passos could not simply sit back to await that propitious moment. He too had adjustments to make involving his relationship to his country's history.

Dos Passos' novel *Chosen Country* ends with the marriage of Jay Pignatelli (Dos Passos) and Lulie Harrington. From the Midwest, Lulie, with her venturesome spirit, her love of life, and her determined individualism, represents the ideality of the American tradition and the American dream. Certainly by 1929, at the time of his marriage to Katharine Smith, as he later indicated symbolically in the novel, Dos Passos had accepted the United States as his "chosen country." But acceptance did not mean belonging. Though his interests were centered here, they were not yet "as deeply rooted here as possible." Failing, despite a diligent search, to discover deep roots in the apparent Sahara of contemporary institutions, he was forced to look for them in the past. If he could re-create his own remembered past and, in artistic form, parallel it with the contemporary past of his country, he would have found the U. S. A. and his own place within it.

By the spring of 1930 he had published *The 42nd Parallel,* the first volume of his major work, which he devoted to this purpose of discovery. In August of 1936 he completed the trilogy with the publication of the third volume, *The Big Money.* In a remarkable coincidence of fact and fiction, the United States at that moment seemed to have achieved simultaneously in Dos Passos' art and in its own political development an intelligible and satisfying form. The explanation of the literary phenomenon lies in the relationship between history and Dos Passos' art.

CHAPTER 8

Architect of History

THE PROBLEM of time and the importance of memory had been persistent themes in Dos Passos' art from the start. One recalls many examples from his early work: the poem in the *Harvard Monthly,* entitled "Memory," and other painful autobiographical reminiscences; the sudden premium put upon time by the war in the lives of Martin Howe and of John Andrews and his friends; Andrews—and Dos Passos— inexorably pursued by the memory of "washing those windows"; Telemachus' haunting memory of "the maxims of Penelope" and his fading remembrance of his quest; and the presentness of the Puritan past in *Streets of Night.*

Dos Passos' quest for form in society was ended when he could identify a group that made the most of time in craftsmanship, and the search for political form also ceased when he could discern an administration with a memory, under a president with a talent for organization and "as richly informed in the history and traditions of his own country as any President since Jefferson."[1] Furthermore, his quest for artistic form was resolved when he discovered how to make of one of the oldest artistic forms one of the newest. This was the documentary, defined by Merriam-Webster as "recording or depicting in artistic form a factual and authoritative presentation, as of an event or a social or cultural phenomenon." This was a form in which his own memories and the re-created memories of his time could serve as commentaries.

I Sense of Past and Present

In *U. S. A.* he made the documentary novel his own. A form committed to historical interpretation, he had been working to perfect it since his college days. His early interest is indicated in his *Harvard Monthly* reviews praising Jack Reed. In "Playboy," his biography of Reed in *1919*, Dos Passos wrote: "Jack Reed was the best American writer of his time, if anybody had wanted to know about the war they could have read about it in the articles he wrote." By 1916, Reed's "sort of writing, half newspaper report and half personal narrative," was already to Dos Passos the one "distinctive and perfected form in American 'near-literature.'" His job was to perfect it and to raise it from the realm of "near-literature" to that of art.

More conscious than most of his contemporaries of the impact of past and present events, his historical training was well under way. In his "Humble Protest" of June, 1916, occurs the following characteristic comment, which reveals a frankly humanistic bias and an ironic or tragic view of history: "In succession, Roman stoicism, Pauline Christianity, and the Ages of Faith have kept prisoner under varying bonds that humanism, that realization of the fullness of man, which was the heritage of the Greeks, and in another form, of Jesus." To Dos Passos, "the most tragic part of modern history" lay in the suppression of humanism by the industrial revolution. And in the paragraph immediately preceding is his insistence upon the vitality of memory and upon self-knowledge, the first and the last concern of the historian: "Haven't we forgotten the *Know thyself* of the Greeks?"

If Dos Passos' artistic efforts have differed from those of most of his contemporaries, it is chiefly because his historical interests have been broader, deeper, more highly conscious than those of most of them. All of the things which contributed to his original rootlessness—as opposed to what Malcolm Cowley called their "deracination"—formed a part of the difference. His "hotel childhood"; his odd, vaguely European accent; and his illegitimacy and lack of a home—all these made him conscious almost from the start of his lack of roots and his need to establish them. And a preoccupation with roots, in that sense, leads inevitably to a concern with the past. His reading in Gibbon and his wide travels reinforced his concern.

As early as August of 1914 with the destruction of Belgium and Brussels, his "earliest known city," history had caught up with Dos Passos. Probably more than most Americans—

even those in the colleges and in government—he was aware of acute personal and historical significance in that event. For this reason, Dos Passos gave to even his earliest work in the *Harvard Monthly* an historical flavor, and he attained an urgency in his editorials, "The Evangelist and the Volcano" (November, 1915) and "A Conference on Foreign Relations" (June, 1916), in which he called upon his readers to wake up to the forces of history engulfing them. It is also why his "Humble Protest" is itself a critical summary of those forces and their effect on the present. It could almost be said that history had claimed Dos Passos from the start and directed his art into a documentary form.

Dos Passos did not, of course, invent the documentary form. As a modern art form it was being developed in the motion pictures by such men as D. W. Griffith, Robert Flaherty, and the Russian director Eisenstein. In essence it is even as old as picture-writing; as a literary form it achieved perhaps its earliest perfection in the Old Testament of the Bible. As a method of reporting and informing, it was as old as the first travel writer, possibly Herodotus. Because its materials are events, its method their interpretation, and its purpose to teach, it was peculiarly adapted to the American frontier experience. From the reports and chronicles of sixteenth-century explorers to the recording of "remarkable providences" and ordinary events by the seventeenth-century Puritan clergy, the majority of our early literature can be classed as documentary. The form had had a long and honorable history "in American 'near-literature'" before Dos Passos discovered it in Jack Reed or perfected it in the novel with *U. S. A.*

Its American tradition alone might have been a good reason for Dos Passos' selecting the documentary as a form. But he chose it because he recognized in Reed's work and later in the motion pictures—he was "enormously stimulated by Eisenstein's 'Cruiser Potemkin'" of 1925[2]—the appropriate vehicle for the expression of his critical commentary and one consistent with his artistic principles. To pursue his "desire to create" as an artist, he chose the novel form; but to pursue his "desire to fathom," he chose the documentary. He achieved their integration by developing an historically oriented theory of art.

II *A Theory of Art*

This theory he announced in an essay in June, 1932—midway through the period of his composition of *U. S. A.*—in the terms of his earliest mature ambition, to study architecture. It was that the novelist should aspire to be "the architect of history." This essay, the "Introduction" to the Modern Library edition of *Three Soldiers,* is a conscious essay in self-evaluation at mid-career. Like his "Humble Protest" at the onset, it is a taking of bearings and a checking of guideposts to be used along the way. But as a re-evaluation it involves thinking of a different kind, which is of the second-degree or philosophic— a pondering of the origins and implications of his ideas about thought and art.

In the "Humble Protest" Dos Passos asked "the inevitable, unanswerable question: what is the end of human life?"; and he answered it in terms not of ends but of aims—"thought and art." In the "Introduction" he asks himself, "What do you write for then?"; and he answers in terms of craftsmanship: "I think there is such a thing as straight writing. . . . The mind of a generation is its speech. A writer makes aspects of that speech enduring by putting them into print. He whittles at the words and phrases of today and makes of them forms to set the mind of tomorrow's generation. That's history. A writer who writes straight is the architect of history." Furthermore, the effect need not be immediate; for "the power of writing is more likely to be exercised vertically through a century than horizontally over a year's sales."

The "twin guide-posts for humanity . . . thought and art" have merged into the single one for the writer, craftsmanship: "straight writing." The old emphasis upon "the breaking down of the modes of thought inherited from the last epoch" has been reversed into the constructive purpose of making of "the words and phrases of today . . . forms to set the mind of tomorrow's generation." Yet beneath these differences is a fundamental consistency; for here is still the insistence on the means, the "path to the fullness of life," in craftsmanship; here is also the meliorative social emphasis—the concern with the mass mind. And in his summation of the years since 1919 is Dos Passos' prevailing sense of immediacy, even urgency, in the last sentence of the essay: "Those of us who have lived through have seen these years strip the bunting off the great illusions of our time, we must deal with the raw structure of history now, we must deal with it quick, before it stamps us out." This appears today as a fairly accurate estimate of America's—or of the world's—situation in June of 1932.

The term "architect of history," then, defines the dual intention, artistic and historical, of Dos Passos' persistent criticism of people and events. All of his art is criticism, and all of it is historically oriented. His first published writing after leaving Harvard, although not intended as art itself, was one of a number of similar essays Dos Passos has since written in criticism of art past and present. In "Against American Literature," already referred to, we see Dos Passos in his characteristic attitude of Janus, looking both forward and backward. In it he looked chiefly forward to a new, indigenous American literature; but he did so only as a "substitute for dependence on the past" and because it had become almost impossible to regain "the lesson of the soil." But even so he suggested a standard from the past: "Shall we pick up the glove Walt Whitman threw at the feet of posterity? Or shall we stagnate forever . . . ?"

In "Young Spain," published in August of 1917, as well as in *Rosinante to the Road Again,* for which the essay served as outline, Dos Passos interpreted the Spanish history and character in terms of its art. His admiration for much of what he found, particularly in the Spanish past, suggests another standard: a nation's art *should* express its character and its history.

Ten years later, under the title "A Great American" in the *New Masses* for December 1927, appeared his review of Paxton Hibben's biography of Henry Ward Beecher, which is one of Dos Passos' most revealing critical commentaries. "History," he observed, "is continually being remade to suit the mood of the present and the immediate past." Questioning as always, he asked, rhetorically, "Why spend years boning up on facts in a library when 'fiction' puts your idea over with more speed than 'history'? I don't think so. It seems to me that history is always more alive and more interesting than fiction. I suppose that is because a story is the day dream of a single man, while history is a mass-invention, the day dream of a race." His conclusion was that a valid work of history "permanently enriches the national consciousness" by providing us with a scale of values—"some sort of standard to measure ourselves by"—without which "any agglomeration . . . of people . . . becomes a mindless and panicky mob."

In the America of 1927 (which was also the year Sacco and Vanzetti were executed), Dos Passos saw "no trace of a scale of values"; but such studies as Hibben's of Beecher might help to provide one, for "Beecher was this utter vacuum that is the American consciousness today, in human form . . . a preacher who could be trusted never to preach against the wind." Such "standards to measure ourselves by" were nothing less than "forms to set the mind of tomorrow's generation. That's history." Both the biographer (or the historian) and the creative artist, or craftsman, should provide the standards: that's criticism. The historian should provide them from "the daydream of a race" and the novelist should obtain his materials from his own experience—"the daydream of a single man."

This task of the artist meant that he must consciously select those materials in his experience from which valid standards might be constructed. That is criticism, not only in the selection of materials, but in the implications of the need for standards; and the creation of the work of art becomes the highest critical function.

The war, Dos Passos hoped in his "Humble Protest" of 1916, would force men, "at least those whose lives and souls are not sucked into the whirlpool . . . to bring their ideals before the bar of criticism, to sift them, to try them, to attempt to discover where they really lead." Since the war not only failed to have that effect, but appeared rather to produce one of the most notoriously uncritical eras in our history, Dos Passos felt obliged to undertake the task himself. This sense of obligation underlies his theory of art as criticism—one which, although nowhere clearly formulated as his own, is everywhere implied in his writing.

III *Preaching against the Wind*

To force people to criticize their ideals was a formidable task, requiring the nicest tact and the most conscious art. It demanded first of all a faith not only in the improvability of men but in their willingness and ability to improve themselves through the use of their reason. It demanded the widest possible audience, yet at the same time one capable of becoming both artists and critics. It required a preacher with a firm sense of responsibility for the effects of his preaching: "Preaching," Dos Passos wrote in his Introduction to *Three Soldiers*, "is part of the business of everybody who deals with words; not to admit that is to play with a gun and then blubber that you didn't know it was loaded." He should be a preacher who could be trusted *always* "to preach against the wind."

The task of preaching self-criticism could best be accomplished if people could be made to see how petty and inadequate or distorted were their ideals, how uncritical in origin, and especially how grotesque and even pernicious their results. The artist should, therefore, be able to discern with the eye of a reporter the results of ideals in contemporary society. He should be able to trace them to their sources with the understanding of an historian. He should express his findings with the acid of the satirist "to sear away the old complacency" and give effect to his criticism.

All of these requirements were implicit in Dos Passos' criticism from the start, for he had started with the humanistic faith and the critical attitude. He found his audience in the novel, which he deliberately limited in style and content to the documentary satire; but with this form he also limited his audience to "the handlers of ideas" and to "men and women of imagination and humanity,"[3] who were most likely to profit from his preaching—and, in turn, to benefit others. He continually sought to trace the events he described to their sources, but until about the time when he began writing *U. S. A.*, history seemed chiefly a *contemporary* force, like that which had taken him by the throat in the war years, and the sources he found were largely contemporary sources. Even in *Streets of Night*, his criticism of a lingering Puritan morality, he went no further back than its contemporary manifestations, except by implication in the oblique criticism of Hawthorne. In *Rosinante*, indeed, he had gone well back into the roots of Iberian culture; but then he was conscious of its roots in the past and of his own among them. Until the later twenties he seemed still to feel that the United States had produced a predominantly contemporary civilization in which—as he had said in "Against American Literature" in 1916—"an all-enveloping industrialism . . . has broken down the old bridges leading to the past."

IV History As Criticism

In the summer of 1926 Dos Passos undertook a deliberately historical investigation of the facts bearing on the Sacco-Vanzetti case. Starting with the ostensible facts of evidence and testimony accumulated since 1920, he then probed the backgrounds of the two principals, both immigrants; the roots of their anarchism; and then the background of the society which condemned them and the causes of its intolerance. Somehow, he found, these met ironically on the shores of Plymouth Bay, Vanzetti's home, where, "about three hundred years before, men from the west of England had first sailed . . . looking for something; liberty . . . freedom to worship God in their own manner . . . space to breathe."[4]

About this time, in his second play, *Airways, Inc.*, Dos Passos went even further into the roots of political idealism, or radicalism. These he presented in the Professor's tragic memories of the defeat of his hopes for Europe in the past and his disillusion with his hopes for America in the present. He presented them also in the racial memories of the Jew, Goldberg. But were there no significant memories in the native stock? As he had written slightly earlier in "The New Masses I'd Like," "Ever since Columbus, imported systems have been the curse of this continent. Why not develop our own brand?" First, Americans would have to discover just what was their "own brand."

This discovery was clearly the task of the historian. But it was also the job of the novelist as artist and critic to discover valid standards. Having expressed the opinion in his review of Hibben's *Henry Ward Beecher* that history, as "the day dream of a race" was "more alive and more interesting than fiction," Dos Passos supplied a supplementary statement the following fall. Under the heading "Statements of Belief," in the *Bookman* for September, 1928, he defined the function of the novelist as that of "a sort of second-class historian of the age he lives in," who is "able to build a reality more nearly out of his own factual experience than a plain historian or biographer can." He concluded that "any novelist that is worth his salt is a sort of truffle dog digging up raw material which a scientist, an anthropologist or a historian can later use to permanent advantage."

These comments, written as he was beginning work on *U. S. A.* and four years before his invention of the term "architect of history," brought the historian and the novelist rather close together. Both were concerned with the interpretation of events: the novelist with the events "of the age he lives in" and the biographer or historian, like Hibben, with "accurate and imaginative studies of the . . . past." Both, therefore, were critics, concerned with the interpretation of the recent or distant past as it affected the present and the future. The theory of history as criticism was simply the corollary of the theory of art as criticism.

CHAPTER 9

U. S. A.

I F AMERICANS were to discover and develop their "own brand" of political idealism, they would have to refurbish their memories—as Dos Passos implied so strongly in his play *Airways*. If they could remember enough within the hectic years they had been living through, perhaps they could discover the elements of a scale of values, without which they would remain a "mindless and panicky mob." If Dos Passos as an artist were to help them, he would first have to stretch his own memory to its limits. In 1927 and 1928, while he was formulating these opinions, Dos Passos was already at work on his manuscript for *The 42nd Parallel*. Early in 1929, just back from Russia, he began digging in earnest into his own and his nation's past. By the fall of that year the stock-market crash had begun to make Americans' mindlessness and panic apparent even to themselves.

I *A Book of Memories*

U. S. A. is first of all a book of memories. These memories, all relating to the United States during the first third of the twentieth century, are presented and developed contrapuntally in autobiography, history, biography, and fiction. The form is that of the associational process of memory itself, by which perceptions are established in the mind and later recalled. And the purpose of the work is equivalent to the function of the memory: to establish in the mind perceptions which, in association with other perceptions from experience such as those of pleasure or pain, develop into attitudes toward certain kinds of experience, frames of reference, or standards by which we judge today.

Dos Passos' intent was to establish for himself and his audience a broad and pertinent framework of memory. This required a maximum selective recall of his own experience, supplemented by the general experience and that of other individuals recorded in documents of the times. It also required an imaginative organization of these materials into a mnemonic unity which could suggest appropriate attitudes toward related kinds of past, present, and future experience.

If he could get a sequence of enough memories, or even a characteristic segment of them, into focus in his camera's eye, he could develop it, edit it, and give it artistic form. Then he could run it through again, stop the motion for a moment if he wished, and present a close-up or a flash-back: "Now who was that, could that have been me in that funny hat?"[1] He could also give a tune or a speech on the sound track. The viewer might even leave the theater wiser than when he went in; at any rate, a few people might risk a nickel to see it. It would probably be misleadingly advertised as one of the "exclusive presentations of the Mesmer Agency" containing comments on "the great and near great" and "a fund of racy anecdotes"—as Dos Passos later satirized the ballyhooing of his books in *The Prospect Before Us* (1950). But for himself, he would present it only as one man's attempt "to add his nickel's worth."

When it was ready, some risked their nickels; and almost the first thing they saw was the producer-director as a little child flitting across the screen, like Alfred Hitchcock sneaking into his own films. As autobiography Dos Passos presented his own story directly in the Camera Eye sequences, in stream-of-consciousness—or more accurately, stream-of-memory—narration. His story in *The 42nd Parallel* is almost entirely separate from the rest of his history of the country in the early years of the century; but, as the novel progresses through the three volumes, there is a continuous tightening in the relationship of its several parts—narrative, Camera Eyes, Newsreels, biographies—as the narrator becomes one with his subject.

In *1919* the autobiography of the Camera Eyes begins to merge with the fictional story of Dick Savage, especially at Harvard and in the war (see above, Chapter Three, section III). Toward the end of the final volume, *The Big Money*, Camera Eyes Forty-nine and Fifty include indirect biography of Sacco and Vanzetti; and in between those two sequences Dos Passos' story merges with the fictional story of Mary

French in her work for the Sacco-Vanzetti defense and with the history of the time as outlined in Newsreel LXVI. Finally, within the last twenty-five pages of the trilogy, the fictional Ben Compton (the prototype of Glenn Spotswood in his next novel, *Adventures* and of Jay Pignatelli in *Chosen Country*), expresses, peering "through his thick glasses," Dos Passos' relationship to the Communist Party: "oppositionist . . . exceptionalism . . . a lot of nonsense." And in the final sketch, "Vag," of the last two and a half pages, the Camera Eye has become the biography of the depression vagrant, a distinctive phenomenon of the times. It is also very nearly the picture of Jimmy Herf hitchhiking west out of Manhattan.

In *U. S. A.* Dos Passos placed himself securely within the history of his country in his time. But he emphasized the history above the importance of his relation to it. As an historian, he did not need to be told that his country's own brand of idealism was "democracy"; the problem was to discover what the word meant. It seemed to have pretty much lost its meaning at about the time the United States had fought a war to make the world safe for it. Taking the word at its pre-war value, Dos Passos devoted his trilogy to a history of the struggle for industrial democracy in America.

As a critic Dos Passos has always been principally interested in the effects of phenomena upon individual men and women. This interest helped to make him a novelist; and it—and not simply his training as a novelist—focuses all of his histories upon personalities and traits of character. The focus of *U. S. A.*, therefore, is upon the twenty-six *actual* persons engaged in the struggle and the twelve principal *fictional* persons also engaged in it and affected by it. The actual people of the biographies are those who influenced the pattern of the struggle— labor leaders, politicians, artists, journalists, scientists, and business leaders. The fictional characters represent average men and women molded by the complex of forces about them.

The fictional characters illustrate more than anything else the dissolution of the once central cohesive institution in American society (the one Dos Passos first achieved with his marriage in 1929, as he began *U. S. A.*), the family. Although most of them come from fairly secure family units, they are unable to form them for themselves. The fictional narrative is filled with pathetic promiscuity, perversion, vague temporary alli-

ances, divorces, abortions. Ben Compton, again, sums up the
need at the end of *The Big Money*. Speaking to Mary French,
who is one of the most sympathetically portrayed of the principal characters and whose maternal instincts have made her
a devoted worker for the oppressed, Ben says, "You know if we
hadn't been fools we'd have had that baby that time . . .
we'd still love each other."

In Dos Passos' picture of the U. S. A., it was essential to
reinstitute the family; but neither of the two larger institutions
in which the forces of the times had become polarized—
laissez-faire capitalism and Stalinist communism—appeared to
permit its free growth. Until people achieved a social system
which would give the average man a sense of participation—
of responsibility for and pride in his work—the smaller, more
vital social units would be ineffective. To achieve that system,
the meaning of the old mercantile-agrarian democracy and
its libertarian phraseology—liberty, equality, pursuit of happiness—must somehow be restored in the scientific, urban-
industrial present.

The makers of that present and those who hoped to remake
it are the subjects of the biographies. Toward each of the
principal fictional characters, each of whom is seen as a child,
the reader shares Dos Passos' affection, which turns to scorn
or pity as they become mere cogs or pulp in the capitalist
or communist machines, or to indignation as their individualism leaves them crushed and dead—like Joe Williams and
Daughter, both killed by accident in France in the aftermath
of the war—or stranded and alone like Ben Compton. Toward
the biographies, however the reader's reaction is principally
a sharing of the burning indignation with which most of them
were written. Of the twenty-six, not counting the two portraits
of the anonymous Unknown Soldier and "Vag," fourteen are
sympathetic and twelve are not.

The criterion of judgment of them as of the fictional characters is the courage or will of the individual to maintain the
faith that most of them were born to in the untarnished meanings of the democratic creed. By this criterion we recognize
them as friends or strangers whatever their births or origins
or ends. If their work is intended to uphold the dignity of the
individual man and woman and the integrity of their language
as Americans, they are friends. If they are scornful or even

like Edison and Henry Ford merely "unconcerned with the results of [their] work in human terms,"[2] they are the "strangers" of Camera Eye Fifty, "who have turned our language inside out who have taken the clean words our fathers spoke and made them slimy and foul."

Dos Passos is not at all mysterious as to his purposes; he even states them directly in Camera Eyes Forty-seven and Forty-nine of *The Big Money*: ". . . shape words remembered light and dark straining to rebuild yesterday to clip out paper figures to stimulate growth Warp newsprint into faces smoothing and wrinkling in the various barelyfelt velocities of time." Or again, reporting his reporting of the Sacco-Vanzetti case: "pencil scrawls in my notebook the scraps of recollection the broken halfphrases the effort to intersect word with word to dovetail clause with clause to rebuild out of mangled memories unshakably (Oh Pontius Pilate) the truth." Here is the meaning of the terms "straight writing" and "architect of history."

Yet the architect of history works not only "to rebuild yesterday" as the foundation of today, but to build of today a sound foundation for tomorrow. By straight writing and with the materials of contemporary speech, the writer provides contexts of meaning for today's speech, which will be the basis of tomorrow's memories. Dos Passos achieves his contexts through the use of dialogue and even of direct narration phrased in the colloquial language appropriate to the character he is treating. The reader sees and hears the speech in conjunction with actions and through the consciousness of the character concerned. We participate in the individual's attitudes toward events.

Further than this, Dos Passos has the reader share, at least for the moment, the attitudes of quite different individuals toward the same or similar events. We see the affair between Dick Savage and Daughter (Anne Elizabeth Trent), for instance, through the eyes and feelings of each of them. To Dick it is simply an affair which becomes awkward and threatens to embarrass him in his career when Daughter expects him to feel some responsibility for her pregnancy. To her it is a tremendous event which results in tragedy. The reader also sees and experiences a variety of attitudes toward business, labor, government, the war, the Sacco-Vanzetti case, and many other institutions and particular events. Since he cannot sympathetically entertain at the same time two opposing attitudes toward a single phenomenon, he is forced to choose, to criticize, to formulate standards.

As a realist Dos Passos reveals his characters in the historical framework of time, place, and social milieu which help to form them. These backgrounds, usually presented through the memories of the characters themselves, are various enough to provide a representative cross-section, geographically and socially, of American society. In the "Introduction" to *Three Soldiers*, Dos Passos remarked that "our beds have made us and the acutest action we can take is to sit up on the edge of them and look around and think." In describing his characters' beds, Dos Passos is an objective reporter of existing phenomena. But in portraying the individuals themselves and their attempts to sit up and look around and think, he is a selective critic. He controls our choice of attitude by creating characters with whom we must at first sympathize, for their beds and their wants are ours. We continue to sympathize as they struggle to express themselves and to satisfy their needs; but we become indignant at the Procrustean forces that chain them prone in their beds or at the individuals as they lose the courage to struggle, refuse to think, or prefer to crawl back under the sheets within the security of the familiar narrow limits of their bedsteads.

II *Tools of Language*

Half of the fictional characters of *U. S. A.* and nearly half of the subjects of the biographies have a special facility with the tools of language, the means with which to build or to restrict human freedom. Of the fictional ones, most are poor or careless keepers of their talents. J. Ward Moorehouse becomes a public-relations executive—a propagandist for big business who exploits language for profit; Janey becomes his expert private secretary and an efficient, warped old maid; Dick Savage degenerates from a young poet to Moorehouse's administrative assistant and contact-man—a sort of commercial pimp. Mac surrenders his principles as an itinerant printer for the labor movement and succumbs to the security offered by a girl and a little bookstore of his own in Mexico; Mary

French and Ben Compton become pawns of communist politics. Only Ben emerges at the end, though rejected and alone,
still looking around him and thinking.

In contrast, only three of roughly a dozen subjects of the
biographies seem to misuse their gifts of language: Bryan,
"a silver tongue in a big mouth"; Woodrow Wilson, "talking
to save his faith in words, talking . . . talking"; Hearst, whose
"empire of the printed word . . . this power over the dreams
of the adolescents of the world grows and poisons like a
cancer." Most of the heroes of Dos Passos' biographies are
chosen from among the heroes and martyrs of the working-
class movement: men who looked around, thought critically,
and developed their abilities in an effort to restore the meanings rather than to exploit the phraseology of American democracy. They were men like Eugene Debs, Bill Haywood,
La Follette, Jack Reed, Randolph Bourne, Paxton Hibben,
Joe Hill, Thorstein Veblen.

Dos Passos' own handling of the language can be demon-
strated in an example from his fictional narrative in *1919*.
Dick Savage at the end of the war is still in Paris; Daughter,
spurned by her "Dickyboy" and carrying his child, goes off
alone in a taxi; Dick, now captain but angling for a public
relations job after the war, goes to bed with a hangover; but
he cannot get to sleep:

> Gradually he got warmer. Tomorrow. Seventhirty: shave,
> buckle puttees. . . . Day dragged out in khaki. . . . Dragged out
> khaki days until after the signing of the peace. Dun, drab,
> khaki. Poor Dick got to go to work after the signing of the
> peace. Poor Tom's cold. Poor Dickyboy . . . Richard . . .
> He brought his feet up to where he could rub them. Poor
> Richard's feet. After the signing of the Peace.

Dick is a Harvard graduate; he had intended to become a
writer. He has nearly lost our sympathy because of his
attitude toward Daughter. Here he gives up the struggle
to sit up and think as he climbs literally and figuratively into
bed, self-indulgent, self-pitying. "Poor Tom" suggests his
subconsicous awareness of his disguise—in part the uniform
of an officer and a gentleman, in part his role of a dedicated
poet; and it also suggests the contrast of his character with
that of Edgar in *King Lear*. "Poor Dickyboy" reveals the

transfer of his pangs of conscience into self-sympathy. "Poor Richard" indicates his falling from critical awareness into the thoughtless selfishness of the old American cliché of success (Franklin's Poor Richard and Horatio Alger's Ragged Dick), as he resumes the foetal position because he lacks the courage to think and to doubt; he has, in the vernacular, cold feet: "By the time his feet were warm he'd fallen asleep."

The picture is at once comic and pathetic and somewhat revolting. Up to about this point we have been sympathizing with Dick as another struggling, wanting human; suffering with him; and enjoying his occasional successes as our own. In this passage, Dos Passos' method prevents our suddenly ceasing to participate. We must share Dick's experience—after all a rather ordinary one, already familiar to us—at the same time that we reject it. We share from within his consciousness; we observe and reject from outside it. By the multiplication of such experiences Dos Passos attempts to establish in the reader something like what T. S. Eliot called the objective correlative of the work of art; but another name for it is a critical standard or part of a frame of reference. Once established, it exists outside of, even independent of, its original source. If Dick Savage's retreat from responsibility, for example, is established as symbolic of all retreat from responsibility, and if we are made to reject it here, then we must reject it whenever we encounter it.

This process Dos Passos once explained in a little-known "Introductory Note" to the first Modern Library edition of his *42nd Parallel* as the destruction and reconstruction of stereotypes. He was aware that it would probably lose him readers: "People feel pain when the stereotype is broken, at least at first." But it was the necessary method of the architect of history. The reaction from the reader is similar to the "grin of pain" that Dos Passos described as the essential response to satire in his essay about George Grosz in 1936.

Yet the reader's reaction to Dos Passos' novels is only remotely and occasionally one of mirth. To *U. S. A.* it is more nearly a grim realization of the sores and weaknesses of our culture which cry out for repair. To some readers, doubtless, it is too bad that Dos Passos is not more nearly the satirist than he is. Perhaps a leavening of humor that could change a grimace to a grin would make him more palatable to both readers and critics and, therefore, presumably more effective because more widely read. But Dos Passos' intent is vitally serious. He does not write to entertain but to communicate, to inform—in brief, to educate. He has always been too close to his materials, too involved personally, to be able to attain the special kind of detachment demanded of the satirist. Like Swift indeed, he heartily loves John, Peter, Thomas, and so forth; but he can by no means manage a principal hate and detestation for that animal called man.

III *Method of Tragedy*

Rather than satire—or rather including the satire and including also his naturalism—Dos Passos' method in *U. S. A.* is that of tragedy, a method based on an ironic attitude toward the past. *U. S. A.* is a great agglomerate tragic history. The protagonist, obviously enough, is the real U. S. A. in the first third of the twentieth century. Its tragic characters are the real subjects of the biographies: Debs, Luther Burbank, Bill Haywood, Bryan, Minor Keith, Carnegie, Edison, Steinmetz, La Follette, Jack Reed, Randolph Bourne, T. R., Paxton Hibben, Woodrow Wilson, and the rest. Merely to read their names is to sense the tragedy of their era: so much talent, ambition, love—all frustrated or misdirected or drained away into war, profits, prohibitions, intolerances, and oppressions.

In the background of the novel, democratic individualism and reliance on the future (pursuit of happiness) are the characteristics which gave the U. S. A. its greatness. A too narrow individualism, a too great reliance on the future— a loss of memory—and a warped interpretation of happiness in purely material terms: these are the characteristics which brought on its apparent downfall in the years Dos Passos wrote of. They are the tragic flaws of the society which rejects its best men. But its failures and its worst men have their own equivalent flaws—Bryan's "silver tongue in a big mouth," Wilson's "faith in words," and the overweening ambition of the Morgans, Insull, and others.

The fictional characters—like the anonymous "Vag" and the Unknown Soldier and the narrator—have not the stature of tragic characters. They are the extras, the *demos* or ordinary citizens like ourselves, or the members of the chorus with whom we can participate as they work and suffer in the shadow of the struggle for industrial democracy. Yet, while we participate, we also watch; and for our capacity as objective audience, there is the more formal chorus of the Newsreels, in which the past provides its own ironic commentary about the past and reveals our recent idiocies to ourselves.

Many Americans in the audience have been unwilling to sit through Dos Passos' documentary tragedy. If they have come to it for entertainment or escape, they have been disappointed. But those who have stayed to see and hear have been exposed to a unique dramatic experience. This experience is one of participating satire; for, as Dos Passos said of the painter Grosz, he "makes you identify yourself with the sordid and pitiful object." This identification, in turn, provides the catharsis, "a release from hatred"—in part because the reader or spectator cannot wholly hate himself and in part because the hatred is already expressed more adequately than most could express it through vitriolic portraits of the villains, real and fictional. The uniqueness, however, is in the partial nature of the catharsis: it might be said to be both catharsis and anti-catharsis. The reader is purged only of the self-indulgent emotions of hatred and self-love, which allow him to forget. He is denied complacency and forced to remember. The tragedy he has witnessed is that of the unfulfilled potential of the individual, including himself, in a society dedicated, ironically, to the possibilities of its fulfillment. He is left with a feeling of incompleteness.

Part of the reason for Dos Passos' unpopularity is probably his lack of sufficient self-esteem for the reader to share. His contemporary, Hemingway, for example, had it both in himself and in his characters. Even in Swift the reader can climb to the heights of satire with the author—Gulliver being only an alter ego, the equivalent of some of the fictional characters of *U. S. A.*—and look down on the puny mass of men with the possibility of self-gratulation that he is not among them. But in Dos Passos' participating satire even the author is satirized; if the reader indulges in any identification (which he can scarcely avoid), he must lose not only his self-esteem but also his complacency.

Dos Passos' self-esteem is almost wholly of the abstract "self," the essential *I, you, me, he, she* of the tragically unfulfilled individual potential. In fact, it is almost the sole object of his esteem. So where another writer—and particularly another autobiographical writer such as Hemingway—might appear to caress his characters, possibly because they contain so much of the author,[3] Dos Passos scorns his, partly for the same reason. He scorns them also because they are not true individuals and because it is not his fault, but theirs. He cannot help them; for, if they are to achieve their individuality, to fulfill their potentials, they must do it themselves. The most he can do is to help define the problem and some of the conditions of its solution. Yet Dos Passos is thoroughly sympathetic, especially towards the fictional men and women who give their names to the narrative sections of *U. S. A.* He shows a pervading pity for his characters, real and fictional, which is evident even in his most acidulous biographical portraits; an example is his quoting from the pathetically presumptuous will of the first J. P. Morgan in his biography of "The House of Morgan" in *1919*.

Both the scorn and the pity come through to the reader. Since one can properly scorn only inevitable weakness or meanness, the reader is left at the end of the tragedy with a sense of awe not so much at the power and authority of the destructive or restricting external forces as at the potential beauty and unity of the thing destroyed, the free personality. Bernard De Voto felt it in "the gusto and delight of American living" whose absence in *U. S. A.* he so deplored.[4]

Yet this sense of incompleteness in the reader—the feeling of having been cheated of some of the ideal goods of life and that something should be done about it—is precisely the reaction that Dos Passos, the architect of history, desired. Unfortunately for his purposes, many readers have felt only the incompleteness and have missed the further implications of his criticism that something can be done about it, but that each individual must do it himself.

IV *Doubt and Affirmation*

Perhaps one reason for the failure of his message is related to the fact that he has had one. As a novelist his chief concern has been, as he wrote in "The Business of a Novelist" for the *New Republic* in April, 1934, "to create characters first and foremost, and then to set them in the snarl of the human currents of his time, so that there results an accurate permanent record of a phase of history." Yet as a man with a message, his chief concern has been with its recipients; and his characters, despite the sympathy of his portrayal, he has left deliberately underdeveloped. Similarly, he has always aimed at discomforting his readers—at stirring them into fresh thought and action by destroying the stereotypes from which they viewed the world. The great antagonist of *U. S. A.* is complacency. Probably most of the adverse criticism of the novel could be traced, like De Voto's, to the critics' protests against Dos Passos' attack on one or another of their complacencies. "When complacency goes," Dos Passos concluded his critical appreciation of Grosz, "young intelligence begins."

The essential first step to the freedom of intelligent action was to doubt. Yet some compromise between doubt and acceptance must be made before real action can begin. Until the early thirties Dos Passos' compromise was in the acceptance of immediate goals: in broadening the range of his own experience and in satisfying chiefly through travel his eager curiosity about the world around him; in participating directly in behalf of the obviously oppressed such as Sacco and Vanzetti, the Scottsboro boys, and, later, refugees from Europe; and in endeavoring to stimulate doubt in others. Then sometime before the fall elections of 1936 he reached the climax of his own doubting: his doubt turned inward upon itself.

The struggle of this moral crisis can be read in Camera Eye Forty-six early in *The Big Money*: "if not why not? walking the streets rolling on your bed eyes sting from peeling the speculative onion of doubt if somebody in your head topdog? underdog? didn't (and on Union Square) say liar to you." From this point on, the reader can trace the development of his Everlasting Yea, which begins with his condemnation of both the capitalistic and communistic viewpoints in *The Big Money* and his enthusiastic vote for Roosevelt in 1936 and which culminates in his novel *Chosen Country*, in his appreciative study of Jefferson, and in his two recent histories of the founders of the republic, *The Men Who Made the Nation* (1957) and *Prospects of a Golden Age* (1959).

In his probing into the meanings of the democratic phraseology and their bearings on his country in his time, Dos Passos found what he sought in an appreciation of the dynamics of his society. From his study of the history of his country and his awareness of the forces of history in action—particularly in the increase of despotism abroad—he came to realize that, for him, the U. S. A. *was* the last, best hope of men.

"The shape of a piece of work should be imposed, and in a good piece of work always is imposed, by the matter," Dos Passos wrote in his "Introductory Note" to the first Modern Library edition of *The 42nd Parallel.* The conscious, organized incompleteness of *U. S. A.* was not merely a device to stimulate the reader; it was the artistic form imposed by the organic necessity of the artist's materials. His study of his matter, American history, had finally revealed to him the secret of form in his society: that the pattern of American society lay where he had intuitively recognized it in the individual—in its potential and incompleteness. Sometime during the composition of his trilogy, Dos Passos became aware of a resurgence of what must have been a still-existing fluidity and dynamic potential in the American social structure. In such a society a man, if he would, could give meaning to his life.

Having intellectually grasped the pattern—or at least one which was satisfying and meaningful to him—and realized its form in his art in *U. S. A.,* Dos Passos had accomplished his major task as an artist. His materials for *U. S. A.* were all historical—the products of his study of the nation's past, his awareness of significant events acting about him, and a mass of painfully remembered detail from his own life. By the effort of his imagination, he constructed from these materials an organic unity which revealed the nation which he had made his own. By his own efforts he had carved out his niche and made himself a citizen.

Believing above all in the responsible and purposeful action of the free individual, Dos Passos was not a man to waste in inaction the freedom he had taken forty years to acquire, or to take lightly the duties of citizenship. However, having achieved the form he sought in his life and in his art, his energies could now take a slightly different direction. History in the service of art had completed the pattern. Henceforth Dos Passos' efforts would be more nearly historical than artistic. Art in the service of history should confirm the pattern and maintain the flexibility of the form.

CHAPTER 10

The Constant Quest

JANUARY 27, 1917, the date of death of Dos Passos' father, can serve psychologically or metaphorically to mark the birth of Dos Passos the artist, the free agent. When *U. S. A.* was first published as one integrated work exactly twenty-one years later, on January 27, 1938, the occasion was an appropriate memorial. It could mark the end of Telemachus' search for his father, and the full maturity of the artist. In the preceding year *The Big Money*, the last novel of the trilogy, had been voted the best of the year by the American Writers Congress; and Dos Passos had had a one-man show of some thirty sketches in New York. The French *Nouvelles Littéraires* for June 5, 1937, had entitled the report of an interview, just before his final return from Spain—which had been, until now, his spiritual home—"The Great Novelist Dos Passos Is in Paris." The interviewer reported that Dos Passos did "not hope to return to Europe before a long time" and quoted Dos Passos' description of himself: "Quant à moi, je suis un Yankee de Chicago." The important words of his statement needed no translation. Back in America, Dos Passos immediately published his "Farewell to Europe."

Thus the occasion of the publication of *U. S. A.* marks also the beginning of Dos Passos' full citizenship in the United States. He had served a long and difficult apprenticeship to acquire the "feeling of belonging to something outside of" himself which he had described in the fall of 1936 as "so necessary to people" under the conditions of contemporary American life.[1] Two questions then remained for him. The first was whether or not the questing which had been his life was now ended. The second was whether he could remain at once fully an artist and fully a citizen. Dos Passos himself has since tentatively answered both questions in the negative.

I *The Integrity of the Artist*

For the moment, all that need be said about his quest is to comment upon the letter from Dos Passos quoted in part at the beginning of this book. When Dos Passos wrote in 1954 that "the danger to survival . . . of personal liberty anywhere in the world has become so patent that those of us who care for liberty more than anything find ourselves continually seeking new ground on which to stand," he was summing up in the phrase "continually seeking" his whole career. Since at least as early as his first trip to Spain in 1916, he has been engaged in a constant, curiously conscious quest. Yet the new ground upon which to stand that he wrote of in 1954 was not at all the same type that he was seeking until the middle 1930's when he found it in the U. S. A.; for he sought literally a homeland where he could establish his roots and a frame-of-reference within which he could flourish as a free man. His search was a personal emotional imperative; and it made him an artist. The new ground he has since been seeking has been more nearly the impersonal one of principle and perspective, an area *apart* from subjective requirements—one from which the historian or critic could appraise the immediate.

Asked his opinion in 1947 of the effect upon young writers of their going to Hollywood, Dos Passos was vehement: "Young writers who believe in themselves should be willing to starve in a garret once more."[2] Literally interpreted, this statement suggests the theory—for which its adherents adduce a certain amount of experimental proof and a great deal of apparent justification from the lives of artists—that the human mind or imagination functions more sharply and clearly under deprivation of physical nourishment because of a sharpening of the various senses by the synesthetic process. Whether or not the theory is valid, the way of the world is such as to provide those of artistic temperament with ample opportunity to go hungry should they propose to earn their livings by their artistic endeavors. And so the theory gains more adherents and less proof.

But this synesthesia was not quite what Dos Passos intended with "starve in a garret." Rather, it is one way of saying that the artist must work from an emotional or ethical position to some degree removed from the culture or social structure of his time: he should be able to look down on it with scorn or compassion; to look up to it with envy or admiration; or to regard it askance with doubt, distrust, or indecision. But he should not be wholly of it—unless imaginatively, perhaps in his art; he should not predominantly accept or acquiesce in it; he must not lose his essential isolation.

In his garret, the artist's denial of man's innate gregariousness and of his need to communicate will stimulate both the emotion and the search for form in content and means of communication that are the essentials of artistic production. And perhaps only thus can they be adequately stimulated. Furthermore, if art is also criticism—thought applied to the perception of discrepancies between what is and what should be—where better than in his garret may the artist achieve the requisite critical perspective?

Thus Dos Passos' meaning was more nearly metaphorical: the spiritual isolation and independence which his phrase suggests comprise the only means of achieving, and even of maintaining, artistic integrity. If his comment of 1947 sounded a bit wistful, it may have been because of his awareness that he had lost his own essential isolation—or, in his metaphor, his spiritual hunger—not because he had not heeded it faithfully, but because he had satisfied it a decade earlier. He had thereby lost his artistic genius.

"Artistic genius" is as equivocal a term as "artistic temperament" (see Chapter Four). Dos Passos' contemporary, John Peale Bishop, however, did not equivocate when he said of the author of *Three Soldiers* in 1921, "Dos Passos is a genius." Between Bishop's assertion and that of the philosopher-critic Jean Paul Sartre in 1938, "I regard Dos Passos as the greatest writer of our time," there is probably sufficient critical unanimity to justify the term, though other critics have been more cautious.[3] Since that time, however, Dos Passos has had but little praise—except as the writer he once was.

I am far from claiming infallibility for Dos Passos' critics. Their conclusions have often been warped by their insistence on political criticism, by their acceptance of one or another of the Dos Passos myths—Dos Passos the communist, the fellow-traveler, or more lately, the reactionary, the apostate— or by their mistaking his naturalistic method for a naturalistic philosophy. But they have correctly observed a difference in quality as well as in kind between his writings preceding and following the publication in January, 1938, of *U. S. A.* as a trilogy.

The difference in kind is the more obvious: before 1938, of fourteen volumes, only two and one half were prose non-fiction (the half is the non-fiction one of *Rosinante*); since January, 1938, of fifteen volumes, only six have been novels and all the rest works of prose nonfiction, four of these explicitly historical narrative—and to these might be added Dos Passos' edition of Tom Paine and his editorial continuity for *Life's Picture History of World War II,* as well as "The General" (1950), a documentary report commissioned by General Mills about the company.

The contrast in quality is less easily defined, but partly it is a function of the difference in kind. With the change in emphasis since *U. S. A.* from the novel to history, there has been a corresponding change in the content and stimulus of Dos Passos' writing: from the imaginative toward the intellectual, from the need to create toward the need to understand and to preserve, from synthesis toward analysis. Dos Passos has not lost sight of his original twin goals of life, art and thought, "the desire to create" and "the desire to fathom"; and the writing of history is still *an art*. But it is not art (no great historian has been accused of artistic genius), and Dos Passos has simply moved nearer one guidepost than the other. He has been less concerned to produce lasting works of the imagination—art—and more concerned to devote his efforts to maintaining a civilization in which art is possible.

II   *History and D. C.*

Dos Passos' American histories began, appropriately, by Plymouth Rock in his investigations in behalf of Sacco and Vanzetti in 1926 (see above, Chapter Eight, section IV). They continued with his study of Tom Paine in 1939, in which he accepted both Paine's philosophical anarchism and his social mission as a pamphleteer. *The Ground We Stand On* was his first full-length study of the historical roots of American democracy; and, if it is not noteworthy as history, it is full of the author's sense of discovery and his enthusiasm for

his subject, and it is significant as his deliberate apprenticeship in his new calling.

The Head and Heart of Thomas Jefferson, like all Dos
Passos' histories, is full of out-of-the-way facts and proba-
bilities which make, if not orthodox history, a living story.
Primarily the book is a study of the shaping of Jefferson's
head and heart, the background of the man before he became
President; and it is a tribute to the great Virginian at a time
when Dos Passos had become a Virginian by choice and was
professing and practicing Jefferson's republican agrarianism
on his father's 1,800-acre farm in northern Virginia. *The Men
Who Made the Nation* treats "the architects of the young
republic"—Washington, Jefferson, Hamilton and their only
less great contemporaries. It is much like the Jefferson biography in tone and intention, and it takes the story a bit
further: the last chapter is Jefferson's, "A Philosopher in the
President's House," although Hamilton, by his death, usurps
the ending.

In his latest history to date, *Prospects of a Golden Age,*
Dos Passos has used materials from all his earlier researches,
including excerpts from the Jefferson study and from *The
Men Who Made the Nation;* it is his nearest approach to an
artistic synthesis of formal historical materials. Having asked in
1920 for a return to "the 'liberty and pursuit of happiness' of
that original, too long forgotten statement of our aims" (above,
Chapter Two, section I), Dos Passos was faced with the long
task of defining his terms. "Happiness," he was able to explain
by 1959, "meant something more than an improved standard
of living. It meant dignity, independence, self government.
It meant opportunity for the young, a serene old age and
fearlessness in the face of death" (p. [vii]). The book, containing over two hundred illustrations, is best described as a
history of the origins of American culture; and its definitions
are those Dos Passos subscribes to today. If he is therefore
described as "reactionary," he accepts the epithet as he
accepted Michael Gold's calling him a "bourgeois intellectual"
in 1926. "Reactionary" was also the epithet applied to General Dean and other uncooperative prisoners of the Chinese
communists in Korea, according to Dos Passos' biography of
the General in *Midcentury* (p. 422). Thus the architect of
history "whittles at the words and phrases of today and

makes of them forms to set the mind of tomorrow's generation" ("Introduction" to *Three Soldiers,* 1932).

Dos Passos' achievements in *U. S. A.* and his increased historical interests since have of course affected his fiction. *District of Columbia,* which comprises Dos Passos' first three novels since *U. S. A.,* is an example. Like *U. S. A.,* it is a documentary trilogy of American life, but it lacks the organic unity of the earlier work. As documentaries, both trilogies are linear in their organization, but whereas *U. S. A.* is marvelously integrated around a central cable of time, *District of Columbia* is three novels spliced together by a rather tenuous tie to the nation's capital and by an equally tenuous thread of family relationship among the Spotswoods, father and sons.

It is true that one can trace evidences of development from *U. S. A.* to *D. C.* The literal autobiography appears least in *D. C.,* for it is used only in the childhood of Glenn Spotswood and in his later general attitude in *Adventures of a Young Man.* The family in *D. C.* achieves a new emphasis: first, among the Spotswoods, where the tie is too weak to sustain its members; and, second, in the lives of the real heroes of the trilogy—Paul Graves and Millard Carroll—who could scarcely have survived without their families. The political attitude, as almost everyone has noticed, has switched from emphasizing the need of change in *U. S. A.* to stressing the necessity to preserve in *D. C.*

Yet all of this apparent development lies principally outside the trilogy as a work of art. The reduction of autobiography in *D. C.* lies with the author, who is now outside his work; for in *U. S. A.* he was at its artistic center in the focusing intelligence of the Camera Eyes. The change in political attitude was both a personal imperative and an historical imperative dictated by political events; but the first relates to *D. C.* as tract, and the second to *D. C.* as documentary—as opposed to *D. C.* the novel or work of art. The family emphasis most nearly hints of artistic development. In *U. S. A.* the very absence of family gave it weight as an invisible counterpoise to the anarchy portrayed. In *D. C.* it is the principal unifying element—and for a number of reasons.

The least important although the most obvious is the Spotswood relationship, which leads some critics to give the novel the misleading subtitle "the Spotswood trilogy." More im-

portant are contrasting successful and unsuccessful family relationships. In *Adventures of a Young Man* the contrast is
between Glenn—lonely, visionary, radical, living under a Communist Party alias as Sandy Crockett—and his friend Paul
Graves, married, expecting a child, practical, confident, com-
petent. In *Number One* it is between the failures of Tyler
Spotswood, who has even less sense of his own identity than
Glenn, and the successes of Chuck Crawford (a transparent
fictional version of Huey Long). Looking frantically for something to belong to, Tyler finds it in Chuck, to whom he is
willing body and soul to belong, as he attempts pathetically,
even comically, to make himself part of Chuck's large and
closely knit family. There is also in *Number One* a significant
gap between what the Spotswoods were and what they might
have been to one another—a contrast raised in the posthumous
letter from his younger brother Glenn which gives Tyler the
courage to survive after the failure at the end of *Number One*
of the demagogue Chuck Crawford.

In *The Grand Design,* the emphasis shifts to the contrasts
between microcosm, the family, and macrocosm, the nation.
Paul Graves, embroiled with the government in the effort
to save the family-sized farm in America, ironically almost
loses his own family in the struggle. Millard Carroll, also
caught up in the idealism of the "Grand Design," never loses
contact with his family or with reality; and he can resign,
worn but intact, when he can no longer hope to stem the
momentum of the governmental macrocosm.

This family emphasis comes close to holding the trilogy together as a work of art, but the reader loses sight of it in the
greater unity given to the work as a study of political forces.
At the end of *Adventures of a Young Man,* Glenn—the idealist,
disillusioned with the Communist Party, but still trying to
work with it for goals he believes in—is sent to his death in
Spain by Communists who are exploiting the Spanish Civil
War for their own political purposes. In *Number One* Tyler
becomes a pawn of Chuck Crawford—as did Glenn of the
Communists—and like him discovers his mistake too late.
In *The Grand Design,* Herb Spotswood, father of Glenn and
Tyler, becomes a pawn of politics in New Deal Washington.
But he is insignificant both as a person (he is a sort of parody
of news analysts Gabriel Heatter and Raymond Gram Swing)

and as a fictional character. For here is where the novel becomes tract: this is not Herb's story but the author's, speaking to us directly in the interchapters. In *The Grand Design* Dos Passos, having noted the failures of communism and American fascism, examines the indigenous middle ground of American politics. What he finds is a vital, experimental, unifying force— a true grand design of American democracy, hardened into dogma and authoritarianism under the pressures of war and its own momentum.

Although the integrity of the work of art is destroyed, or dissipated in this intrusion of the author, the trilogy attains real unity both as documentary and as tract in its presentation of contemporary history—history of and for the contemporary world. For the imaginative synthesis of *District of Columbia* consists in the broadening of Dos Passos' own philosophic code, *lo flamenco*, into a premise of American democracy. Its basis is an historical insight: that democracy is a process, not a form of government, a means, not an end; that when we treat it as an end or form, it becomes one and regiments us; it becomes no longer democracy but an institution, stronger than the individuals who comprise it; and the state, no longer the individual, becomes sovereign. The first lesson in institutionalizing force, in over-preoccupation with ends, was from American and European communism: "We are not interested in the fates of individuals," the party boss explained to Glenn in *Adventures of a Young Man*. The second was from European and American fascism, the picture of an average man like Tyler struggling vaguely toward a better life for himself and others, putting his faith in the illusions and promises of a demagogue, and being double-crossed in the end. The final lesson was from democracy in action perverted into an institution by its commitment to an end—the winning of World War II, at any cost.

If the reader protests today, "Well, we won the war, didn't we? And how much democracy would have been left if we hadn't?"—he poses precisely the kind of question, with its assumption that the end justifies the means, to which Dos Passos as historian of our democracy directs his studies. He answers it with another question: How long and how often can we acquiesce in institutionalizing democracy, trusting that later, somehow, it will again become a flexible, dynamic *process?*

As history, then, if not as art, *District of Columbia* is well worth reading—as are Dos Passos' other, more explicit histories, his introduction to *Tom Paine, The Ground We Stand On, The Head and Heart of Thomas Jefferson, The Men Who Made the Nation,* and *Prospects of a Golden Age.* All of these are studies by an amateur (in the true sense of the word) of the men who made the nation what it is and of their hopes and plans, their frustrations, their defeats, and their successes as they helped to shape the foundations of our democracy, the ground we stand on today.

These five explicit studies of history, all written since *U. S. A.,* simply confirm Dos Passos' expressed opinion of 1927, when he was just beginning *U. S. A.*: "It seems to me that history is always more alive and more interesting than fiction." Certainly these works are more alive and more interesting than Dos Passos' recent fiction—*Chosen Country, Most Likely to Succeed, The Great Days*—in which the author's self-satire is often embarrassing and in which his political thesis, the anti-communist warning that the end never justifies the means, though valid in itself, is often an unwieldy club. Both of these weaknesses apply as well to Dos Passos' later travel books of reporting and opinion: *State of the Nation, Tour of Duty, The Prospect Before Us, The Theme Is Freedom.*

But the chief weakness of all but the histories is their lack of perspective. In 1927, the same year that Dos Passos proclaimed the superiority of history to fiction, Lindbergh's achievement had already shrunk the globe, and by 1938 there was no longer a place to stand from which to view the United States—except the United States itself. So the only perspective possible had become a temporal one. In his recent novels and reportorial commentaries, Dos Passos is too oppressed by the immediate and also too conscious of the writer's duty to inform and to teach before it is too late. Only in the histories, in which he is looking back a century and more, does the reader feel the aesthetic distance of the artist from his materials: the possibility of a view broad enough to be comprehensive and meaningful, and of a serenity permitting him to be wise and undidactic.

III *The Perspective at Midcentury*

Dos Passos' latest novel, like his latest history, is probably his best performance since *U. S. A.* in the genre. In fact it is deliberately patterned upon *U. S. A.*, and his publishers (Houghton Mifflin, who had previously published *D. C.*) and the *New York Times* evidently thought well enough of it to give it a front-page review.[4] *Midcentury*, according to its dust-jacket subtitle, is a "contemporary chronicle," and Dos Passos' purpose, he has said, was the same as in *U. S. A.*—to "organize the chaotic whole of American life into an artistic pattern."[5]

To a considerable degree, the novel does just that. It begins and ends, like so many of his better novels, with the picture of one man alone, who is faced with the central problem of communication. As in the better novels (*Three Soldiers, Manhattan Transfer, U. S. A.*), the one man alone in *Midcentury* is autobiographical—Dos Passos, walking with his dog on his farm in tidewater Virginia, an identification made explicit in the smell of "the cold loblollies" (which one must know is a type of pine, the principal business of Dos Passos' farm) and the use of the first person singular in the opening autograph. Unlike many of his novels, this one has no further autobiography—except perhaps for the six "Investigator's Notes," which seem to have been devised as a substitute for the Camera Eyes of *U. S. A.* and which concentrate on the workingman being interviewed, presumably by an agent of the McClellan Committee.

The novel itself traces the period since the forties through the intermeshing lives of four or five principal characters. Blackie Bowman, an old-time Wobbly and philosophical anarchist, tells his own story—which is independent of the others—by almost total recall from the veterans' hospital where he is dying. Terry Bryant, a young man oppressed first by management and then by labor as he tries to support his family, turns finally to driving a taxicab in a gesture of independence. Frank Worthington, a well-intentioned man who rises to the top in a career in labor, gradually loses touch with the rank-and-file union members such as Terry Bryant as institutionalized Labor controls even its executives. Jasper Milliron, a business executive (who was introduced in

Chosen Country as a boy and later as a beribboned combat veteran of World War I), is forced out of his proper role in life by executive and financial conniving. Will Jenks, Jasper's son-in-law, a combat veteran of Korea, tries to break a taxi monopoly with his own cab company until his traffic engineer, Terry, is killed and Will succumbs to a compromise with the monopolists.

Interlarded with the fictional narrative are biographies of prominent figures of the period—five labor leaders (Bridges, John L. Lewis, Reuther, Tobin, Beck, and Hoffa), two generals (MacArthur and Dean), two senators (McClellan and the younger La Follette), five shapers of contemporary opinion (Eleanor Roosevelt, Sam Goldwyn of the movies, financier Robert Young, physicist Robert Oppenheimer, movie idol James Dean), and one molder of the mass mind, Sigmund Freud. Replacing the Newsreels of *U. S. A.* are the "Documentaries" of *Midcentury*—clippings from newspaper headlines, from technological advertising, and from recent revelations in *Scientific American*, which Dos Passos reads "passionately."[6]

Midcentury is indeed a "contemporary chronicle" which organizes much of the chaos of American life into some kind of pattern, chiefly that which traces the growth of Labor into a corrupt and corrupting institution. The dominant thread in this pattern is intended to be the activities and findings of the McClellan Committee investigating union malpractices. They are clearly seen in several of the biographies, in all of the Investigator's Notes, in over a third of the Documentaries, and in the fictional narrative. But instead of a unifying thread, they become links in a steel chain binding all the parts rigorously to the anti-union thesis and almost obscuring the true warp and woof of midcentury American life.

Dos Passos has perhaps wisely turned from autobiography in this latest novel, but he seems not yet to have discovered an adequate substitute for the focusing intelligence of the Camera Eyes. The view of contemporary America is comprehensive but distorted. The primary purpose seems not, after all, to have been to create "an artistic pattern," but rather, as so often of late (and with just cause, we may feel constrained to add), to save his readers from themselves.

Despite the distortion in perspective, *Midcentury* does help us to see more clearly some of the relations that exist today between American ideals and practice. The old themes are here—the struggle of the individual (Blackie, Terry, Jasper, Will) amid industrial warfare set against a background of political war; the tragic failures in communication which isolate the individual (MacArthur, La Follette, Oppenheimer) from his kind: "When a man's function in society is gone he sometimes just plain wants to die" (p. 362); the importance of the family as a psychological necessity (sustaining Terry and Will, lacking to La Follette, who succumbed to suicide) and as the central cohesive social unit. Here too is the emphasis upon conscious memory as a vital humanizing activity, and upon the distinctions between means and ends.

And there are new emphases as well. One is the threat to individualism of over-reliance upon psychiatry—revealed in the contrast between the satirical portraits of the analysts Drs. X and Y (in the Freud biography) and Terry Bryant's diagnosing and curing his own battle-fatigue after World War II. Another is the similar challenge of the limitless vistas of theoretical physics too easily divorced from human considerations, which is exemplified by the personal predicaments of Robert Oppenheimer. And as a counterbalance is a new explicitness of religious reference—"The still small private voice that is God's spark in man" ever on the verge of extinction.

If the perspective of Dos Passos' novel seems warped, that of the man is constant and whole. But it is still the perspective of the citizen rather than of the isolated artist. To many readers trained in the liberalism of the 1930's, Dos Passos' perspective as a citizen is also warped. But it would be fairer and truer to say that theirs is if they have not been so ready as he to refocus as contemporary problems and the institutions which reflect them constantly change and take new forms.

Today Dos Passos supports Senator Goldwater on the same principle that aligned him with the communists in the 1920's and early 1930's and with the McCarthy hearings (though not with "loudmouthed young Joe McCarthy . . . a simple minded demagogue"—*Midcentury*, p. 361) in the early 1950's. The reason is that each has represented the leadership for the direction Dos Passos has felt the United States must take *at the moment*. This is not to say that the means (communism, McCarthy, Goldwater) justify the end. Quite the reverse is true: the means are what must be done now to swing the ever-shifting balance of institutionalizing forces back into an equilibrium in which the individual can make his own way. Thus, on April 18, 1961, at least, Dos Passos was optimistic. He had voted for Nixon for President, ". . . but Kennedy might just turn out to be extremely good for us. . . . I'm absolutely cheering for him 100 percent right now, and he's up against terrific problems. Right now I'm optimistic about his chances. And I thought Adlai Stevenson's speech the other day on the Cuban situation was excellent. . . . There's no question we have a fighting chance in the world."[7] The casual reviewer of *Midcentury* is likely to miss that optimism and the emphasis on the fighting chance—unless he recognizes that the novel itself is part of the fight in its forthright indignation at oppression.

Like Terry Bryant, Dos Passos has been his own best psychoanalyst and has conquered by vigorous self-expression his old sense of isolation and inadequacy. In 1896 Dos Passos' essential isolation was presented him in a hotel in Chicago at his birth. With both the occasion and the mental equipment to develop his awareness, he was not long in feeling his isolation and suffering by it: "four eyes," "Frenchy," "The Man Without a Country." In 1916 he started out into the world along the paths of art and thought as a virtual vacuum of unfulfilled longings, omnivorous, voracious, seeking raw experience—the war, Spain, Italy, the Near East, Manhattan. Whatever he encountered he devoured avidly. But he was only feeding the tapeworm of doubt; it left him unsatisfied, his essential hunger unappeased.

Though he was "willing to starve in a garret" to maintain his moral freedom, neither his spiritual hunger nor his isolation created his art. Their function was to provide the opportunity for the development of his genius. He achieved its first expression in *Three Soldiers*, his first book to be accepted by an American publisher and to be widely acclaimed. But in retrospect, it is evident that Dos Passos would not stop with this novel. For his search for form was for a significant and acceptable pattern in his own society, and he knew it.

Three Soldiers was only an early step in a series of books which reveals a thoroughly rational and even methodical progression. First came his investigations of his own activities outside the society (in Martin Howe); next were his studies of his society's then dominant institution, the army; and of another, older society (Spain's) with an established pattern that he could accept. There followed his story of a narrow segment of the United States (Cambridge), which was succeeded by a vertical cross-sectional view of America's representative metropolis (Manhattan) and its most obvious social pattern, the struggle for economic success. Finally Dos Passos arrived at the three-dimensional view of the entire society and his own relation to it in *U. S. A.* In it he studied his society horizontally across the country, vertically through its social-economic strata, and temporally to the furthest reaches of his own memory. Each of these novels, with the possible exception of *Streets of Night*, was technically superior to the one before it. In fact so successful was Dos Passos in his imaginative exploitation of the possibilities of his materials that much of what critical reputation remains to him is as a technical innovator and virtuoso, rather than as the artist he unquestionably was.

IV   *"The Duty of the Writer"*

If the artist had won relief from the rigors of his garret by the middle 1930's, it was partially through his own efforts— through his achievement in form—and partially through developments in external circumstances. Most important among external changes were, first, what Dos Passos calls "the parallel, but, fortunately for us still diverse, development of industrial society in the U. S. and the U. S. S. R.";[8] and, second, the similar contrasts between the hope and vigor of New Deal America and the increasing stagnation and despotism he saw in Europe. So the artist made his peace with his times; but his era drove a hard bargain as it abandoned peace and demanded much of a citizen.

In effect Dos Passos renounced the responsibilities of his genius in favor of those of a citizen; but he did not thereby lose the moral freedom which he had so jealously guarded as an artist. Rather he enlarged it by accepting the larger framework (society) for the smaller (his garret) in which to work. He could in fact no longer have retained his moral freedom in any other way. Since such liberty consisted in his right to think and then to do what he thought right, he could not ignore the claims upon his moral judgment of what he called, in his letter to Fitzgerald in the autumn of 1936, "the general conflagration . . . one of the damndest tragic moments in history."[9]

A year and a half earlier in "The Writer as Technician"—written for the American Writers' Congress in April, 1935—he had devoted his whole paper to an exposition of the moral and practical responsibilities of the writer "in his relation to society." What he was saying to the largely communist-sympathizing audience of the Congress was that they had to remember that as writers and technicians they depended absolutely on the existence of "a situation in which a technician can . . . be free to give rein to those doubts . . . that are at the root of invention and discovery and original thinking." If they did not devote their whole efforts to maintaining that freedom—and especially, because most insidious, freedom from "the imperial and bureaucratic tendencies of the groups we believe in"—they would find their own moral freedoms gone.

Although he distinguished in his paper between a writer's "function as a citizen and his function as a technician," he spoke of the writer's "obligation, like any other citizen, to take part in the struggle against oppression." The difference was only in the more compelling responsibility of the writer toward moral freedom: "I don't see how it is possible to organize effectively for liberty and the human values of life without protecting and demanding during every minute of the fight the liberties of investigation, speech and discussion that are the greatest part of the ends of the struggle."[10]

The chief difference between "The Writer as Technician" and "The Duty of the Writer"—which he delivered to another group of writers, the P. E. N. Club, in London in September, 1941—is in the added emphasis in the latter upon the writer's duties as a citizen. "The next war," which Dos Passos had clearly anticipated as early as 1934,[11] was in progress. To him, the insistence of the previous speakers upon the writer's primary obligations to his muse was sheer irresponsibility:

"Well, Mr. Poet-Writer, I am all for you, if you can get away with it, but the type of writer I am interested in now is the writer who is also a good citizen." He then defined the duties of the good citizen and the specific responsibility of the citizen-writer. He made it quite clear that he felt that in times of emergency the writer's duty was to write and act first as a citizen and only secondarily, if at all, as an artist:

> The average factory worker or clerk or college professor is only dimly aware of what kind of society he is living in. It is the business of the writer to tell him. There are endless ways of doing the job . . . , but that is the job that has got to be done and it has got to be done quickly. When you say *quickly* literature and the *aere perennius* fly out the window. Great works of the imagination are not produced quickly nor do they take quick effect on the popular mind. Well, Milton put off *Paradise Lost* to slave for the Commonwealth."[12]

Dos Passos himself, then, would first of all be a good citizen. It had been his lifelong ambition, but first he had had to find something that he could conscientiously be a good citizen of. His program for fulfilling his responsibilities was little more than a restatement of the platitudes of democratic citizenship: the eternal vigilance of an intelligent and informed electorate. The trouble with platitudes, though, was that they had already lost their meaning when they became platitudes. They needed restatement. At this moment, the fall of 1941, Dos Passos had just finished a few more lessons in his "course in American history" of which he had written Fitzgerald in the fall of 1936. *The Living Thoughts of Tom Paine* had appeared the year before; *The Ground We Stand On* was just off the press. He was in a position to restate American principles.

These principles were the basis of the "modern industrial society" of which the electorate must become more than "dimly aware." When he, one of the electorate, became aware, his duty was to inform the rest—and "quickly." This feeling of urgency, rather than tiredness or "disillusionment" or even loss of inspiration, explains why the *aere perennius* has not flown back in the window of Dos Passos' garret and why he would not have been there to capture it if it had.

In that same letter to Fitzgerald of 1936, he was urging his friend to use his perfected talents, "as long as the murderous forces of history will let you." Those forces, and in fact their very murderousness—in Russia, Italy, and Germany, and finally in Spain and France—contributed largely to expelling Dos Passos from the luxury of his isolation in his garret into the community of responsible citizenship. They have not permitted his return. By 1941, when he addressed the P. E. N. Club in London, they had become obviously and immediately murderous. Since 1936, while he has watched the very bases of our society and even of all society continuously and increasingly threatened, for Dos Passos it has not been literature but the practical foundations of the social order that must be made "more durable than brass" (*aere perennius*). This is also why he has become apparently permanently involved in the study of American history, not so much as the "truffle dog" digging up facts for historians to use later—or even as the "architect of history" of *U. S. A.*, content with long-range results—but more nearly as an historian himself, an amateur with a novelist's bent, who still hopes, as he wrote in *U. S. A.*, to "bring back (I too Walt Whitman) our storybook democracy" (Cam. Eye 46). It seems unlikely that he will escape the imperatives of his citizenship.

In "A Note on Fitzgerald," published early in 1941, Dos Passos explained, in a way, why he cannot—though Fitzgerald did—regain the essential isolation of the artist. Both, as it happened, had lost it at about the same time and largely through their own efforts. Fitzgerald had suffered his "crack-up" in 1936 because of his schizophrenic attempt to be at once an artist and "the moneyed celebrity" of public acclaim. But, Dos Passos says, "No durable piece of work . . . has ever been accomplished by a double-minded man. To attain the invention of any sound thing . . . demands the integrated effort of somebody's whole heart and whole intelligence." Fitzgerald, enjoying but never really believing in his role of celebrity, managed by determined effort to unite the two "in *The Great Gatsby* and to a greater degree in *The Last Tycoon*," by *being* the artist and writing about the moneyed celebrity.

Dos Passos, whose citizenship is not even a role but a vocation, cannot so much as make the effort to be instead an artist. That does not mean, of course, that he must be a double-minded man. He may well produce durable pieces of work to follow *U. S. A.*—may in fact have already produced them; for example, his recent *Prospects of a Golden Age* or *Mid-century*—and they may even turn out to be works of art; but they will not be produced primarily *as* works of art, but, more probably, as history. For the role of historian is fully complementary to that of citizen; it might even be called an essential part of it. The role of citizen, however, as a consciously participating—not merely protesting—member of society, Dos Passos felt to be antithetical to that of artist. Milton, he noted, had to "put off" the role of artist to work for the Commonwealth. When Dos Passos urged his fellow writers to do likewise, it was probably not with the expectation that the forces of history would prevent their resuming the role.

Dos Passos also says of Fitzgerald that "as a man he was tragically destroyed by his own invention," the rich celebrity, and "as a writer his triumph was that he managed . . . to weld together again" his "two divergent halves." Almost the opposite may be said of Dos Passos. As a man his triumph is that he has managed to weld together, once and permanently, his two divergent halves, the lonely romantic seeker and the gregarious practical man, the idealist and the realist. As an artist he destroyed his painful isolation—in *Manhattan Transfer* and to a greater degree in *U. S. A.*—by his own art. Most of his critics agree that this is tragic: that the "complete cessation of his creative energy," "the tragic exhaustion of a once formidable talent," is "one of the saddest things that [has] happened in recent literary history."[13]

Regarded from any other point of view than that of literary history, Dos Passos' development since the middle thirties is neither tragic nor sad. To say that it is, is almost to say that the artist *should* die young, that his best work should be his last. Yet these same critics would doubtless agree that the best work of many artists has been far from their last. Would they kill off the man to avoid the "tragedy" of a lingering artistic demise? From the viewpoint of the man, it would have been more nearly tragic if he had *not* attained the inner peace—relieved the spiritual hunger of which his art was the expression. From the viewpoint of the society, are we prepared at this time to renounce the citizen for the artist, the historian for the novelist? For as the novelist Dos Passos has diminished, the historian has grown. Having asked, as a novelist, the first question of the historian, "Who am I?" he has been pursuing it to its roots in the hope of helping Americans discover who they are, too, before it is too late.

Dos Passos himself characteristically saw first the tragedy of the man Fitzgerald, which was only mitigated by the triumph of the artist; that is, although he was writing of a fellow artist and even writing of him *as* an artist, he never lost sight of him as a man, as a living and breathing and suffering human being. This is precisely the central characteristic of all of Dos Passos' work—as artist, reporter, critic, historian, and citizen. It is a characteristic which many of his literary critics would do well to emulate.

When Dos Passos first began his search for pattern and form and unity which would give meaning to the apparently chaotic world in which he grew up, he was forced by his isolation into a kind of practical solipsism—the belief that he alone existed. His transient boyhood, combined with his real and imagined differences from others, left him only himself whom he could know well (his mother was a familiar goddess, his father an unfamiliar god) as a nucleus from which to construct a meaningful order. Like Thoreau at the beginning of *Walden*, he might have observed at any time that he should not talk so much about himself if there were anybody else he knew as well. And so John Dos Passos became the first object of his search and the first center of his work.

But the intent of his pursuit of self was never, after childhood, merely solipsistic. Rather, it was to discover the common humanity of living and breathing and suffering individuals and his relation to them. His search, as Telemachus, for his father was for the man behind the symbol, for the identity of the relationships which should give meaning to both lives.

His role as a novelist was always conditioned by his conception of his relationship to his audience which he defined in December of 1927 as part of his definition of the theater: "By theatre . . . I mean a group of people, preferably a huge group of people; part of the group puts on plays"—or writes a novel—"and the rest forms the audience, an active, working audience." If many of the characters of his fiction have been stillborn as social entities, they were such so that Dos Passos and the individuals in his audience might live.

Thus Dos Passos' search for a society was for a group of individuals who could corroborate his intuitive faith in human nature and confirm the testimony of the vitality he felt within him. Yet as Skinny had told him, "If you'd never been baptized you couldn't be confirmed." Dos Passos' real baptism to membership in society, for all the metaphoric ones in his early life and fiction, was in the fire of his own genius. His confirmation was in his acceptance of his citizenship and of its privileges and responsibilities at a time when "the general conflagration" had consumed parts of the social fabric on three continents and threatened it elsewhere.

By January, 1938, Dos Passos had forged, chiefly in *U. S. A.*, his own link in the social chain. He had written the major work of his vast *apologia pro vita sua*. Yet neither his quest nor its story would likely be finished before his death. Starting from Spain in 1917, with only imagination and courage and the convictions of his quest, he discovered America. Unlike its first discovery, this one was no mere accident. He was not looking for any Cathay or for "the land where the streets are paved with gold of the immigrant's dream," but for "a land where . . . in a certain elemental freedom of thought and action the foundations [had] been laid for a life" in which people could "enjoy . . . 'liberty and pursuit of happiness.'"14

He found it. But since his discovery, he has only searched the deeper: locating the boundaries and foundations marked out and established by earlier explorers and builders—Roger Williams, Tom Paine, Joel Barlow, Thomas Jefferson—in whom, not surprisingly, he has found his own spiritual ancestors. And so the story of his quest continues, in his histories as well as in his fiction.

If it has been predominantly his own story, it is because, like Thoreau, Whitman, and Henry Adams, and less obviously Melville and Twain—all of whom he admires15—he has used the self to explain the universe. Starting on the undefined ground of his common humanity, he made of himself the representative man, seeking to define himself and his integrity. When he stood upon the firmer ground of democratic citizenship, he had defined in that symbol a man's freedom to act as he will and his responsibility for his actions. In his continuing efforts to establish that ground for every individual, he has been seeking to create in his fiction and to revitalize in his history, other models for Americans of the free and responsible individual.

Of his recent history, *The Men Who Made the Nation,* he has remarked, "I have been trying to bring people to life as a novelist would."[16] This statement epitomizes his career as a writer. Possibly his most significant achievement as a craftsman is his perfected ability to present events in perspective: to make his reader perceive an event as an isolated historical phenomenon and simultaneously experience it in the human context of one or more characters whom it affects. In fiction his greatest success in this direction was in *U. S. A.;* in history it is in *Prospects of a Golden Age,* in which he makes of early American history an immediate and extraordinarily integrated human experience. The reader, finally, must breathe life into the fictions which the artist has drawn, into the historian's stiff canvas and marble likenesses of our forefathers (*Prospects of a Golden Age* is illustrated with these.)

If Dos Passos' critics occasionally protest that he has not wholly succeeded in his attempt "to bring people to life," they should judge his attempt by his own terms. For the people he has been trying to bring to life are not so much those of his fiction, or of his histories, as everyman. Insofar as he has provided his readers with a memory, with frames of reference by which to judge today, he has, in his own terms, made his readers live. Without a memory, they are but "a mindless and panicky mob," a subhuman thing. It is impossible in 1961 to estimate whatever success he may ultimately have had, but it is equally impossible to conceive of a road more significant or more nearly identical with its destination.

"The cool detachment of a writer," Dos Passos noted in 1941, "is hard to keep in middle age."[17] At forty-five, he was explaining, in effect, the loss of his own artistic genius—peculiarly conscious, as always, of his precise position. Yet he was offering neither excuses nor regrets. Though he has by no means renounced his role as novelist, he has seemed to find more congenial his role as citizen-historian. If he has lost the cool detachment essential to the artist, he has retained the warm humanity essential to the man. If his readers regret the passing of the artist, they may applaud the enlightenment of the historian and the triumph of the man.

Notes and References

1. Dos Passos (see back of title page).
2. These brief annotations appear as marginal comments on a MS I once sent to Mr. Dos Passos for his corrections (1950). See also the account of Jay Pignatelli's maternal grandfather in Dos Passos' autobiographical novel, *Chosen Country* (1951), pp. 40-42; Dos Passos' fullest account of his mother is the portrait of Kathryn Jay Isham in this novel.
3. Dos Passos, in *Portraits and Self-Portraits*, ed. Georges Schreiber (1958), p. 25.
4. Samuel E. Morison and Henry Steele Commager, *The Growth of the American Republic*, Vol. II, 3rd ed. (1942), 423, 428.
5. "Satire as a Way of Seeing," *Interregnum* [drawings by George Grosz], ed. Caresse Crosby (1936), pp. 9-10. Most of this Introduction appeared as "Grosz Comes to America," *Esquire*, VI (Sept., 1936), 105, 128, 131.
6. For Pegler, see J. F. Powers, quoted in Alfred Kazin, ed., *F. Scott Fitzgerald: The Man and His Work* (1951), p. 182; the "recent critic" is Henry Dan Piper, "Fitzgerald's Cult of Disillusion," *American Quarterly*, III (Spring, 1951), 73.
7. "Constructive pacifism" is from "A Conference on Foreign Relations," *Harvard Monthly*, LXII (June, 1916), 126. The references to his father's concern about his "block being blown off," and to Spain as a compromise are among Dos Passos' marginal comments in the MS mentioned in n. 2. The comments in French are quoted in Armand Pierhal, "Le grand romancier Dos Passos est à Paris," *Nouvelles Littéraires* (June 5, 1937), p. 9. Pierhal notes that Dos Passos' French, in which the interview was conducted, was "un français non seulment aisé mais choisi" (not only fluent but select).
8. Camera Eye 2; this second Jack in the Camera Eyes is of course John R. Dos Passos, Jr. (Jay, in *Chosen Country*).
9. Jack Potter in his *A Bibliography of John Dos Passos* (1950), pp. 68, 69, attributes to Dos Passos two additional editorials, "The World Decision," *Harvard Monthly*, LXII (March, 1916), 23-24, and "The Amateur Spirit," *Harvard Monthly*, LXII (April, 1916), 56. Both signed "D. P.," they conflict in tone and signature with

other items attributed to Dos Passos; they are probably the work of Dudley Poore ('17).

10. The names are from Greek and Spanish story: Telemachus was the son of Odysseus and Penelope; Lyaeus, Telemachus' companion in *Rosinante,* is better known in myth as the god Bacchus or Dionysus; Rosinante (or Rocinante) will be remembered as Don Quixote's horse.

11. *One Man's Initiation—1917* was reprinted by the Philosophical Library for the market of the second World War with a new and less cumbersome title, *First Encounter* (1945), and with no mention of the earlier printing. This second edition contains an original preface by Dos Passos written for the new edition from his home in Provincetown (not "Providence" as in the date line), Mass., in which he is fairly explicit about his method and materials in the book: "In *reporting* a conversation *we* had. . . ." (italics mine), p. [9].

12. This rather clear Oedipal image may very well never have been noticed before, although the mature reader can scarcely read any of Dos Passos' novels (or other modern fiction) without coming across hints of this nature. Naming the envied friend Tom Randolph was no mere Freudian slip, just as it was not two years later in *Rosinante* when Dos Passos gave us a clear Telemachus and an ambiguous Lyaeus—a name almost no one recognizes as the Greek Bacchus, although most of us are familiar with a very similar Greek name—at least in English pronunciation—Laïus, the natural father of Oedipus.

13. The preface to *U. S. A.* is labeled "U. S. A." and is an integral part of the trilogy, added upon publication of the three volumes as a single work in 1938. It is the equivalent of a first and generalized Camera Eye. The other two quotations here are from Camera Eyes 28 and 36 of *U. S. A.*

14. See, for example, nearly any letter or personal essay by nearly any member of the "lost generation" written at about this time. A good sample review of these opinions may be found in Alfred Kazin, ed., *F. Scott Fitzgerald: The Man and His Work* (1951).

Chapter Two

1. "To report the class war we launched the *New Masses.* I forget who put up the money," Dos Passos reminisces in his recent book *The Theme Is Freedom* (1956), p. 4. According to Granville Hicks in "The Politics of John Dos Passos," *Antioch Review,* X (March, 1950), 89—it was "with the aid of a subsidy from the Garland Fund." The names of some of the writers listed in the first issue are interesting: Michael Gold, editor and president;

Dos Passos on the executive board; contributing editors—Sherwood Anderson, Carleton Beals, Van Wyck Brooks, Stuart Chase, Floyd Dell, Max Eastman, Waldo Frank, Susan Glaspell, J. H. Lawson, Claude McKaye, Lewis Mumford, Eugene O'Neill, Elmer Rice, Boardman Robinson, Carl Sandburg, Upton Sinclair, Genevieve Taggard, Louis Untermeyer, Mary Heaton Vorse, Walter F. White, Edmund Wilson, Jr., Art Young; writing for the first issue were Robinson Jeffers, William Carlos Williams, Whittaker Chambers.

2. Most of Dos Passos' reporting of this period is collected in his non-fiction travel book, *In All Countries* (1934). The editorial appears with minor changes in *The Theme Is Freedom* (1956), pp. 7-10.

3. Hicks, "Politics of John Dos Passos," p. 89.

4. Dos Passos' marginal comment on my MS. See above, Chap. One, n. 2.

5. Dos Passos, *Facing the Chair* (Boston, 1927); "They Are Dead Now," *New Masses*, III (Oct., 1927), 7; "An Open Letter to President Lowell," *Nation*, CXXV (August 24, 1927), 176; Cam. Eyes 49, 50, *The Big Money*, pp. 435-37, 461-64. The last of these is quoted below in the text.

6. Wilson, "The Literary Consequences of the Crash," *Shores of Light* (1952), p. 498; "Marxism and Literature," *The Triple Thinkers* (revised and enlarged ed., 1948), p. 208. The attitude toward Dos Passos' reliability in September, 1929, which Wilson expressed in the article first cited was, of course, understandable on the part of the *New Republic*, which could not investigate minutely the philosophical positions of its correspondents. It is more difficult to know what to make of Wilson's phrase "reliable from our point of view," considering his personal acquaintance with Dos Passos—except to note that earlier in that year of the crash he had strongly disparaged the literary expression in the U. S. of "the emotions and the points of view appropriate to bankruptcy and exhaustion . . . [in] a country full of money and health" ("Dostoevsky Abroad" [dated Jan. 30, 1929], *Shores of Light*, p. 412).

7. "Back to Red Hysteria," *New Republic*, LXIII (July 2, 1930), 159; "Whom Can We Appeal To?" *New Masses*, VI (Aug., 1930), 8; "Wanted: An Ivy Lee for Liberals," *New Republic*, LXIII (Aug. 13, 1930), 371, 372.

8. *The Left*, I (Summer, 1931), 100 (on the committee were Sherwood Anderson, Roger Baldwin, Waldo Frank, Michael Gold, Robert Morse Lovett, Upton Sinclair, and others); *New Republic*, LXVII (August 5, 1931), 318.

9. *Theme Is Freedom*, p. 86. The Kentucky experience, like the Sacco-Vanzetti one, is the subject of much of Dos Passos' writing:

three magazine articles, repeated with variations in three non-fiction books, and employed in three novels.

10. See *In All Countries*, pp. 112-16.

11. "An Appeal," *Student Review*, II (Oct., 1932), 21. This last was signed by Newton Arvin, Sherwood Anderson, Roger Baldwin, Malcolm Cowley, H. W. L. Dana, John Dos Passos, Theodore Dreiser, Max Eastman, Waldo Frank, Michael Gold, Oakley Johnson, Corliss Lamont, Scott Nearing, Mark Van Doren.

12. "Four Nights in a Garden: A Campaign Yarn," *Common Sense*, I, No. 1 (Dec. 5, 1932), 20-22; the staff of contributors included Dos Passos and Stuart Chase, A. J. Muste, V. F. Calverton, John T. Flynn, John Chamberlain, Ernest Boyd, James Rorty, and others.

13. "Tom Paine's 'Common Sense,' " *Common Sense*, VIII (Sept., 1939), 3-6; "Tom Paine's 'Rights of Man,' " *Common Sense*, VIII (Oct., 1939), 12-15.

Chapter Three

1. See "Passport Photo," *In All Countries*, pp. 3-6; this experience is reviewed with a firmer emphasis in *Theme Is Freedom*, p. 66. For Calypso, see above, Chap. One, n. 10.

2. "In Portugal," *Liberator*, III (April, 1920), 25; dated four months before its publication.

3. Michael Gold, "The Education of John Dos Passos," *English Journal*, XXII (Feb., 1933), 92, 97.

4. There would be no need to go into all this at this late date if Hicks and others had not been so successful in establishing and perpetuating the existence of the mythical (communist or fellow-traveling) Dos Passos, or if they had not been so successful in establishing the supposed validity of political criticism of an artist. The result of their effort has been that even a younger critic such as Martin Kallich devotes his energies to proving the Hicks thesis. See his "John Dos Passos: Liberty and the Father Image," *Antioch Review*, X (March, 1950), 100-5, which is cheek by jowl with Hicks's article, and "John Dos Passos Fellow-Traveler: A Dossier with Commentary," *Twentieth Century Literature*, I (January, 1956), 173-90; the "Dossier" here is a valuable piece of Dos Passos biographical research for the years 1923-1936, but the "Commentary" is frankly an elaboration of Hicks's article—a search for proofs rather than explanations.

5. Dos Passos, in "Whither the American Writer? A Questionnaire," *Modern Quarterly*, VI (Summer, 1932), 11, 12. Some other answerers, following Dos Passos, are Sherwood Anderson, Edwin Seaver, Clifton Fadiman, Ernest Southerland Bates, John

Chamberlain, H. S. Canby, Percy H. Boynton, Henry Hazlitt, pp. 12-19.

6. *Theme Is Freedom* (1956), pp. 101, 161.

7. Bernard De Voto, "John Dos Passos, Anatomist of Our Time," *Saturday Review of Literature,* XIV (Aug. 8, 1936), 12. For other criticisms of Dos Passos' handling of characters, see T. K. Whipple, *Study Out the Land* (1943), pp. 88-90; James T. Farrell, "Dos Passos and the Critics," *American Mercury,* XLVII (Aug., 1939), 492 [concerning a later Dos Passos book]. With these, cf. Maxwell Geismar, *Writers in Crisis* (Boston, 1942), p. 125; Mason Wade, "Novelist of America—John Dos Passos," *North American Review,* CCXLIV (Dec., 1937), 364; these last two praise his characterization; Wade's is one of the more perceptive articles about Dos Passos.

8. The narrator and Dick attended Harvard; and Herf, Columbia; Herf's walk with the minister's wife (not in *Manhattan Transfer*) occurs in the excerpt "July," republished from *Transatlantic Review* in *Transatlantic Stories* (1926), pp. 129-64. For other similarities between Dick Savage and Dos Passos, such as the error of getting a room in the Yard as a freshman at Harvard, cf. *1919*, pp. 88 ff., and Charles W. Bernardin, "John Dos Passos' Harvard Years," *New England Quarterly,* XXVII (March, 1954), 3-26. Dos Passos disguised Dick slightly and made him more representative by giving him a part of the background of his own good friend and fellow *Monthly* editor, Robert Hillyer: his schooling at Kent (rather than at Choate), his becoming an officer after the breakup of the Norton-Harjes unit, and his serving as courier at the Peace Conference; see Fred B. Millet, *Contemporary American Authors* (1944) s.v. "Robert Hillyer."

9. *U. S. A.,* Cam. Eye 28; "U. S. A." (preface to trilogy); Cam. Eyes 37, 42, 38, respectively. See also *Chosen Country,* p. 354, for Jay Pignatelli's experiences with scrap iron and a lost service record; and *Three Soldiers,* pp. 401 ff., for similar experiences by John Andrews ("Skinny") before *he* escaped the army.

10. *Theme Is Freedom,* p. 161. He was too young to vote for Wilson in 1916, although he may have favored his candidacy, as did Dick Savage (*1919*, p. 91); according to Bernardin, "Harvard Years," p. 26, Dos Passos' friend Stewart Mitchell remembers him as favoring Wilson's reformism but objecting to his war talk; he would scarcely have voted for any of the succeeding presidents until F. D. R. under any conditions. His voting record from 1932 to 1948 may be constructed from *Theme Is Freedom*: 1932—Foster (pp. 101-3); 1936 and 1940—F. D. R. (p. 151); 1944 and 1948—Dewey (as a "protest" vote, like that in 1932, p. 101).

11. "A Letter from John Dos Passos [October ?, 1936]"

[sic], in Edmund Wilson, ed., *The Crack-Up—F. Scott Fitzgerald* (1945), p. 311.

12. "America and the Pursuit of Happiness"; see above, Chap. Two, sect. I.

13. "A Case of Conscience," *Common Sense,* IV (May, 1935), 17; this article, "bitterly non-fiction" (p. 16), is the story of Ray Becker, in jail in Walla Walla, Washington, because, like Dos Passos, he was a conscientious objector who acted according to his conscience.

14. "Statement of the Committee for Cultural Freedom," in "In Defense of Free Minds [letter and statement from Sidney Hook]," *American Mercury,* XLVII (July, 1939), 375-76. See "Humble Protest," above, Chap. One, sect. III; Dos Passos' signature to the statement in *American Mercury* is not generally known, probably because it appears under "P" in the alphabetical listing.

Chapter Four

1. "Two American Novelists," [London] *Times* Literary Supplement (anon. review), Oct. 27, 1950, p. 669.

2. Or one can call it the artistic *temper*—insofar as its source was more nearly environmental than innate. The above ideas are based upon the premise of the existence in every man of a need for some kind of satisfying pattern or form in his life. In most of us it may remain forever below the level of our consciousness as it is satisfied by an already established order. But in periods of disruption of the established order, or of the introduction of new and urgent unassimilated elements, we become conscious of the need for new forms and patterns of our own or another's making. If the sensitive and perceptive individual is relatively free to seek or create his own, if an absolute order is not imposed arbitrarily from above, then the widespread efforts in the direction of new organizations will tend increasingly to be expressed in art, which is perhaps the characteristic expression of the civilizing process.

3. Dos Passos, "Looking Back on 'U. S. A.,'" *New York Times,* Sunday, October 25, 1959, sect. 2, p. 5, cols. 1-3.

4. "July," *Transatlantic Stories* (1926), p. 138. This story, first published over a year before *Manhattan Transfer* (Nov., 1925), treats a brief but important period in the life of Jimmy Herf, spending a stagnant, yearning summer with the family of his mother's sister, Aunt Emily, before going on to college in the fall. The family names, Herf and the Merivales, are those of *Manhattan Transfer;* the local names and incidents recur much later in *42nd Parallel* (1930), condensed into four pages of autobiographical narrative in Cam. Eyes 19 and 21.

5. "Phases of the Moon: X," *Pushcart,* p. 206. This is the last of the six sections into which the book is divided: "Winter in Castille" (dated Nov., 1916-Feb., 1917, the first trip to Spain), "Nights at Bassano" (dated 1918-1919, treated in the life of Dick Savage in *1919,* pp. 200 ff.), "Vagones de Tercera" (dated 1919-1920, the second trip to Spain), "Quai de la Tournelle" (dated 1919, wartime Paris), "On Foreign Travel," and "Phases of the Moon" (both undated).

6. See, however: W. M. Frohock, "John Dos Passos: Of Time and Frustration," *Southwest Review,* XXXIII (Winter, Spring, 1948), 71-80, 170-79; Malcolm Cowley, "The Poet and the World," *New Republic,* LXX (Feb. 2, 1938), 303-5; and John Peale Bishop, "Poets in Prose," *Collected Essays,* ed. Edmund Wilson (1948), pp. 272-74.

7. See, e.g., Edmund Wilson, "Dos Passos' Reporting," *New Yorker,* XX (July 29, 1944), 57-84. Wilson here poses this very problem.

8. This phrase occurs as the title of Chap. I of *Adventures of a Young Man* (1939) and again in *The Ground We Stand On* (1941), p. 254.

9. See last illnesses of Lily Herf (*Manhattan Transfer,* 86, 113, *passim*), Kathryn Jay (*Chosen Country,* pp. 54-57), Aunt Em (*Streets of Night,* p. 287); see also *1919,* pp. 9-10.

10. Dos Passos, "The Making of a Writer," *New Masses,* IV (March, 1929), 23.

Chapter Five

1. "Book Reviews: *The War in Eastern Europe* by John Reed," p. 149. There is no mention of Henry James here, but in "Young Spain" (Aug., 1917), 482-83, Dos Passos compares Baroja's attitude toward Spain with "the attitude toward America of the early Henry James, though as artists there is no comparison between them." In *Journeys,* p. 337, he describes some French fascists in terms of characters in a James novel, "one of those chronicles of gradually diminishing interest. . . ." Probably the phrase "near-literature" exempted James in his review.

2. Besides "July" (see above, Chap. Three, n. 8), there are two related stories published in inverse chronological order, in separate periodicals, in different years, which did not become parts of a larger work. These are "Tin Can Tourist," *Direction,* I (Dec., 1937), 10-12, and "Migratory Worker," *Partisan Review,* IV (Jan., 1938), 63. Probably originally intended to conclude *The Big Money* (1936), they take up the later career of Ike Hall, Mac's friend early in *42nd Parallel* (1930): in "Worker" he marries, loses his job in the depression, takes a "scabbing" job; in "Tourist"

his wife dies, and he takes to the road again, as we had last seen him, hopping a freight in *42nd Parallel* (p. 79).

3. While this statement appears to refute the opinion of Maxwell Geismar and others, that "it was from . . . Pío Baroja, that Dos Passos gained his early intellectual concepts" (Geismar, "A Cycle of Fiction," *Literary History of the United States*, ed. Robert E. Spiller *et al.* [1949], p. 1302), there is no documented proof. Bernardin, however, in his analysis of Dos Passos' Harvard reading, ("J. D. P.'s Harvard Years") does not mention Baroja, although he was being read in American college literary circles at the time. It now appears likely, as I have implied, that Baroja was more nearly a corroboration and an example than a source. See also the implication of an opinion similar to Geismar's in Edmund Wilson, "Dos Passos' Reporting," *New Yorker*, XX (July 29, 1944), 58.

4. Dos Passos, "Introduction: Why Write for the Theatre Anyway?" *Three Plays* (1934), p. xiii.

5. [Longhand presentation-note] *U. S. A.*, University of Pennsylvania Library "rare book."

6. Dos Passos in "Whither the American Writer? A Questionnaire," *Modern Quarterly*, VI (Summer, 1932), 12.

7. Bernardin, pp. 11-12. Of the writers named in the above three paragraphs, Bernardin does not mention Dreiser, London, Anderson, or Reed. He does not mention Zola, perhaps because Dos Passos had read him earlier.

Chapter Six

1. This is the tradition represented by, among others, Compton MacKenzie and James Joyce in Great Britain, Pío Baroja in Spain, and Scott Fitzgerald—whose first novel, *This Side of Paradise* (1920) was published in the same year as Dos Passos' first, *One Man's Initiation—1917*—in America.

2. The classic expression of this last idea is in T. S. Eliot's essay, "Tradition and the Individual Talent" (1917), published in his collection *The Sacred Wood* (Alfred A. Knopf, 1920) and the lead essay in his *Selected Essays, 1917-1932* (Harcourt, Brace, 1932).

Chapter Seven

1. *Manhattan Transfer*, pp. 155-56, 340-43, *et passim; U. S. A.* (in Cam. Eye 31; in the story of Margo Dowling; in the biography of Valentino: "Adagio Dancer"); *The Garbage Man* (1923), and *Most Likely to Succeed, passim.* See also comments in *Theme Is Freedom*, p. 42.

2. Produced under that title in 1925 and 1926 and published

as *The Garbage Man* in 1926. This play, as well as Dos Passos' two others, *Airways, Inc.* (published and produced in 1928) and *Fortune Heights* (first in *International Literature*, No. IV, April, 1933; produced in the Soviet Union only), is in his *Three Plays* (1934). I refer to each of them in this latest revised edition.

3. The date 1923 is conjectural. *The Garbage Man* was first written as the composition of a fictional character in an early unpublished novel. In "Looking Back on 'U. S. A.'" (see Chap. Four, n. 3), Dos Passos notes that the play was first produced "years later" (*i.e.,* 1925) by Ed Massey.

4. "American Theatre: 1930-31," *New Republic*, LXVI (April 2, 1931), 74; also in a revised reprint of this article: "Why Write for the Theatre Anyway?"—the Introduction to *Three Plays*, p. xx.

5. "Towards a Revolutionary [American] Theatre," p. 20. Noting the omission of an obviously intended key word in the title, we suspect the motives of the editors. After his publication in this issue, Dos Passos no longer contributed as a member of the Executive Board of the *New Masses*.

6. "Wanted: An Ivy Lee for Liberals," *New Republic*, LXIII (Aug. 13, 1930), 371; see also his "Back to Red Hysteria," *New Republic*, LXIII (July 2, 1930), 168-69. Both of these are similar to "Whom Can We Appeal To?" in the *New Masses*.

Chapter Eight

1. Henry Steele Commager, *The American Mind* (1950), p. 434.

2. *The Theme Is Freedom* (1954), p. 41.

3. "Whom Can We Appeal To?" *New Masses*, VI (Aug., 1930), 8; and "The Two Youngest," *Nation*, CXXXV (Aug. 24, 1952), 172, respectively.

4. *Theme Is Freedom*, p. 25—reprinted from his *Facing the Chair* (1927), p. 58.

Chapter Nine

1. Dos Passos, *In All Countries* (1934), p. 16.

2. "Edison and Steinmetz: Medicine Men," *New Republic*, LXI (Dec. 18, 1929), 104. See also *1919*, pp. 297-301, 325-28, for contrasting biographies.

3. W. M. Frohock, "John Dos Passos: Of Time and Frustration," *Southwest Review*, XXXIII (Spring, 1948), 177, ascribes to Hemingway this characteristic, but he does not develop the contrasting characteristic in Dos Passos.

4. "John Dos Passos, Anatomist of Our Times," *Saturday Review of Literature*, XIV (Aug. 8, 1936), 12.

Chapter Ten

1. "Big Parade—1936 Model," *Nation*, CXLIII (Oct. 3, 1936), 393.

2. [Reactions to Questionnaire] *Time*, L (Aug. 4, 1947), 83.

3. "Three Brilliant Young Novelists," *The Collected Essays of John Peale Bishop*, ed. Edmund Wilson (1948), p. 233; first in *Vanity Fair*, Oct., 1921; "Apropos de John Dos Passos. . . ," *Situations* (1949), I, 25, article dated: "*Août* 1938."

4. Harry T. Moore, "Proud Men in an Age of Conformity," February 26, 1961, pp. 1, 51. A review of *Midcentury*.

5. Cherrill Anson, "Dos Passos: Changing with the Times," Sunday *Sun* [Baltimore] Magazine, January 22, 1961, p. 7. A report of an interview with Dos Passos just before release of *Midcentury*; the material quoted is not quoted directly in the article.

6. Robert L. Perkin, "Dos Passos Retains Hope for Humanity," *Rocky Mountain News* (Denver, Colorado), April 19, 1961, p. 71. A question and answer interview.

7. *Ibid.*

8. Letter to the author (March, 1954), p. 2.

9. In *The Crack-Up*, ed. Edmund Wilson (1945), p. 311.

10. "The Writer as Technician," *American Writer's Congress*, ed. Henry Hart (1935), pp. 79, 80, 81, respectively.

11. See "The World's Iron, Our Blood, and Their Profits," *Student Outlook*, III (Oct., 1934), 17; "Two Views of the Student Strike," *Student Outlook*, III (April, 1935), 5.

12. Quotations in this paragraph from "The Duty of the Writer," *Writers in Freedom*, ed. Hermon Ould [1942], pp. 25-26.

13. These opinions of Dos Passos are from Maxwell Geismar, "The Theme Is Fear," *Nation*, CLXXXII (April 14, 1956), 305; [book review of *Most Likely to Succeed*], *Commonweal*, LXI (Oct. 8, 1954), 20; Granville Hicks, "Dos Passos: The Fruits of Disillusionment," *New Republic*, CXXXI (Sept. 27, 1954), 18, respectively.

14. "America and the Pursuit of Happiness," *Nation*, CXI (Dec. 29, 1920), 778.

15. For Thoreau, Whitman, Melville, and Twain, see "The Situation in American Writing" [Dos Passos' reply to questionnaire], *Partisan Review* VI (Summer, 1939), 26; for Henry Adams, see "Hicks and 'Forgotten Frontiers,'" *New Republic*, LXXXIV (March 29, 1933), 190.

16. Quoted in "The Novelist as Historian," anon. commentary, *Newsweek*, XLIX (Feb. 11, 1957), 106.

17. Quoted in Robert Van Gelder, "An Interview . . . Nov., 1941," *Writers and Writing* (1946), p. 237.

Selected Bibliography

I PRIMARY SOURCES

Books by Dos Passos

Adventures of a Young Man. New York: Harcourt, Brace, 1939. First vol. of *District of Columbia.*

Airways, Inc. New York: Macaulay, 1928.

The Big Money. New York: Harcourt, Brace, 1936.

Chosen Country. Boston: Houghton Mifflin, 1951.

District of Columbia. Boston: Houghton Mifflin, 1952.

Eight Harvard Poets. New York: Laurence J. Gomme, 1917. Contains seven Dos Passos poems.

Facing the Chair. Boston: Sacco-Vanzetti Defense Committee, 1927. A defense of Sacco and Vanzetti.

Fortune Heights. 1933. First in *International Lit.* (April, 1933); next in *Three Plays.*

The 42nd Parallel. New York: Harper and Brothers, 1930. First vol. of trilogy *U. S. A.*

The Garbage Man. New York, 1926. The first of *Three Plays.*

The Grand Design. Boston: Houghton Mifflin, 1949. Last vol. of *District of Columbia.*

The Great Days. New York: Sagamore Press, 1958.

The Ground We Stand On. New York: Harcourt, Brace, 1941.

The Head and Heart of Thomas Jefferson. New York: Doubleday, 1954.

In All Countries. New York: Harcourt, Brace, 1934.

Journeys Between Wars. New York: Harcourt, Brace, 1938.

Life's Picture History of World War II. New York: Time, Inc., 1950.

The Living Thoughts of Tom Paine: Presented by John Dos Passos. New York: Longmans, Green, 1940.

Manhattan Transfer. New York: Harper and Brothers, 1925.

The Men Who Made the Nation. New York: Doubleday, 1957.

Midcentury. Boston: Houghton Mifflin, 1961.

Most Likely to Succeed. Englewood Cliffs, N. J.: Prentice-Hall, 1954.

1919. New York: Harcourt, Brace, 1932. Second vol. of *U. S. A.*

Number One. Boston: Houghton Mifflin, 1943. Second vol. of *District of Columbia.*

One Man's Initiation—1917. London: Allen and Unwin, 1920 (New

Selected Bibliography

York: Geo. H. Doran, 1922); reprinted as *First Encounter*, New York: Philosophical Library, 1945.
Orient Express. New York: Harper and Brothers, 1927.
The Prospect Before Us. Boston: Houghton Mifflin, 1950.
Prospects of a Golden Age. Englewood Cliffs, N. J.: Prentice-Hall, 1959.
A Pushcart at the Curb. New York: Geo. H. Doran, 1922.
Rosinante to the Road Again. New York: Geo. H. Doran, 1922.
State of the Nation. Boston: Houghton Mifflin, 1944.
Streets of Night. New York: Geo. H. Doran, 1923.
The Theme Is Freedom. New York: Dodd, Mead, 1956.
Three Plays. New York: Harcourt, Brace, 1934.
Three Soldiers. New York: Geo. H. Doran, 1921.
Tour of Duty. Boston: Houghton Mifflin, 1946.
U. S. A. New York: Harcourt, Brace, 1938. First appearance of introductory sketch "U. S. A."
The Villages Are the Heart of Spain. Chicago: Esquire-Coronet, 1937. First in *Esquire* (Feb., 1937).

Selected Articles (including errata in Potter's *Bibliography*—see below, Selective Secondary Sources) *by Dos Passos.*

(?) "The Amateur Spirit," *Harvard Monthly*, LXVI (April, 1916), 56. Listed in Potter (p. 69), this editorial conflicts in tone and signature with Dos Passos' other contributions and is probably the work of Dudley Poore ('17).
"America and the Pursuit of Happiness," *Nation*, CXI (Dec. 29, 1920), 777-78. Vol. given erroneously in Potter (p. 69) as CLX.
"American Theatre: 1930-31," *New Republic*, LXVI (April 2, 1931), 171-75.
"An Appeal," *Student Review*, II (Oct., 1932), 21.
Autobiographical note of four paragraphs and signature (with portrait), covering whole of back cover of dust-jacket, *District of Columbia* (Boston, 1952).
"Big Parade—1936 Model," *Nation*, CXLIII (Oct. 3, 1936), 392-93.
"Books," *New Masses*, V (Dec., 1929), 16. A rev. of Hemingway's *Farewell to Arms*.
"Book Reviews," *Harvard Monthly*, LIX (Nov., 1914), 67, 68. Rev. of Jack Reed's *Insurgent Mexico*.
"Book Reviews," *Harvard Monthly*, LXII (May, 1916), 89. Revs. of *The Catholic Anthology* and *Georgian Poetry*.
"Business of a Novelist," *New Republic*, LXXVIII (April 4, 1934), 220.
"A Case of Conscience," *Common Sense*, IV (May, 1935), 16-19.

"Cardinal's Grapes," *Harvard Monthly*, LXI (Feb., 1916), 152-55.

"Carlo Tresca," *Nation*, CLVI (Jan. 23, 1943), 123-24.

"Caucasus Under the Soviets," *Liberator*, V (Aug., 1922), 5-8.

"A Conference on Foreign Relations," *Harvard Monthly*, LXII (June, 1916), 126-27.

"Duty of a Writer," *Writers in Freedom*, ed. Hermon Ould. London: Hutchinson and Co., 1942. Address delivered Sept., 1941.

"Edison and Steinmetz: Medicine Men," *New Republic*, LXI (Dec. 18, 1929), 103-4.

"Evangelist and the Volcano," *Harvard Monthly*, LXI (Nov., 1915), 59-61.

"Farewell to Europe," *Common Sense*, VI (July, 1937), 9-11.

"Four Nights in a Garden: A Campaign Yarn," *Common Sense*, I (Dec. 5, 1932), 20-22.

"The General," *The Modern Millwheel*, XIV (Jan.-July, 1950). Originally commissioned as a book, this series appeared in seven issues of this employee publication of General Mills, Inc. I have not discovered a copy in book form.

"Grandfather and Grandson," *New Masses*, XXI (Dec. 15, 1936), 19.

"Great American," *New Masses*, III (Dec., 1927), 26.

"Grosz Comes To America," *Esquire* VI (Sept., 1936), 105, 128, 131.

"Help the Scottsboro Boys," *New Republic*, LXXII (Aug. 24, 1932), 49.

"Hicks and 'Forgotten Frontiers,'" *New Republic*, LXXIV (March 29, 1933), 190.

"Honor of a Klepht," *Harvard Monthly*, LVII (Feb., 1914), 158-63.

"Humble Protest," *Harvard Monthly*, LXII (June, 1916), 115-20.

"Incarnation," *Harvard Monthly*, LXII (May, 1916), 89.

"In Portugal," *Liberator*, III (April, 1920), 25.

"In the Tents of the Agail," *The Arts*, III (March, 1923), 214-17. Has a book appearance not listed in Potter: *Orient Express*.

"July," *The Transatlantic Review*, II (Sept., 1924), 154-79.

"Les Lauriers Sont Coupés," *Harvard Monthly*, LXI (April, 1916), 48-49. Potter (p. 68) has p. 48 only.

"Lèse Majesté," *New Masses*, III (July, 1927), 3.

Letter to the author (3 pp.), March 15, 1954.

Longhand presentation note [in Theodore Dreiser's copy of *U. S. A.*] University of Pennsylvania Library "rare book."

"Looking Back on 'U. S. A.'" *New York Times*, Sunday, Oct. 25, 1959, sect. 2, p. 5.

"Making of a Writer," *New Masses*, IV (March, 1929), 23.

Marginalia, March, 1954 [penciled comments and corrections], in "Politics and History and John Dos Passos," unpubl. report (Univ. of Pennsylvania, 1950) by the author.

"Memory," *Harvard Monthly*, LXII (April, 1916), 38-40.

"Migratory Worker," *Partisan Review*, IV (Jan., 1938), 16-20.

"The New Masses I'd Like," *New Masses*, I (June, 1926), 20.

"A Note on Fitzgerald," *The Crack-Up*, ed. Edmund Wilson. New York: New Directions, 1945, pp. 338-43.

"An Open Letter to President Lowell," *Nation*, CXXV (Aug. 24, 1927), 176. Potter (p. 72) has "August 4."

"Poor Whites of Cuba," *Esquire*, V (May, 1936), 110. Not listed in Potter, though he lists under "Miscellany" (p. 90) a critical commentary by Dos Passos on the paintings of Luis Quintanilla, similar to this item.

Reactions to a questionnaire, *Time*, L (Aug. 4, 1947), 83.

"Satire as a Way of Seeing." Introduction to *Interregnum*, ed. Caresse Crosby. New York, 1937, pp. 9-19. Cited in Potter (p. 64); he also lists (p. 77) "Grosz Comes to America," *Esquire*, VI (Sept., 1936), 105, 128, 131, but he does not mention the near identity in these publications of this important material.

"The Shepherd," *Harvard Monthly*, LXI (Jan., 1916), 115-21.

"The Situation in American Writing," *Partisan Review*, VI (Summer, 1939), 26-27.

"Spain Gets Her New Deal," *American Mercury*, XXXI (March, 1934), 343-56.

"Statements of Belief," *Bookman*, LXVIII (Sept., 1928), 26.

"Thank You, Mr. Hitler," *Common Sense*, I (April 27, 1933), 13.

"They Are Dead Now," *New Masses*, III (Oct., 1927), 7.

"They Want Ritzy Art," *New Masses*, IV (June, 1928), 13.

"Tin Can Tourist," *Direction*, I (Dec., 1937), 10-12. Not in Potter.

"Tom Paine's 'Common Sense,'" *Common Sense*, VIII (Sept., 1939), 3-6.

"Tom Paine's 'Rights of Man,'" *Common Sense*, VIII (Oct., 1939), 12-15.

"Towards a Revolutionary [American] Theatre," *New Masses*, III (Dec., 1927), 20.

"Two Views of the Student Strike," *Student Outlook*, III (April, 1935), 5.

"The Two Youngest," *Nation*, CXXXV (Aug. 24, 1932), 172.

"Wanted: An Ivy Lee for Liberals," *New Republic*, LXIII (Aug. 13, 1930), 371-72.

"Washington and Chicago," *New Republic*, LXXI (June 29, 1932), 177-79.

"Whither the American Writer? A Questionnaire," *Modern Quarterly*, VI (Summer, 1932), 11-12.

"Whom Can We Appeal To?" *New Masses,* VI (Aug., 1930), 8. Listed under "Intellectuals In America" in Potter (p. 73).

"The World Decision," *Harvard Monthly,* LXXI (March, 1916), 23-24. Potter (p. 68); see comment on "The Amateur Spirit," above.

"The World's Iron, Our Blood and Their Profits," *Student Outlook,* III (Oct., 1934), 17-18.

"The Writer as Technician," *American Writers Conference.* ed. Henry Hart. New York: International Publishers Co., 1935, pp. 78-82.

"Young Spain," *Seven Arts,* II (Aug., 1917), 473-88.

II SELECTIVE SECONDARY SOURCES

To the scholar interested in checking or pursuing further references in this book, I recommend Jack Potter's *A Bibliography of John Dos Passos* (1950), listed below. Because of their distractions to the general reader, I have tried to keep bibliographical paraphernalia to a minimum (I should have been unable to do so without the general availability of Potter's *Bibliography* in research libraries). But I have also tried to include sufficient bibliographical information (chiefly dates and names of periodicals) in the text so that the interested reader may track down any of the references with little difficulty.

Potter's *Bibliography* contains selected bibliographies of secondary studies in both books and articles. As far as I know, no full-length study of Dos Passos has yet appeared, except in dissertation form. Some recently completed studies which may soon appear as books follow:

BERNARDIN, CHARLES W. "The Development of John Dos Passos." Unpubl. diss. (Univ. of Wisc., 1949). Potter mentions "his book to be published in 1950," p. 11. It has not yet appeared.

DONNELL, RICHARD S. "John Dos Passos: Satirical Historian of American Morality." Unpubl. diss. (Harvard, 1960).

GORMAN, THOMAS R. "Words and Deeds: A Study of the Political Attitudes of John Dos Passos." Unpubl. diss. (Univ. of Pa., 1960).

LANDSBERG, MELVIN D. "A Study of the Political Development of John Dos Passos from 1912 to 1936 with Emphasis upon the Origins of *U. S. A.*" Unpubl. diss. (Columbia Univ., 1959); diss. withheld pending publ.

NELSON, F. WILLIAM. "An Analysis of John Dos Passos' *U. S. A.*" Unpubl. diss. (Univ. of Okla., 1957).

NEWMAN, PAUL B. "The Critical Reputation of John Dos Passos: 1920-1950." Unpubl. diss. (Univ. of Chi., 1958-59).

Writers who seem to me to have expressed the fullest understanding of Dos Passos are Edmund Wilson, Jean Paul Sartre,
James T. Farrell, John Peale Bishop. Others are Mason Wade,
W. M. Frohock. Malcolm Cowley, Maxwell Geismar, and Granville Hicks are provocative.

Except for contributions by Wilson, Sartre, Farrell, and Bishop,
I have not found secondary studies of much help. The great majority are simple or extended book reviews. Their greatest value
is as a gauge to contemporary reactions to Dos Passos' work and
as sources of biographical information. The two most useful biographical studies I have consulted are, for Dos Passos, son and
father, respectively,

BLOCK, MAXINE, ed. *Current Biography*. New York: H. W. Wilson,
1940.

JOHNSON, ALLEN, and DUMAS MALONE, eds. *Dictionary of American Biography*. New York: Scribners, 1930.

The following is a list of all secondary materials I have cited
not included in Potter's *Bibliography*. The reader may locate any
reference in the present work by consulting the Index under the
name of the author. Included in the following list, with brief
annotations, are items unlisted or listed erroneously or inadequately
in Potter. Further annotations, of course, are in the text and notes
of the present volume (see Index).

Anon. Rev. of *Most Likely To Succeed, Commonweal,* LXI (Oct.
8, 1954), 20.

ANSON, CHERRILL. "Dos Passos: Changing with the Times," *Sunday Sun* [Baltimore] *Magazine,* Jan. 22, 1961, p. 7. A report
of an interview with Dos Passos just before release of *Midcentury.*

BERNARDIN, CHARLES W. "John Dos Passos' Harvard Years," *New
England Quarterly,* XXVII (March, 1954), 3-26.

Biog. note on Dos Passos, *The Arts,* III (March, 1923), 214. Potter
(p. 71) lists only "In the Tents of the Agail," pp. 214-17,
but does not list it *as* a poem (with prose portions), nor its
book appearance under "Table D'Hôte" in *Orient Express.*

————. *Seven Arts,* II (August, 1917), 473. Potter (p. 69) lists
only the article, "Young Spain," pp. 473-88.

COMMAGER, HENRY STEELE. *The American Mind.* New Haven:
Yale University Press, 1950. Describes the background, the
social, intellectual, and moral climate of Dos Passos' era.

COWLEY, MALCOLM. *Exile's Return,* rev. ed. New York: Viking
Press, 1951. This study by the critic and historian of his
generation forces Dos Passos into the "exile" mold.

CRANE, STEPHEN. *The Red Badge of Courage.* New York: D. Appleton Century Co., 1895. Contrasted with *Three Soldiers* in Chapter VI, section one, above.

DOS PASSOS, JOHN RANDOLPH. *The Anglo-Saxon Century and the Unification of the English Speaking People.* New York: G. P. Putnam's Sons, 1903.

DREISER, THEODORE. *Sister Carrie.* New York: Doubleday, Page, 1900.

ELIOT, T. S. *Poems: 1909-1925.* London: Faber and Gwyer, 1925.
————. *Selected Essays, 1917-1932.* New York: Faber and Faber, 1932.

GEISMAR, MAXWELL. "The Theme Is Fear," *Nation,* LXXXII (April 14, 1956), 305-6.

HAWTHORNE, NATHANIEL. *The Complete Works of Nathaniel Hawthorne . . . ,* ed. George P. Lathrop. 12 vols. Boston: Houghton Mifflin, 1883.

HEMINGWAY, ERNEST. *A Farewell to Arms.* New York: Scribners, 1929.

HICKS, GRANVILLE. "Dos Passos: The Fruits of Disillusionment," *New Republic,* CXXXI (September 27, 1954), 17-18.
————. "The Politics of John Dos Passos," *Antioch Review,* X (March, 1950), 85-98.

Holy Bible. Authorized King James Version. Dos Passos has several times complained that his is the first generation of American writers to write for an audience unfamiliar with the Bible (see "Introduction" to *Three Soldiers*); the Newsreels of *U. S. A.* and Documentaries of *Midcentury* are attempts to provide a substitute for this common background of ideas and symbols. Yet there remain too many biblical references in Dos Passos' canon for citation here though I have not been concerned to trace them in this study. See, *e.g.,* in *Three Soldiers,* the dialogue quoted above in Chapter Six, section I, and the virtual baptism of "Chris" by "John" Andrews in the same novel ("Machines," III).

HOOK, SIDNEY, JOHN DOS PASSOS, *et al.* "Statement of the Committee for Cultural Freedom," *American Mercury,* XLVII (July, 1939), 375-76.

"Individual Uppermost to John Dos Passos." Anon. interview, *Rocky Mountain News,* July 29, 1956, p. 72.

KALLICH, MARTIN. "John Dos Passos: Liberty and the Father Image," *Antioch Review,* X (March, 1950), 100-5.
————. "John Dos Passos Fellow-Traveler: A Dossier with Commentary," *Twentieth Century Literature,* I (January, 1956), 173-90.

Selected Bibliography

KAZIN, ALFRED, ed. *F. Scott Fitzgerald: The Man and His Work.* Cleveland: World Publishing Co., 1951.

MOORE, HARRY T. "Proud Men in an Age of Conformity," *New York Times* Book Rev., Sunday, Feb. 26, 1961, pp. 1, 51. Review of *Midcentury.*

MORISON, SAMUEL E. and HENRY STEELE COMMAGER. *The Growth of the American Republic,* 2 vols. New York: Oxford Univ. Press, 1942. Still the best standard American history.

"The Novelist as Historian." Anon. commentary and interview [?], *Newsweek,* XLIX (February 11, 1957), 106.

"Open Letter to the Communist Party," *New Masses,* X (March 6, 1954), 9.

PERKIN, ROBERT L. "Dos Passos Retains Hope for Humanity," *Rocky Mountain News* (Denver, Colo.), April 19, 1961, p. 71. A question and answer interview.

PIPER, HENRY DAN. "Fitzgerald's Cult of Disillusion," *American Quarterly,* III (Spring, 1951), 69-80.

"Platform" [of *Common Sense*], *Common Sense,* I (April 13, 1933), 1.

POTTER, JACK. *A Bibliography of John Dos Passos.* Chicago: Normandie House, 1950.

SHAKESPEARE, WILLIAM. *Hamlet.* Like the Bible and Greek myth, a common source of symbol and idea.

————. *King Lear.*

STEINBECK, JOHN. *The Grapes of Wrath.* New York: Viking Press, 1939.

"To John Dos Passos." Open letter, *New Masses,* X (March 6, 1934), 8, 9.

"Two American Novelists." Anon. rev., [London] *Times Literary Supplement,* October 27, 1950, p. 669.

WILSON, EDMUND. *Shores of Light.* New York: Farrar, Straus and Cudahy, 1952.

————. *The Triple Thinkers.* Rev. ed., New York: Oxford Univ. Press, 1948.

Index

American Mercury, The, 68, 193
Anderson, Sherwood, 105, 106, 191, 195
Andrews, John, 47, 48, 51, 69, 72, 73, 79, 93, 102, 103, 108-16, 122, 126, 145, 192
Antioch Review, 65, 189
Arts, The, 46

Baroja, Pío, 91, 92, 115, 194, 195
Bernardin, Charles W., 192, 195
Bishop, John Peale, 194, 197

Catholic Anthology, The, 98
Clemens, Samuel, 28, 48, 72, 107, 186, 197
Common Sense, 61, 67, 74, 77, 191
Communism, [7], 43, 45, 53, 55, 56, 57, 58, 60, 61, 62, 63-69, 76, 141, 156, 169, 173
Compton, Benny, 94, 160
Conrad, Joseph, 94, 95
Cowley, Malcolm, [8], 19, 29, 36, 39, 40, 146, 191, 194
Crane, Stephen, 106, 107, 109, 131
Cummings, E. E., 29, 42

Daily Worker, The, 55, 56
De Voto, Bernard, 164, 165, 196
Dos Passos, John Randolph, 19, 21, 22, 25, 31, 32, 33, 38, 40, 41, 46, 53, 80, 87, 127
Dos Passos, John Roderigo

WRITINGS OF:

Adventures of a Young Man, 72, 73, 74, 77, 172, 173, 194
"Aesthete's Nightmare, An," 30
"Against American Literature," 53, 88, 90, 115, 152
"America and the Pursuit of Happiness," 45, 193, 197
"American Theatre," 196
"Appeal, An" (list of signers), 60, 191
"Back to Red Hysteria," 190
Big Money, The, 68, 74, 144, 155, 157, 158, 165, 167, 190, 194
"Big Parade—1956 Model," 75, 197
"Book Reviews: *The Catholic Anthology* and *Georgian Poetry*," 97

"Book Reviews: *The War in Eastern Europe* by John Reed," 194
"Books" (rev. of *Farewell to Arms*), 58
"Business of a Novelist, The," 164
"Cardinal's Grapes, The," 82
"Carlo Tresca," 128-29
"Case of Conscience, A," 74, 193
"Caucasus Under the Soviets, The," 44
Chosen Country, 22, 23, 24, 30, 32, 37, 41, 42, 53, 72, 73, 83, 101, 107, 128, 143, 156, 165, 175, 177, 188, 192, 194
"Conference on Foreign Relations, A," 46, 100, 147, 188
District of Columbia, 84, 172, 175
"Duty of a Writer, The," 181, 197
"Edison and Steinmetz: Medicine Men," 59, 196
"Evangelist and the Volcano, The," 147
Facing the Chair, 190, 196
"Farewell to Europe," 167
First Encounter (see *One Man's Initiation—1917*)
42nd Parallel, 23, 41, 57, 69, 72, 144, 154, 155, 161, 166, 193, 194, 195
"Four Nights in a Garden," 191
"General, The," 170
Grand Design, The, 173, 174
"Grandfather and Grandson," 68
"Great American, A," 149
Great Days, The, 88, 175
"Grosz Comes to America," 75, 81, 86, 161, 163, 165, 188
Ground We Stand On, The, 77, 112, 127, 170, 175, 182, 194
Head and Heart of Thomas Jefferson, The, 34, 94, 171, 175
"Hicks and 'Forgotten Frontiers,'" 197
"Honor of a Klepht, The," 28
"Humble Protest," 34, 52, 53, 77, 81, 85, 88, 99, 115, 116, 121, 146, 147, 148, 150, 193

In All Countries, 44, 56, 66, 68, 84, 190, 191, 196
"Incarnation," 97
"In Portugal," 44, 45, 191
"In the Tents of the Agail," 46
Journeys Between Wars, 44, 78, 84, 194
"July," 83, 122, 192, 193, 194
"Les Lauriers Sont Coupés," 82, 96, 101
"Lèse Majesté," 55
Letter to Fitzgerald, 75
Letter to the Author, [6], 19, 168
"Looking Back on 'U. S. A.,'" 133, 193, 196
"Making of a Writer, The," 58, 194
Manhattan Transfer, 47, 51, 55, 70, 84, 94, 98, 108, 121-32, 176, 184, 192, 193, 194, 195
Marginalia (Wrenn MS), 22, 31, 188, 190
"Memory," 82, 97, 145
Men Who Made the Nation, The, 165, 171, 175, 186
Midcentury, [8], 98, 171, 176, 178, 179, 184, 197
"Migratory Worker," 194
Most Likely To Succeed, 55, 88, 117, 175, 195
"New Masses I'd Like, The," 52, 64, 152
1919, 42, 43, 47, 71, 94, 97, 155, 194, 196
"Note on Fitzgerald, A," 183
Number One, 173
One Man's Initiation—1917, 40, 41, 71, 88, 92, 102, 106, 107, 108, 120, 126, 189, 195
"Open Letter to the Communist Party, An," 68
"Open Letter to President Lowell, An," 55, 58, 59, 108, 190
Orient Express, 44
"Propaganda in the Theatre," 55
Prospect Before Us, The, 155, 175
Prospects of a Golden Age, 165, 171, 175, 184, 187
Pushcart at the Curb, 46, 82, 84, 93, 193
Reactions to Questionnaire (*Time*), 197

Rosinante to the Road Again, 36, 37, 44, 69, 71, 78, 83, 84, 86, 87, 89, 90, 91, 92, 93, 94, 95, 103, 104, 105, 115, 125, 140, 149, 151, 170, 189
"Satire As a Way of Seeing," (*see* "Grosz Comes to America")
"Shepherd, The," 82, 95, 98
"Situation In American Writing, The," 197
State of the Nation, 175
"Statements of Belief," 152
Streets of Night, 46, 49, 51, 70, 93, 95, 98, 108, 116-21, 126, 130-31, 137, 145, 151, 180, 194
"Thank You, Mr. Hitler," 67, 74
Theme Is Freedom, The, 19, 55, 57, 66, 76, 85, 87, 128, 133, 175, 189, 190, 191, 192, 195, 196
"They are Dead Now," 190
"They Want Ritzy Art," 56
Three Plays: "Moon Is a Gong" ("Garbage Man"), "Airways, Inc.," "Fortune Heights," 54, 67, 132-44, 152, 154, 195, 196
Three Soldiers, [8], 39, 40, 41, 46, 47, 93, 102, 103, 105, 106, 108-17, 120, 126-27, 131, 148, 151, 159, 169, 172, 176, 179, 180, 192
"Tin Can Tourist," 194
Tour of Duty, 47, 62, 175
"Towards a Revolutionary [American] Theatre," 55, 141, 196
"Two Views of the Student Strike," 197
"Two Youngest, The," 196
U. S. A., [7], 22, 23, 24, 33, 42, 54, 68, 70, 71, 72, 73, 74, 75, 84, 88, 98, 105, 125, 145, 147, 148, 151, 153-66, 167, 170, 172, 175, 176, 177, 180, 183, 184, 186, 187, 189, 195
"Wanted: An Ivy Lee for Liberals," 190, 196
"Whither the American Writer? A Questionnaire," 191, 195
"Whom Can We Appeal To?", 142, 190, 196

"World's Iron, Our Blood and Their Profits," 197
"Writer as Technician, The," 181, 197
"Young Spain," 87, 89, 91, 149, 194
Dreiser, Theodore, 60, 105, 106, 125, 126, 131, 191, 195

Eight Harvard Poets, 84, 93
Eliot, T. S., 29, 98, 118, 161, 195
Esquire, 75, 76

Fitzgerald, F. Scott, 29, 75, 76, 181, 183, 185, 188, 189, 195
Frohock, W. M., 194, 196

Geismar, Maxwell, 192, 195, 197
Gibbon, Edward, 26, 30
Gogol, Nikolai V., 106
Gold, Michael, 54, 58, 59, 65, 171, 189, 191

Harvard Monthly, 28, 29, 30, 31, 34, 35, 37, 46, 49, 64, 71, 81, 82, 93, 94, 96, 97, 99, 100, 101, 105, 145, 146, 147, 188, 192
Hawthorne, Nathaniel, 106, 116-21, 131, 151
Hemingway, Ernest, 30, 48, 57, 58, 76, 142, 163, 164, 196
Herf, Jimmy, 51, 71, 72, 74, 83, 121-32, 136, 156, 193
Hibben, Paxton, 149-53, 160, 162
Hicks, Granville, 53, 65, 66, 189, 190, 191, 197
Howe, Martin, 40, 41, 43, 44, 51, 69, 70, 71, 74, 87, 102, 103, 108, 120, 122, 126, 145, 180

"Individual Uppermost to John Dos Passos," quoted, 117
Ivens, Joris, 76

Jefferson, Thomas, 165, 186
Joyce, James, 106, 195

Left, The, 60, 190
Liberator, The, 44, 45, 92, 191
Life's Picture History of World War II, 170
lo flamenco, 89, 90, 104, 136
Lyaeus, 36, 37, 62, 63, 73, 78, 91, 104, 125, 189

Man Without a Country, The, 55, 70, 179

Nation, The, 45, 55, 59, 60, 75, 128, 196, 197

New Masses, 44, 53, 54, 55, 58, 59, 60, 64, 65, 66, 68, 141, 142, 149, 194, 196
New Playwrights Theater, 54, 55, 56
New Republic, 53, 58, 59, 60, 88, 89, 164, 190, 196, 197
Norton-Harjes, 31, 38, 42, 71, 72, 84, 92
"Novelist as Historian," 197

Odysseus, 38, 47, 56, 70, 78
O'Neill, Eugene, 105, 133

Paine, Tom, 61, 77, 170, 175, 182, 186, 191
Partisan Review: A Quarterly of Literature & Marxism, 77, 194
Pierhal, Armand, 9, 188
Pignatelli, Jay, 24, 30, 37, 42, 53, 128, 143, 156, 188, 192
Piper, Henry Dan, 29, 188

Reed, Jack, 64, 94, 101, 106, 146, 147, 160, 162, 194, 195

Sacco-Vanzetti Case, 54, 108, 133, 150, 152, 155, 158, 165, 190
Sartre, Jean Paul, 169, 197
Savage, Richard Ellsworth, 71, 72, 73, 74, 79, 97, 158, 159, 160, 161, 192
Schreiber, Georges, 25, 188
Scientific American, The, 177
Seven Arts, 87
Smith, Katharine F., 57, 62, 143
Spotswood, Glenn, 73, 77, 172, 173
Sprigg, Lucy Addison, 22, 23, 35, 73
Student Outlook, 74, 197

Telemachus, 36, 37, 38, 47, 51, 62, 63, 69, 70, 73, 74, 78, 83, 91, 104, 125, 145, 189
Thoreau, Henry David, 184-86, 197
Transatlantic Review, 83, 192
"Two American Novelists," 193

Vag, 156, 157, 162
Veblen, Thorstein, 30, 160

"Washing Windows," 42, 47, 103
Wenny, (David Wendell), 49, 51, 70, 72, 116-22, 134
Whitman, Walt, 106, 116, 149, 183, 186, 197
Wilson, Edmund, 29, 58, 190, 191, 192, 193, 194, 195, 197